A Good Forest for Dying

A
Good
Forest for
Dying

THE TRAGIC DEATH

OF A YOUNG MAN ON THE FRONT

LINES OF THE ENVIRONMENTAL WARS

Patrick Beach

DOUBLEDAY
New York London Toronto Sydney Auckland

333.72

Bea

PUBLISHED BY DOUBLEDAY
a division of Random House, Inc.

DOUBLEDAY and the portrayal of an anchor with a dolphin are
registered trademarks of Random House, Inc.

Book design by Richard Oriolo

LIBRARY OF CONGRESS CATALOGING-IN-PUBLICATION DATA

Beach, Patrick.
A good forest for dying : the tragic death of a young man on
the front lines of the environmental wars / Patrick Beach.—
1st ed.
p. cm.
1. Chain, David, d. 1998. 2. Environmentalists—Texas—
Biography. 3. Radicals—Texas—Biography. 4. Earth First!
(Organization) I. Title.

GE56.C43B43 2004
333.72'092—dc22
[B]
2003055346

ISBN 0-385-50617-1

PRINTED IN THE UNITED STATES OF AMERICA

[May 2004]

♲ Printed on recycled paper

FIRST EDITION

10 9 8 7 6 5 4 3 2 1

FOR ALLISON

CONTENTS

"Justice?—you get justice in the next world, in this world, you have the law."
—WILLIAM GADDIS, *A Frolic of His Own*

DAVID CHAIN'S DEATH AT THE HANDS of an angry logger in September of 1998 was shocking and darkly ironic, and
the story was, briefly, international news. Members of the media from
all over descended on Humboldt County, California. I was one of
them. Because Chain was a Texan—and most recently an Austinite—
his death was a local story for my newspaper, the *Austin American-
Statesman*. I expected the familiar journalist's routine: spend a few days
reporting in the area, file the best story I could for the Sunday paper,
move on to the next assignment. Like David Chain, I had no idea that
I was wandering into a war zone.

It was a story that could and had been cartoonishly rendered. In
this corner: the radical environmental movement-not-a-group Earth

First!, composed of a bunch of unwashed, apocalyptic, animist forest dwellers and self-appointed saviors of the Earth. And in this corner: Charles Hurwitz, the Machiavellian, planet-raping takeover artist from Houston, a scorched-earth businessman who had turned the bucolic Whoville of Scotia, California, into a place where both the local economy and the environment were being destroyed at blinding speed. Then there were certain law enforcement agencies that seemed itching to play the heavy in this long-running serial drama.

There's a grain of truth to many a stereotype. I did meet Earth First!ers who said the trees talked to them, young kids who had meandered into the movement because it was the best way they could most deeply annoy their parents. I also met people who'd put their professional obligations on hold and come from hundreds of miles away when they heard that one of their own had been killed. Like David Chain, they had thought long and hard about the imprint their actions left on the world, and they put their philosophy into daily practice. Their idealism resonated with me even if some of their ideals didn't. On the other side, there was a credible case to be made that Charles Hurwitz was cheerfully logging his company out of existence, and to hell with Humboldt County and the region after that. I also met with residents whose families had produced generations of proud loggers, people who spoke about the respect they felt for the land and the pride they took in doing what is, according to 2000 data from the Bureau of Labor Statistics, the most deadly job in America. A good number of them told me Humboldt County would have been better off if its residents had never heard of Earth First! or Charles Hurwitz.

It seemed an untenable situation, and yet the standoff at the time of Chain's death was in its thirteenth year. Both sides donned the cloak of righteousness, and both had an abundant capacity for and history of behaving badly at times. While the jagged edge of the environmental movement liked to paint its cause as the moral equivalent of the civil rights struggle of the 1950s and 1960s—a comparison that African

Americans who fought and died in that movement would hotly dispute—the truth was plainly more nuanced.

I couldn't quite shake off the story and the larger questions it posed. Chain had wanted to live every bit as much as you or I. And yet at the hour of his death he had been doing something he believed in—perhaps too much. The way he died seemed a passion play of sorts: the passion of David Nathan Chain. And the struggle for which he died, taken to its extreme (this is, after all, a debate that rarely accommodates moderation in deeds or rhetoric), couldn't be higher: it was nothing less than the American way of life versus life itself.

In the spring of 2001, as she waited for her wrongful-death lawsuit to go to trial in federal court, Chain's mother, Cindy Allsbrooks, was keeping tabs on what was happening with the North Coast activists, a number of whom had been her son's friends and had been with him when he died. At the time, there were reports—not exactly unbiased ones—of loggers and law enforcement once again roughing up Earth First!ers in the woods, and Allsbrooks feared it was just a matter of time before somebody else's child got killed. She called me to see if I had any ideas about whom to call in the California press, hoping to get some media exposure on the continuing controversy that might cool things down. I told Allsbrooks that she was the only person I'd had even sporadic contact with in the interim—we'd spoken maybe once or twice a year—but that perhaps the subject demanded something larger than another article in the newspaper. The book that began with that conversation is the one you're reading now.

Research for this project commenced before the events of September 11, 2001, after which the story I had to tell seemed to pale in significance. I now believe, however, that both stories represent possible paths to destruction. And it's quite possible that long after we have stopped talking about the threat of terrorist cells, shoe bombs, and death delivered via the U.S. Postal Service that what we do or don't do with respect to the environment will be the paramount issue. And, being a fan of both clean air and the right of working people to earn a living wage, I continue to struggle with questions that defy easy answers. Over the course of my research, I confessed to one source that I had no idea who was right in this struggle. Her response was striking: "Why does anybody have to be right?"

A Good Forest for Dying is the product of more than one hundred interviews, examinations of previously published material, court documents, evidence collected by the Humboldt County sheriff's and district attorney's offices, videotapes, audiotapes, and depositions. Exact quotes in quotation marks come from at least one of those sources and, when possible, were verified with a second or third source. As is commonplace among witnesses to a traumatic event, many of those with David Chain when he died offer sometimes conflicting statements about what happened on September 17, 1998. In instances where the record is less than clear, I have weighed the disputed details and endeavored to produce the most credible account of the events described. Truth is subjective, especially in the woods where much of this story unfolds.

A Good Forest for Dying

A
Good
Place
to Die

ONCE, THE TREES WERE NUMBERLESS. In the Jurassic Era, the sheer surreal scale of the forest might have been appropriate—redwoods rocketing well over 350 feet; ferns more than half again as tall as a grown man today; the morning fog a force of nature in its own right, obliterating the canopy overhead, draping down practically to the huckleberry. And in the archipelago of ancient forests that remain today, when the fog yields to the sun, the trees appear not to be reaching for the sky so much as holding it up.

The coastal redwoods, or their forebears, have been there for some 160 million years. As recently as a million years ago, they grew in Europe, Asia, and North America. Now they're found only in a narrow band hugging the coast of the Pacific Northwest. They are the tallest living things on Earth, and through the ages humans have attached a spiritual resonance to this forest, this basilica of redwoods. In thick stands, when there is sun, the light refracts through tentatively, and the forest floor is dim and damp. It can make visitors unexpectedly solemn, strike them suddenly silent and contemplative. As John Steinbeck wrote: "The most irreverent of men, in the presence of redwoods, goes under a spell of wonder and respect."

As any surviving species must be, they are resilient and adaptable. Growing in one of the most geologically unstable regions in the country—though not one prone to frequent catastrophic earthquakes such as those that afflict the Bay Area and southern California—redwoods developed shallow but multitiered root systems. For strength, the roots of neighboring trees intertwine like fingers. Each tree circulates thousands of gallons of water daily, and even today—when only between 3 and 4 percent of what was there just a century ago remains—stands of redwood can be thick enough to make their own weather. The area in which they grow in Humboldt County, along the coast in extreme northern California, is a temperate rain forest, with annual precipitation of about forty-five inches. Strongly resistant to fire, flood, and insects, the trees also endured all manner of prehistoric chaos—shifting tectonic plates that heaved mountain ranges into existence, ice ages. If lightning detonated the trunk, it wasn't uncommon for saplings to rise out of the truncated monster or for a bird to begin work on a nest there. And when trees blew down or simply rotted and died, they became habitat and food. The only things the primordial skyscrapers never developed an effective resistance to were saws and the demands of a ravenous nation gorging itself on its natural bounty, pushing westward and thumping its chest along the way.

Until the 1980s, the tallest living tree on record was a tree named, with a spectacular lack of imagination, Tall Tree, in what is now Redwood National Park in northern Humboldt County. Tall Tree grew to 367.8 feet. Logging in the Redwood Creek basin subjected the grove in which Tall Tree lives to more wind and hotter and drier conditions, and the tree's crown snapped off. (A tree named General Sherman, a giant sequoia in Sequoia National Park in the Sierra Nevada, is the world's largest tree by volume but, at 272 feet, not close to the height of some coastal old-growth redwoods.) Around the fourth century A.D., along a river that would come to be named the Eel in Humboldt County, a sapling grew to more than 350 feet—almost 50 feet taller than the Statue of Liberty from the ground to the tip of its torch—and a yard shy of 20 feet in diameter. The Dyerville Giant, as it came to be known, fell in 1991.

By then, Humboldt County had become a battleground. Everybody there loved trees, the saying went, just some folks preferred them horizontal. The joke attempted to take the edge off an intractable truth: the timber industry believed that its forest land was to be maintained, harvested, and capitalized upon. Those stands might be pretty, but they were also private property and, when the trees were marked for harvest, that property became an industrial workplace. Radical environmental activists said the loggers were ripping out the lungs of the planet, that the eco-apocalypse was nigh. The lines were well drawn, the opponents hardened by years of skirmishes and acrimony. Felling timber had been the lifeblood of Humboldt County's economy since before the Civil War, when the redwood belt filled half a million acres in the county alone, and now that way of life—hard, proud, and the very marrow of the area's history—was under attack by a bunch of self-appointed forest defenders. If you weren't against them, you were with them. Stenciled signs appeared on half of the houses in the county, bearing a message of pride, defiance, and pragmatism: THIS FAMILY SUPPORTED BY TIMBER DOLLARS. The protesters kept at it. Warning of an imminent and wholly man-made environmental collapse, they put their bodies between the chain saws and the trees they held sacred. To logging families, these were people whose organizing principle in life was opposition—opposition to the way ordinary guys made their wages.

Thousands of protesters had been drawn to the conflict over the years. Some of them had been threatened, beaten, cut out of trees they were occupying to save from the saws, doused with pepper spray, or thrown in jail.

One of the lucky ones was David Chain, who'd come from a working-class suburb of Houston to save the forest. True, the previous year, 1997, he'd gotten arrested at a protest in San Francisco. And once he'd had to run to stay ahead of the Pacific Lumber thugs in the woods. As his second protest season began, however, he hadn't been on the receiving end of any serious heaviness. Although he'd shaved off his brown dreadlocks from the year before, many of the veterans at the Earth First! action camp recognized his crescent eyes alight with mischief and purpose. The one they knew as Gypsy was back. Gypsy, who had helped out at the Bell Creek tree sit the year before, who had taken his nonviolence training and later learned to climb trees. Gypsy was always ready to pitch in—haul supplies or somebody's crummy rain gear, fix vegetarian meals, whatever the moment called for. He was twenty-four years old and had long searched for something to give his life definition and a tangible sense of purpose. With Earth First! and its brand of full-contact environmental protest he had found it, and the discovery was a gift and a transformation. He'd gone back to Texas the previous winter, when the rains came to the North Coast and the protesters' ranks typically thinned, and he'd worked two jobs in Austin to save for the return trip. This time he was here for good. This was where he was going to stay. This was where he was going to make his stand.

His mother and stepfather, Cindy and Ron Allsbrooks, could hardly have missed the pronounced change in him when he went home to the East Texas town of Pasadena the previous Thanksgiving. At his aunt Pam's house, he'd showed up in ratty clothes, smelling a little funky—but fairly glowing. He sat on a swing in the backyard with his sisters, Bridgett and Sarah, rolling a cigarette as he rolled out his story.

"My forest name is Gypsy," he began.

He'd told them he had been working to save the forest from wanton, wholesale destruction. That there was a logging company running roughshod over the environment in the name of almighty profit. That the last of the paternalistic capitalist timber companies had been swallowed whole by a rapacious, junk-bond-wielding robber baron from Houston. He showed them pictures of himself in trees he had occupied to save from the saws. Even his appearance had changed. He looked a good bit like Keanu Reeves gone native. His body had filled out from climbing. Most striking, the black moods that sometimes had beset him seemed to have fled. He practically vibrated with a sense of mission. The young man they knew as Nathan—his middle name, used to distinguish him from his father, David Allen Chain—had been transformed. Cindy had understandable maternal worries about her boy climbing 200-foot trees, and she knew nothing of the fight to save the redwoods, but Nathan was now focused on saving the world, one tall tree at a time. He was an adult, and she saw that, for him, not standing up to the enemy was tantamount to hastening the extinction of life on Earth.

His uncle Mike thought the young man was sinewy, as if taking a leave after finishing basic training. He told him he was proud of him. He never saw his nephew again.

THE BUZZING OF THE SAW shredded the morning. Gypsy and the rest of the Earth First!ers could hear it up on the mountain from where they were gathered at Grizzly Creek Redwoods State Park, a de facto DMZ bordering a piece of Pacific Lumber's timber empire. To the people stirring in their sleeping bags, the noise meant that another day of planet-raping had commenced. It meant the loggers were back on the scene, felling trees, wreaking havoc, destroying habitat for endangered species, cutting away so that soon the holy redwood forest would be as lifeless as a moonscape.

It meant that Gypsy and the other activists were late for work. But if the Earth survived this incomprehensible assault, some of Gypsy's fellow activists believed, its spirit would thank them for saving it.

Mike Avcollie, Gypsy's best friend among the Earth First!ers, shook the tent in which Gypsy and his friend Jennifer Walts slept. Gypsy crawled over Walts and out of the tent. They'd both been exhausted when they moved from the action camp at Williams Grove to Grizzly the night before. He was going to let Jennifer sleep. But the rest of them should have gotten up earlier, should have hatched a firm plan before they'd crashed out at the campground the night before. As the other Earth First!ers pulled on extra layers, unzipped their tents, yawned, and shook off a mid-September daybreak chill around the fire, they knew they had to stop the killing until the California Department of Forestry crew could get up to the site and properly investigate. CDF had promised as much a day earlier when the First!ers laid siege— again—to the CDF office in Fortuna. CDF had said it would check out the claim that Pacific Lumber was illegally logging up at Grizzly. And yet the company sent the crews out anyway, knowing they could get the jump on the bureaucrats, knowing that once those great old redwoods and Douglas firs were on the ground and loaded onto trucks and sent down to the mill, CDF could tsk-tsk all it wanted, add another citation to the company's growing collection, maybe, but those trees—some stretched 150 feet into the Pacific sky—were not going back up. And the cash from the sale of that timber was headed to the Pacific Lumber Company, in Scotia—one of the last honest-to-God company towns in America.

Carey Jordan wasn't crazy about humping up the hill again, but she told the group around the fire she'd do it. While the bulk of the Earth First! troops had been concentrating on the scene in Fortuna the day before, she and a small group had walked up the mountain toward the sound of the saw, being careful to stay out of sight of the Pacific Lumber workers until they got to where the active logging was. If they were caught before they made it there, they would have accomplished nothing, but if they sat down in front of the yarder—the gurgling, diesel-fired crane that dragged the felled trees up the steep, unstable slope to the flat landing—they knew the workers would cuss them out and shut down the heavy equipment. And then the cutting would stop, at least for as long as it took for the crew to radio base camp that it was time to call the sheriff's department again, tell them that there were protesters in the area, that they couldn't safely log with those goddam hippies running around.

Which is what most of Jordan's companions did that day. She thought she might try a little worker outreach, as it was euphemistically called. Jordan, a dark-haired registered nurse from Maine with more surety and composure than most twenty-six-year-olds, walked toward the sound of an idling Stihl chain saw and met a short, stout timber faller. He had a face cut with smile lines and eyes the color of blue ice. It was getting on toward the middle of the afternoon, hot, close to quitting time, and the faller, a mustachioed man in his middle years named A. E. Ammons, didn't consider it a grave imposition to while away the rest of the waning day casually flirting with a hippie chick. Any chance he had to educate one of these ying-yangs was an opportunity, he figured. Jordan told him that what the loggers were doing was illegal; he told her that was crap, that she didn't know what she was talking about. Then, although he creeped her out, she turned up the charm: "What do you do? What kind of beer do you like?"

Ammons said his nickname was "Big A," now an accidentally ironic handle from his school days when so many people had trouble with his name: "Big A, big E . . ." He told her that his dad—stepdad, actually—had committed suicide: the old man was sticking a shotgun into his mouth when the four-year-old boy happened to pad into the room. Big A told her he'd been in Vietnam, which he hadn't. He told her he liked to drink beer after work, had child support to pay, was convinced the protesters were wrong and he was right. And he told her that if she were sitting in a tree trying to save it, he'd go ahead and fell that tree and kill her.

"Come on, Big A," Jordan said. "If I was up there, you'd kill me?"

"Yes, I would."

The fact that a logger was taking so much time to talk with a protester was not lost on Jordan, but she kept him jawing for an hour or more. Before it was over, she'd given him a hug and posed for a picture, Big A with his saw slung over his shoulder, his arm around Jordan, who all the while couldn't figure out why Big A and his spotter were still visiting with her.

"Don't you know?" Big A asked. "Your friends are all up there blocking the road. The cops are coming any minute. You better run now if you don't want to get arrested."

Just then the sheriff's car came to the bottom of the mountain, and Jordan dutifully went to join her seven comrades sitting on the ground, waiting to get hauled down the logging road. On the way, the driver asked which one was Jordan and then handed her a scrap of paper. Big A had passed along his phone number, just in case she wanted to go to dinner after she got booked for trespassing and processed out of the jail in Eureka.

CONFRONTING PISSED-OFF LOGGERS, of course, wasn't the only hazard one might encounter in the woods. The night before Jordan's encounter, Gypsy and Jennifer Walts were helping to bring in ropes and food to protesters squatting in trees on Pacific Lumber land above Grizzly Creek. It was crucial if unsexy labor. As dark was coming on, they heard a frightful crack. Gypsy threw himself over Walts on the ground. When the dust settled, Walts switched on her flashlight and saw a branch about ten feet long and nine inches in diameter that had just fallen a few feet away from them.

"Oh my God, Gypsy, that almost killed us," Walts said as she tried to catch her breath.

Gypsy took a look around and said, "This looks like a good place to die."

They spent the next day at the tree sit—a tactic in which protesters perch on platforms high in trees as a last line of defense to keep them from being cut—after enduring a restless night, one of those when you can't wish the sun up but never stop trying. Gypsy had forgotten his sleeping bag. Again. The two of them had to wedge themselves into Walts's. They were both exhausted all the following day, the day the bulk of the activists were in Fortuna trying to get the CDF to commit to investigating the allegedly illegal logging.

It was a typically colorful piece of Earth First! street theater. They'd made papier-mâché masks and carried banners: CDF: DO YOUR JOB! TREES HAVE LIFE TOO—ALL LIVING THINGS ARE EQUAL. WHO CLEAR-CUT CDF'S BACKBONE? The CDF man who came outside and spoke to them, John Marshall, had been drafted in so many of these dramas that they ran together in his memory, but he listened with resigned patience. The protesters registered their concerns: Timber Harvest Plan 172 was on a steep grade. It was possibly an unfinished survey area for the marbled murrelet, an endangered seabird. There'd been activity in the area before the allowable time.

Marshall said, "We're looking into that."

The protesters wanted to know a time frame for looking into that. Marshall told them he had a call in to the inspector in Bridgeville. It'd probably be today or tomorrow, he said.

The Earth First!ers asked variations of the same question over and over: Why can't you just stop them? Marshall told them that Pacific Lumber's record of compliance for the year so far was much better than in years past. He told them that, in an agreement almost without precedent, the CDF had keys to all of Pacific Lumber's gates and could enter the property at any time without notifying the company ahead of time. The Earth First!ers asked if they might accompany the inspector on such occasions. Marshall said no, it wouldn't be possible.

A carful of hippie-haters drove by, throwing eggs and screaming, "Cocksucking motherfuckers, get outta here!"

"Probably in the interest of all of us, we ought to call this good, huh?" Marshall suggested. "I mean, in view of people driving by and throwing eggs and yelling stuff out."

They kept at him: "How many watersheds do you need? How many mudslides do you need? How many fish going extinct do you need?"

When Marshall finally retreated to his office, the Earth First!ers danced. Somebody banged on a drum and a guy with a clumpy beard picked a mandolin.

Back at the park where Earth First! was having its action camp, where volunteers took training and strategized on how best to screw with PL's plans, there was talk about going back up the mountain the following morning. The activists knew that, historically, what little goodwill the loggers had for Earth First! tended to be pretty much burned up after the first standoff. Gypsy was wary of a showdown, but he and the others were also convinced that they had no choice: PL *was* logging too close to an off-limits nesting area for the marbled murrelet—a latter-day spotted owl in terms of environmental symbolism. The company *was* also putting roads where it shouldn't and building them prohibitively early. And the company most decidedly *was* going to go to town on that timber before CDF got around to investigating the protesters' claims.

"Well," Jordan said, "if you guys are all going to go up, I'll go again."

Jake Wilson, who drove a beat-up white van held together with hope and a Phish bumper sticker, had hauled part of the crew back over to Grizzly to be closer to the logging site in case the Earth First!ers did, indeed, decide to go back in the morning. Jordan's boyfriend, Erik "Ayr" Eisenberg, who'd been at the CDF protest the day before, was up for it. So was Mike McCurdy. Gypsy was a maybe when he crawled into the tent with Walts, weary beyond description.

As people from disparate backgrounds who are flung into intense and hazardous experiences frequently do, Avcollie and Gypsy had bonded fast the year before at the Bell Creek tree sit. Avcollie was a product of the southern California middle class, an educated, charismatic radical who spoke in torrents, with eloquence and clear-eyed passion, about establishment lies, corporate greed, and the lopsided distribution of wealth. Short-haired, with a neatly trimmed beard, he was in many respects an exception to the convenient stereotype of an Earth First!er as a shoeless transient in desperate need of a clue, a haircut, and a hot bath. His friend with the forest name that suggested a nomadic life was less seasoned but just as sharp. Gypsy had seized on activism as a means to shape his existence into something more than hanging out with his friends at the mall, listening to the Fugees, and smoking dope. Both had helped the new recruits this year. Gypsy handled the tree-climbing workshop, while Avcollie taught nonviolence. This morning, September 17, 1998, Avcollie's hope had been to blockade the logging road to keep the workers from getting anywhere close to the cutting site, but by the time the Earth First!ers were up and ready to move out, it was too late. Gypsy and Avcollie also had little hope that CDF staffers would get around to actually doing their job. The protesters would have to do it for them.

The day was coming on, and the saw was merciless. In the end, nine activists decided to go. Acting on chivalry, Gypsy told the others Walts wasn't feeling well. In fact, she was so deeply asleep that she didn't even feel Gypsy crawl over her, unzip the tent, and get ready to roll. By the time she woke up, he and the rest were long gone up the mountain.

They packed a little food and water, just enough for a day trip. The camcorder was vital, too, an essential in documenting the company's destruction and the workers' history of getting heavy with the activists, especially if events were disputed after the fact. Jordan stuck a few cloves of garlic in her pocket. Wilson toted water. Somebody had a crust of bread; someone else had a radish or two. The activists made a circle and spoke of remaining strong and calm no matter what happened. Then they started the climb, made longer and more circuitous because they needed to avoid being spotted before they got to the site. Zoe Zalia's asthma came on and slowed her down. Gypsy went back to check on her. Mike McCurdy stayed with her, and Gypsy moved back up to rejoin the others.

The hike was stealthy but urgent. The Earth First!ers heard trees crashing all the way up the mountain, into the conifer air.

The war between Earth First! and Pacific Lumber had developed rules of engagement since the troubles started back in 1985, and Gypsy knew today's exercise in potent protest was supposed to go something like this: if approaching a faller, wait until his saw is off or at least idling to be sure he can hear you. Yell out that you're there. An active timber-felling site is one of the most dangerous workplaces in America, and fallers know they can't safely fell trees when people, even hippies, are nearby. Then the worker outreach begins: Hi. What's your name? Do you know that what you're doing is possibly illegal? Do you know you're an unwitting participant in a ruinous plot? Do you know the company doesn't care about you since it was taken over by a corporate raider from Houston who's going to cut every one of these trees down, bankrupt the company, and wreck the entire economy of Humboldt County? What will you do for a job then? Turn burgers? Keep them talking, force them to see you as something more than a Birkenstock-wearing freak with nothing better to do with your life since Jerry Garcia died.

THAT HAD BEEN JORDAN'S TACTIC the day before. Use calm, measured tones and nonconfrontational speech and body language. Defuse, de-escalate. If the guys are pissed off, let them be pissed off. The crews are supposed to radio security. If they beat you up while waiting for the sheriff to arrive, don't fight back. In a part of the world where the passions are as oversized as the redwoods, this conflict, especially during the protest season that traditionally began in mid-September, had precedent in abundance. In a sense, it was almost business as usual.

Today would not be business as usual.

The Earth First!ers stepped into the logger's sight. Big A again. Big A working the Stihl with the thirty-inch bar. Big A saw them. Big A tweaked. Big A thundered like an Old Testament prophet.

"Get the fuck out of here!" he bellowed. "You've got me hot enough now to fuck!"

Some of the activists scattered back into the dense brush. Ayr Eisenberg held his ground, said they didn't want to cause him any problems.

"You already have! So get out of here! You cocksuckers! I mean it!"

Eisenberg said when the CDF came out they'd tell him to stop.

"When the motherfucker shows up and tells me to stop, I'll stop!"

Eisenberg said, "Well, we should give them a chance to show up."

"Why weren't they here early this morning?"

"Because they're in the company's pocket . . ."

"They're in the company's pocket? That's why they're fuckin' with us every day, yeah?"

"They're not fuckin' with you every day. Otherwise they'd be out here this morning."

"Get outta here! Otherwise I'll fuckin', I'll make sure I got a tree comin' this way."

"All right, well, let's not talk about that. You know we're not gonna—"

"Cocksucker!"

Big A's spotter, a twenty-one-year-old guy named Rhett Reback, suggested in language almost as searing as Big A's that the hippies go harass another crew away from the active logging. But Big A wasn't done yet.

"Oh, fuck! I wish I had my fuckin' pistol. I guess I'm gonna just start packin' that motherfucker in here. 'Cause I can only be nice so fuckin' long. Go get my saw, I'm gonna start fellin' into this fuckin' draw!"

Big A dropped his saw and gave chase, throwing rocks and whatever else he could grab off the ground. Eisenberg, hearing a rock zing past his ear, knew he wasn't interested in letting Big A get hold of him.

Panting hard after running up the slope, the Earth First!ers hooted in the dense brush to locate each other. No way was one of them, Patrick Seelie, sticking around—he'd endured some scary threats and mind games when trying to intervene on an action the year before. "This is just how those guys sounded," he said. "This guy is dangerous." And then he was gone. McCurdy and Zalia were hiding with the video camera farther away.

Jordan decided to give it a go. The six approached again. Gypsy saw Jordan get as close as fifty feet from Ammons, and when Big A recognized Jordan he cooled off, or at least didn't seem quite as enraged. "Oh. What are you doing back out here?" Big A asked. "I told you not to come back out here." Then his voice changed and he unleashed a hailstorm of rage: "Get the fuck out of here, you stupid cocksuckers. I'm going to knock your fucking head off with the next one if you're around here. This one's coming your way. You better get the fuck out of here or somebody's going to get hurt."

"You don't mean that, A.E.," Jordan said. "You wouldn't want to kill anybody. We live here. This is our home."

"This is my *job*," Big A spat back. "You know, I can't talk to you all day. You better get the fuck out of here. You better have your hard hat on, because this one's coming your way. This one will reach you for sure."

They scrambled again and, as threatened, Big A started felling trees in their direction. On that nearly vertical mountainside, if a tree happened to get away from a saw jock and shoot downhill, it'd be an unguided missile straight to Highway 36. Anybody in the path of the tree wouldn't have a chance to get out of the way. So the Earth First!ers regrouped uphill and slightly sidehill—unwittingly right in Big A's line of fire, close enough to be good and scared. Jake Wilson felt shaking when Big A felled the trees, but Jake couldn't tell if it was the ground or his legs. Another protester, a sixteen-year-old with the forest name Farmer, could hear his companions stomping around in the woods, trying to gain footholds on the slope. The forest floor was so loose it was like trying to climb a mountain of marbles.

Gypsy joined his companions as they regrouped, six of them now crouching uphill from Big A and Reback. They shared a meager lunch of the crust of bread, the garlic, and the radishes. They needed to figure out what to do next, and it wasn't safe to approach with trees falling. This was beyond belief—that maniac kept felling in their direction. If anything, he seemed to be ripping through the trees faster, as if the interruption to his work had made him want to teach the Earth First!ers a lesson.

Whenever a tree would fall, the protesters would yell out, either in fear or to vocalize the tree's death wail—another bit of Earth First! theatricality. Big A was hollering, too, giving a "Yee-ha!" or "Up the hill! Up the hill!" when a tree was about to come down. That's what he was supposed to do. But he wasn't supposed to be cutting if he knew people were around. And Jordan was sure that Big A and Reback were deliberately talking loudly enough for the protesters to hear them.

Another hoot went up—McCurdy somewhere, maybe? Zoe? Big A said, "Who the hell's that?"

"Oh, hippies," Reback said. "They're everywhere. They're all over the place."

The hippies squatted in their snack spot for fifteen minutes or more, talking about what to do, hoping the break would calm this guy down. Gypsy wasn't interested in sticking around, but he knew to wait until the saw was shut down to make a move. "Big A was really mad," he said. "Maybe we should leave." Avcollie agreed—cede the day to the enemy, hang out at camp, try for a good blockade the following morning. Jordan and Eisenberg said no, that letting Big A win with the explicit threat of physical harm would send the wrong message to the company—maybe even ratchet up the violence.

Downhill, Big A had just about had it. On top of working this steep, shaley piece of PL real estate, on top of the fact that it was by now hotter than a sonofabitch, on top of the fact that the wind was picking up from above them and the brush was so thick he had to cut a trail wherever he and Reback went . . . now he's dealing with all that *and* hippies? "You know what? Fuck it," he told Reback. "I'm gonna fell this last redwood tree and I'm packing up all my tools and I'm out of here. I'm gonna go in and talk to McLaughlin tonight, tell him either he's got to do something or get a new timber faller out here 'cause I'm not dealing with this anymore."

Big A went to work on the twentieth tree of the day by putting in a back cut. At about 130 feet, the tree had maybe 3,000 board feet in it, worth $7,000 to the company if it landed in one piece. With the wind blowing down the hill, he wanted the thing to lean uphill a little more. Then he had Reback take his ax and beat a wedge into the cut. He was damn near through the face cut—that baby just hanging by a thread— when the wind died and the tree leaned back down and sat on his bar and chain. "Aw, shit," he said. He'd gotten an $800 saw hung up in a tree that was about to go in whatever direction it wanted. He sent Reback down to where their backpack was to get the extra bar and chain, by which time, of course, Big A had the bar and chain out and was putting the saw back together. He finished the face cut, told Reback to knock in another wedge and beat the thing over.

One final time, the Earth First!ers had decided as a group, they would try to approach. If Big A went off on them again, they'd clear out.

They figured they'd be safer in two groups of three, one going high and one low. Gypsy and Jordan were among the first out of the circle, ducking under a previously fallen log on their way out. They went high. No way did they want to be low.

They yelled and stepped out. Then Avcollie heard the loud thwack of metal hitting plastic—the sound of a wedge being hammered into a thirteen-story tree about to topple. Then he heard the tree's stem crack, like a string of firecrackers popping on the Fourth of July.

Jordan looked up and saw a quivering tree, a faltering giant.

"Holy shit, that's coming toward us," she said to Gypsy. "We better run."

She clawed her way up. Gypsy didn't. She turned around and Gypsy wasn't with her. She ran down, said, "Gypsy, you've got to run. That tree's falling. Go high. Go up the hill." She went back up.

Maybe Gypsy froze. Maybe he tried to get away and slipped.

It was hard to tell which way the thing was going, much less which direction to run. Farmer jumped back the way he'd come, hiding beneath the tree they'd just walked under. He rolled over on his back and saw the redwood coming down.

The crash was as loud and sharp as a thunderclap. The impact stole the breath from their lungs and the ground shuddered for hundreds of feet around them. The hail of dust and debris from the forest floor made it seem like one of Humboldt County's famously impenetrable fogs had descended in the blink of an eye. Jake Wilson thought the white light and the debris hitting his head meant he was dead.

Avcollie had been able to scramble only ten feet from where he'd been standing a second before, but he was alive. Then they were all on their feet and screaming. "What the fuck are you doing?" Avcollie shrieked. "You're going to fucking kill somebody."

Big A ran up the trunk of the tree he'd just felled, bellowing back at the activists who were screaming at him.

Jordan cut the cacophony with a panicked question. "Shut up! Shut up!" she said. "Where's Gypsy?"

Big A: "Who's Gypsy, your fuckin' dog?"

Then Big A found him. He dropped to his knees, which some of the protesters took as a gesture of horror or grief or prayer.

"Holy fuck," Big A said. "He's right there. His brains are falling out."

Jordan's first impulse was to try to put Gypsy's head back together. Eisenberg thought to check for a pulse, but when he saw Gypsy's skull gaping in a silent howl, he simply put his hand on the dead man's back. In mourning, Wilson threw dirt on his back. Avcollie—the best friend Gypsy had on that mountain—cried, screamed, and threw up.

Back at the campsite, Jennifer Walts was showing an activist how to play Johnny Cash's "Big River" on the guitar: "Now I taught the weeping willow how to cry / And I showed the clouds how to cover up a clear blue sky." Farmer ran down and told the Earth First!ers something had happened. "His brains fell out," Farmer kept saying. "I saw his brains." Walts ran up the mountain. By the time she got to the landing, she was hysterical.

"Murderers!" she shrieked at the loggers. "You killed my boyfriend! You killed my boyfriend!" She tried to make it down to Gypsy's body. A worker grabbed her ankle and brought her to the ground. An older man rubbed the back of her neck and said, "Calm down, honey. You don't want to see that." That infuriated Walts all the more. She fought them, flailing on the ground.

Thirteen years into the battle between the hippies and the planet-rapers, Earth First! finally had a martyr. Above a creek named for a bear not seen in those parts for generations, this piece of forest would become hallowed ground for its defenders, consecrated in the blood of one of their brothers. And Pacific Lumber—which some believed had shrewdly manipulated the protesters' presence to its own advantage—had, at minimum, an unprecedented public-relations disaster.

IN A RURAL SUBDIVISION OUTSIDE Coldspring, Texas, Cindy Allsbrooks parked her pickup and went inside her modest, well-kept, three-bedroom house. She'd been to her first weight-loss meeting that day and was feeling a little buoyant. All the other women in the group were a lot bigger than she was. Work was going just fine. She sold incentive packages to companies looking to beef up their safety programs. The East Texas timber industry was her biggest client. Aside from wanting to lose a few pounds, she was as content and comfortable as she'd ever been in her adult life. It was mid-September, time to start thinking about Christmas. Her Nathan had said he wouldn't be coming home for the holidays. He was going to stay in California and continue his work to save the redwoods. His mother was going to have to get him something he could use in the forest.

Allsbrooks got out of her work clothes and settled into her recliner. Ron was at work. It would be just she and the Thursday night sitcoms.

She heard the dog barking outside. Her oldest daughter, Bridgett, was walking across her front lawn. This wasn't right. Bridgett lived more than an hour away and had a family of her own to mind. Showing up unannounced at her mother's on a weeknight telegraphed that something was wrong, news too grave to be delivered in a telephone call. Their eyes locked.

"Who was it and what happened?"

"Mom, it's Nathan."

"Is he dead?"

"Yes."

Seeds

DAVID CHAIN'S PARENTS MET AT A roller rink. *That boy's looking at me*, Cindy Trimm thought, *and he's so fine*. It was a Friday night in 1967 at the rink next to the bowling alley in Pasadena, Texas, hormones hanging in the air. Cindy was twelve going on thirteen and a regular heartbreaker in her fringed outfits. But this boy exuded cool. He was two classes ahead of her in school. He wasn't there to skate, he was there to check out girls. When that same boy turned up at Cindy's surprise birthday party a short time later at the park pavilion behind Pasadena High, Cindy didn't pay him much attention until he got in a fistfight with another boy, nearly knocking him out. Then it was love. Cindy spent the rest of her own party swooning, ministering to a cut on the bad boy's face, basking in the certainty that David Allen Chain was the one.

At fourteen, Cindy was engaged. Her mother laughed, but her mother was also distracted working full-time and raising six children in a one-story tract home. Her father was a beloved man who had fought and been wounded in the invasion of Normandy in World War II. Cindy had had a boyfriend or two already, and she'd sneak out at night to meet them or to walk to the Dairy Queen. But David Chain was something else. In May of 1969, she wrote in her schoolgirl's hand, "I love David Allen Chain more than anything in the world and I always will."

On April 4, 1970, a justice of the peace in Pasadena put the matter to rest, and sixteen-year-old Cindy Trimm became Mrs. David Chain. She wore a miniskirt and was three months pregnant. After the wedding, the newlyweds went shopping at Kmart to furnish their apartment, and that night they went to a German restaurant with David's sister and her husband. The three of them drank beer while Cindy threw up in the bathroom.

Greater Houston was humming: the Astrodome, "the eighth wonder of the world," opened in 1965. Before that decade's end, NASA—the embodiment of America's fervor for adventure, technology, and grasping for the next great something—was depositing men on the moon. Office towers gleamed, their occupants sealed off from the heat and the reek of oil, the smell of their money being made for them. Houston boomed. Traffic snarled. Petro-alchemy in action. At the butt end of the economic spectrum, in adjacent suburbs such as Pasadena, education wasn't much of a priority, but who needed school when you could walk across the road and get two jobs before lunchtime? You woke up in your tract house; breathed air the color of sweet East Texas tea; pulled on your work boots; clocked in at the tank farm or the chemical plant or one of the spewing, sprawling oil refineries; cashed your paycheck at the end of the week; and headed for the auto parts store or the beer joints. At least Pasadena wasn't quite as bad as nearby Texas City, where hundreds died in 1947 when two tankers loaded with fertilizer exploded. Texas City's own luckless inhabitants called the town "Toxic City."

David, for one, didn't need school. He needed a job. And, lucky for him, the army was hiring. David and Cindy's first child, Bridgett, was born just after David had cleared basic training. He sat up all night polishing his boots and waiting for Cindy to go into labor, then, after his two-week leave, it was back to the base. David's draft number was bound to come up, everybody knew it was black kids and working-class white boys who were fighting this war, and David figured he'd be better off beating the service to the punch. He sorely hoped the army would teach him a trade, and his family would have insurance. Although Cindy was opposed to the war and even wrote a poem about it, David volunteered for a tour in Vietnam and eventually spent three years in the service. Once back home in Pasadena, David was hired by Armco Steel along the Houston Ship Channel, working in the electric melt shop, where men sweated like blacksmiths, pouring ladles full of molten steel into molds. It was a good, steady job for a Pasadena workingman, a union job with free Blue Cross.

Cindy was two weeks late with her second child. In those days before sonograms, her doctor had predicted that the baby would be a boy. On June 17, 1974, the day after Father's Day, with the nation riveted to the downward spiral of Nixon's presidency, David Nathan Chain entered the world at Pasadena Bayshore Hospital. Cindy was, per her custom, a vigilant note-taker, most certainly not one of those mothers whose children's baby books go blank after the first few well-intentioned pages. " 'David' means beloved," she wrote. " 'Nathan' means a gift from God, and he is both." Bridgett was three and a half when her parents brought the funny-looking little boy home to steal all the attention from her.

The following year—the same year that Pacific Lumber Company was listed on the New York Stock Exchange—little David was learning to say "dada" and suffering from a series of ear infections that kept his parents pacing the floors of their apartment at 315 Richey Street.

The doctor told Cindy that when her little boy had been taken to be circumcised, he was livid at being held down. He'd hollered with indignation much more loudly than he did when he was being cut. He was like his father that way, stubbornly and almost recklessly willful. As he grew, he also appeared to have inherited his father's worldview, which could be wildly pessimistic, as if even the forces of nature were conspiring against him. When it rained, the elder David Chain would think, *Well of course it's raining. I was going to change the spark plugs in the car this afternoon.* The boy also inherited some of his father's unflinching resolve. If David was going to be in a war, he was going where he could look the enemy in the eye.

As a vet, David was able to get a VA loan for the family's first house, down the street from the washateria and a stone's throw from the freeway and the Houston Ship Channel. The family was poorer than dirt—they'd floored the den of their first house with remnants of carpet from the Dumpsters behind carpet stores and used a large wooden spool as an end table—but all the kids' friends thought the Chains were gentry because they had a trampoline *and* a pool table. (The pool table would develop into, as all flat surfaces must in a busy house with children, a place to fold clothes.) There was a big oak in the backyard with a rabbit cage underneath. One year, Bridgett tried to grow carrots in the sandy soil. There was a vacant lot between their house and the neighbor's where touch football games would break out.

In July of 1976, Sarah Joy Chain made them a family of five. There was never much money, but Cindy was at home during the day and the family took its pleasures simply. They would walk to the park in the neighborhood to feed the ducks. Squirrels would eat out of Sarah's hand.

Nathan was a classic middle child, a born conciliator, yet one who wasn't afraid of mixing it up with his sisters—or, alternately, defending them—when circumstances called for it. His boyhood was typical for kids growing up along the coastal lowlands and bayous—Little League, weekend getaways to the lake. There is a picture of David Nathan Chain as a little boy of three or so, holding up a tiny fish he'd caught.

His expression is less proud than pensive, as if he's contemplating the fate of the fish, a creature that took the bait without knowing what it was getting into.

Out on the ship channel, the Armco plant had become the site of one of the young Environmental Protection Agency's first high-stakes showdowns with big-time corporate polluters. The plant, a federal judge ruled, had over several decades dumped more than half a ton of cyanide and other toxic chemicals into the channel, with a chaser of as much as six tons of ammonia every day. The result was numerous fish kills; the shellfish beds in Galveston Bay were as lifeless as boneyards. The company faced shutting down its furnaces in Houston—the source of the Chain family's daily bread—to comply with a cleanup order. The boys at the plant, David included, thought that was pretty damned ironic: Armco had been a big contributor to Nixon's campaign and now his EPA had the stones to go after them? A *Washington Star* exposé on the company's curry favoring, however, embarrassed the administration and forced a squeaky-clean settlement. David was soon painfully cognizant that the government had the power to mess with a man's job, which it did by shutting down the plant. David Chain and the rest of the workforce were laid off.

Any fool could find some kind of job in those days, and David got work as a mechanic, contracting with garage owners to split his hourly take. The money and the benefits weren't like they had been at the plant, and the family's pinched finances exacerbated existing strains in the marriage. David started spending more time in bars. Cindy—who'd been aching to begin her adult life fifteen years earlier, before she could even vote—got a job and a single-mom-with-kids apartment in Pasadena. The marriage had succumbed to the long odds against it.

BEFORE THE INVASION OF MARAUDING Caucasians with no concept or history of living in harmony with their environment, wildlands such as redwood forests were single, static beings that did not suffer human alteration. That, at least, is the romantic and enduring myth, perhaps induced in part by the undeniable "spell of wonder and respect" of which Steinbeck wrote. In fact, aboriginal peoples are now believed to have radically changed the landscape to suit their needs. Stands of old-growth trees didn't provide habitat for many large mammals, and Indians consistently burned woods to gain cropland. Some contemporary academics even go so far as to suggest that white settlers, as they wiped out the native population through smallpox and slaughter, actually hastened reforestation of lands that natives had once used for agricultural purposes.

But a handful of spots in far coastal northern California still contains vestiges of forest that look, in some sidelong approximation, as they must have before recorded history, before the arrival of bipeds with a knack for making tools and trouble. Most of it has been developed as parkland.

Native tribes hugged the coast, as did the redwood forest. Using heated stones, elk horns, and not a single metal implement, the Yurok and Tolowa made dugout canoes and sweat lodges out of redwood. Natives netted or harpooned salmon and smoked it over alder, and made wicker baskets woven tightly enough to hold water. Spanish eyes first reconnoitered the area in 1542 and Russian fur traders had passed through, but it would be almost three hundred years before nonnatives had anything but a token presence in the area. With ample game, tribes were able to establish permanent settlements, and intertribe disputes were rare. Aside from the occasional Spanish missionary, the natives' existence was unmolested by encroaching white settlers.

That peaceful existence would come to a brutal end in a procession of events that repeated itself wherever white settlers encountered natives: at first, both sides were eager to trade and coexist, but eventually the settlers' demands exhausted the Indians' patience. Inland, away from the coast, the catalyst for the bloodshed was gold. In the first month of 1848—the same year the United States ended its war with Mexico, claiming California and other Mexican territories—James Marshall found a few gold nuggets in the American River not far from Sacramento. In a flash, half a million fortune hunters were stricken with gold fever. Among them was Pierson B. Reading, a rancher in the upper Sacramento valley who in May 1849 discovered gold on the banks of the Trinity River. Josiah Gregg established an overland route from the Trinity deposits to the coast. And in 1850, the first American ship came into the harbor closest to the mines, a place that settlers would name Humboldt Bay, near the site of a town they would call Eureka. As the inevitable conflicts with Indians broke out, frantic settlers appealed to the government for help, claiming the native peoples had a curious aversion to being massacred. In January of 1853, the government dispatched a company of army soldiers, who established Fort Humboldt on a high bluff, its rectangular clearing bordering a virtual wall of trees.

The isolation, coupled with the weather—ceaseless winter rains and oppressive summer fog—could annihilate the spirits of homesick exiles. At Fort Humboldt in the winter of 1853–54, one disconsolate soldier's letters home were torrents of lamentations on the cruel fate that had driven him to the country's most remote garrison, into an abyss well past the edge of civilization. According to Leigh H. Irvine's 1915 *History of Humboldt County*, "It was during this period that he sought consolation in the flowing bowl and seemed happy only when under the exhilaration of a few drinks." By some accounts, the fort's commanding officer demanded the soldier resign from the army or stand trial for drunkenness. The soldier resigned. His name was Ulysses S. Grant.

Meanwhile, as the gold rush dried up, a few of the more resourceful forty-niners looked to the fog belt along the coast and saw in those breathtaking woods what they hadn't seen in the streams inland and to the south: a new industry with the potential for sustained revenue, turning trees into dollars. The redwoods stretched in a band more than a hundred miles long and as much as twenty miles wide, 500,000 acres of largely untouched forest in country ranging from flat bottomlands to vertiginous mountainsides. But the settlers had packed along with them Eastern perceptions of what merchantable timber was—pine and spruce—and they didn't know what to do with the unwieldy redwoods, a few of which could have been saplings when Christ was born. Logging in Humboldt began in 1850, but it was a few years before anybody had fabricated the hardware and undertook the staggering effort to bring the big daddies down. Mills rose along the waterfront, enormous mills built to handle the thickest logs in the world. Before long, Eureka was, indeed, in the throes of a boomlet. The waterfront became clustered with saloons and whorehouses; the effluvia of whiskey and horse dung hung in the bay air. Shipbuilding, whaling, and fishing operations came and went, but spinning trees into "red gold" would be the area's dominant enterprise.

To the south, San Francisco was bursting with newcomers, and lumber, shingles, and other building materials were scarce. Redwood was well suited for such uses for the same reasons it had survived in the wild for so long: it was strong, lightweight, and resistant to fire and insect infestation. A local businessman named Harry Mason went to work cutting the big redwoods in the East Bay. In 1852, Mason built a massive mill in Mendocino County, and the following year a staggering 20 million board feet of timber were shipped out of Humboldt Bay to the north. The efficiency of Mason's enterprise changed the landscape forever. A decade after he started cutting in the East Bay, there was nothing left, not a single mature tree.

It was an age wedded to the notion that the wild world could be subjugated to serve the needs of man and in which the resources seemed as limitless as the work was backbreaking—if the East Bay didn't have redwoods anymore, there were plenty up in Mendocino, and if not in Mendocino, then on up to Humboldt. Because a redwood trunk could be twice as wide at its base as it was just ten or so feet up, fallers would take an ax to bite out a chunk of the tree and jam in a plank called a springboard. Sometimes several springboards made portable scaffolding on which the fallers perched while they worked. It could take days to bring the biggest ones down, and sometimes all that was left was three hundred tons of kindling. On luckier days, the crews maneuvered intact fallen trees around stumps and hitched them to oxen teams, which dragged logs down skid roads—trails made of fallen timber, slicked up with grease or water—to the nearest stream or waterway, and from there on down to the mill. Later, "steam donkeys" did the work of the oxen, and railways penetrated deep into the dark woods to haul out trees from locales too remote for water transport. The amount of infrastructure the companies were willing to install on their lands—bridges, trails, railroads—testified to the profitability of the enterprise. In photographs the working woodsmen are hard-eyed and extravagantly mustachioed, exuding a redwood-sized pride.

THE BEGINNINGS OF WHAT WOULD become a robust quarter-million-acre timber empire came in 1863, when two Mendocino County timber company bosses, A. W. McPherson and Henry Wetherbee, looked north and decided to get in on the action in Humboldt. They bought six thousand acres at $1.25 each on the banks of the Eel. Six years later, after buying an additional four thousand acres, the Pacific Lumber Company incorporated, with headquarters in San Francisco. In 1884, the company began construction of Mill A in a town the company first called Forestville, along a fishhook in the Eel. There was, however, another town to the south called Forestville. At the suggestion of the lumberjacks, many of whom came from easternmost Canada, the town was renamed Scotia. By 1888, the company was the biggest logging concern in the county, with three hundred men on the payroll, growing to five hundred just two years later. The company built its own power plant and houses for workers.

The "cut 'em all" ethic prevailed, but Pacific Lumber received the rise of the conservation movement more warmly than did many of its corporate contemporaries. In the early 1920s, the company established a seedling nursery to reforest lands cut so bare they looked like a head shaved with a dull razor. But even in those days the company on occasion found itself at odds with local conservationists. In 1924, Laura Mahan, the wife of a prominent Eureka attorney, learned that a rail spur was being built to log part of the forest. Mahan physically put herself in the path of the workers, the story goes, while her husband got an injunction to stop the work and the logging that would follow. A few years later, the Save-the-Redwoods League, thanks largely to a gift from John D. Rockefeller, got the money to buy the disputed land, which was named the Rockefeller Forest. In all, Pacific Lumber donated or sold below market value almost twenty thousand acres—today that figure stands at more than twenty-seven thousand acres—of old-growth redwood to form five parks in the area, including the Avenue of the Giants, a narrow strip of monstrous redwoods that today stands as a symbol of what the area looked like before men went into the woods with their beasts of burden and crosscut saws—"misery whips," they called them.

In the early days, the standard timberman's uniform started with a union suit, preferably black to avoid frivolous laundering. To wash an item of clothing before it was too stiff to bend was to invite speculation about one's manhood. The men worked hard, ate plain food in volume in the cookhouse, and collapsed into their racks in the bunkhouse. Because food was fuel, they were fed well and amply: sides of beef and bacon, sacks of beans and potatoes, coffee and tea that never ran out. On weekends there was female company for hire and other manly entertainment to be had across the Eel in Rio Dell.

As hard and potentially lethal as working in the woods and the mills could be, paternalistic, conservative Pacific Lumber was close to a timberman's paradise—if indeed such a place could exist. Men there worked consistently in a business already notorious for booming and busting with alarming regularity. The company kept labor organizers at bay by offering better pay and benefits than existing union shops. It built churches and a movie house and a sewage plant, put a bank where a saloon had once been, raised its own cattle, and threw a big picnic for the workforce every Labor Day. It offered free life insurance, a pension plan, and Christmas bonuses, and gave away millions in scholarships for workers' kids. Scotia was the town, the company, the life, the law. A self-contained, self-sufficient operation. If you were casting about for a place that would become the Birmingham of the environmental movement, the setting for a chronic internecine battle, the placid little hamlet of Scotia, California, would be a laughable choice.

Aside from unpredictable calamities such as fire, flood, and earthquake, from which the company recovered and rebuilt—bigger without fail, and with state-of-the-art technology—change came slowly to Scotia and Humboldt County, about as slowly as those offshore tectonic plates shifted. The Murphy family had a nearly unbroken dynasty running the company, and by most accounts they ran it well. Pacific Lumber bought its competitors, went on acreage-buying binges, became the largest private employer in the county. It was the engine of the local economy. The saw jockeys hacked their way deeper into the woods and felled more trees, including, over the decades, millions the company itself had planted. Damn redwoods, they grew like weeds, especially in a clear-cut where young saplings had plenty of room to grow even faster because they didn't have to compete with mature trees for sunlight. The crews felled and bucked and yarded the trees, loaded them onto trucks and sent them off. At the end of the day on autumn afternoons during hunting season, the men would drink beer and plink off their deer rifles as they rode back to camp.

The town's history was long in years but short on notable events, in part because of its and the county's isolation, even after U.S. 101 to San Francisco and the little airstrip in McKinleyville made the world outside Humboldt more accessible. Since the early days, when the seasons determined whether the overland route to the area was passable, folks joked—half joked, anyway—about living behind a redwood curtain.

In 1985, a Houston man parted the curtain and discovered Scotia and Pacific Lumber, a somnambulant, undervalued operation that time had forgotten, a property just begging to get snatched by some savvy takeover artist. What days those were. A new generation found itself revving the throttle of the new economy, having survived the corrupt ideology and unfortunate fashions of the 1960s followed by Nixon's immolation and the self-flagellating "malaise" of the Carter years. Then Reagan dropped the green flag, and it was go-go days. Become a master of the universe. Put on a red tie. Make money. Spend $300 on dinner and . . . Is that a platinum card?

The man who parted the curtain was the son of a small-town purveyor of men's furnishings, which perhaps is why he always wore a fine dark suit and why his hair was so perfect it looked as if it had been styled and then baked in a kiln. The man's name was Charles Hurwitz, and he was a player in this new economy.

By that time, less than 4 percent of the old-growth forest was left. The last stands were like precious emeralds being chipped ever smaller.

CHARLES HURWITZ—WHO EVENTUALLY WOULD be the subject of a Web site devoted to the pursuit of imprisoning him for alleged trespasses against humanity and the environment, complete with a $50,000 bounty—was born in 1940 in Kilgore, in the piney woods of East Texas. Ten years earlier, wells had begun gushing oil in the area, which was by the time of Hurwitz's birth flooded with speculators, profiteers, and new money. Hurwitz's parents, Hyman and Eva, were a prominent local couple. Hyman—who had a pair of haberdasheries and built Kilgore's first shopping center—inculcated in young Charles a love of work and forged the boy's destiny as a man of commerce, finance, and striving. Charles was your stereotypical young man in a hurry, and it didn't take long for him to figure out you could get rich using other people's money. After college and then the service, he spent barely a year employed as a stockbroker at Bache and Company in San Antonio, where he used to draw crowds when he worked the phones. He was piloting a hedge fund worth more than $50 million before he was thirty. Turning up in the society columns of the Houston papers was more his wife, Barbara's, deal; Hurwitz was about business and not much else. A *Texas Monthly* article called him "aggressively colorless." Another magazine said he was in possession of a "reptilian calm." While hardly terms of endearment, both qualities helped Hurwitz do what he did best: make big, bold deals without fear. Even in the heyday of junk bond finance, it took balls to move around in Hurwitz's world. Junk bonds paid like crazy when they hit, and the proceeds were invariably used to finance company takeovers, but they were risky, too.

By 1981, Takeover Charlie was adroit at putting together deals of daunting complexity, big enough to have play with Michael Milken of Drexel Burnham Lambert. And in the year of Ronald Reagan's reelection, Drexel again ponied up junk bonds for the creation of Maxxam Group Inc., whose business, put very simply, would be to invest in or run other companies. In the go-go days before the bubble burst—before Milken and Ivan Boesky were handcuffed and packed off to prison for their misdeeds, before Drexel went down in flames, before the savings-and-loan bust left taxpayers holding the bag for billions—the captains of the new American finance were kings. And they gained and consolidated power by feasting on new companies. From this historical remove, it seems obvious that the masters of the universe spelled their own doom. But at the time? That disreputable, redheaded stepchild of finance, the junk bond, was, in Milken's genius hands, no less a powerful and ill-understood tool than atomic energy. The go-go days were going to last forever.

In the abstract, the sleepy little timber company on the fogbound coast of California was a peach of a target. Because of the company's history of relatively conservative cutting, its major asset—vast swaths of prime, uncut timberland—was comically undervalued. Drexel—that is, Milken—whispered to a few prospective buyers that the joint was practically asking for it, but there was, to anyone who more than blinked at the numbers, a hell of a catch: to pay off the bonds used for a successful takeover, the new owner would be forced to drastically ratchet up the cut rate and sacrifice an enormous number of trees to service the debt, thus reducing the company's value. Hurwitz sat in his utilitarian office in Houston and took a look at what Drexel was saying about Pacific Lumber. He didn't think it looked good. Then he looked again.

CHARLES HURWITZ WAS MAKING THE tectonic plates move now, putting together a campaign that would have him sitting on more merchantable redwood than anybody in the world. He was already in charge of some $400 million worth of enterprises, most prominently in oil and gas and real estate. In the summer of 1985, he went to see Milken, the Mr. Big of junk bonds, the man who arguably had more control over the American economic juggernaut than anyone else. Milken was Hurwitz's best hope for putting together a rapid-fire strike before Pacific Lumber had a chance to mount a credible defense. Milken had helped Hurwitz take over United Savings Association of Texas, the fattest savings and loan in the state, three years earlier. (United Savings would eventually crash and burn, costing taxpayers $1.6 billion.) It was time for them to do business again.

To say Hurwitz was inscrutable in his business dealings would be an understatement. The face of a cadaver would be easier to read. Nobody, not even insiders, knew what his next target would be until he'd already dropped it with a clean shot, gutted it, and field-dressed it. "Charles Hurwitz doesn't bark, he just bites," *Business Week* wrote. And the takeover of Pacific Lumber, which at the time had its corporate offices in San Francisco, was a textbook Hurwitz chomp: a campaign against a torpid, gloriously undervalued company. By the time the company noticed its stock price was going up, it was over.

And some stockholders were frankly delighted, particularly old-line board members who saw their paper worth shooting for the moon as some mysterious figure out in the wide world far from Scotia was buying up shares of Pacific Lumber stock. Then-CEO Gene Elam—an effete San Francisco accountant with no business running the show, according to some in Scotia—saw it happening, but he was distracted steering the company through a recession. Timber, it seemed, was an old-fashioned boat immune to being lifted by the rising tide of the new economy. By the end of September, Hurwitz had tipped his hand, offering—via a predawn phone call to Elam—to buy outstanding shares of PL stock for $36, more than $10 higher than the price at which the stock had been trading in June. In no time, Elam was on the phone to Salomon Brothers, which he'd retained in a consulting capacity only days before to help PL figure out just what the hell was going on. Salomon's mergers-and-acquisitions boys in New York were well aware of who Charles Hurwitz was, correctly guessed that Drexel Burnham Lambert was the muscle behind the move, and promised to start parachuting lawyers in to put together a desperate defense strategy to save the company as Elam and the Murphys knew it.

The fact was, the old Pacific Lumber Company faced a doom as inexorable as that of the dinosaurs or David Chain's Armco job, and nobody—not Gene Elam, not even Charles Hurwitz—knew the intricacies of the web being spun to snare the company. Ever since going public, the company had known nothing but a dull, steady burble of trading. By the end of the workweek following Hurwitz's tender offer, almost 2.8 million shares of PL—one tenth of the company—had changed hands on the New York exchange. Behind much of that activity was the other dark star of the 1980s bull market, Ivan Boesky.

In the days when greed was regarded as a virtue, Boesky's dubious forte was buying shares of companies in the crosshairs as takeover targets, sitting on them until the stock got white-hot, and then cashing out. Because securities law put a kibosh on Drexel buying Pacific Lumber shares, Milken and Boesky schemed to have Boesky buy shares for Milken. Quite illegal, quite lucrative. Every day, according to *The Last Stand*, a book by David Harris on the Pacific Lumber takeover and its aftermath, Boesky would call one of Milken's cronies and "settle up that day's accounts." Milken was fishing with two hooks on his line. As long as Boesky kept buying, money was coming in to Drexel. And if that activity was driving up the stock price above Hurwitz's offer, well, everybody knew $36 wasn't his *final* offer. It was a beautiful situation as long as Hurwitz didn't stroll downwind of it: Drexel was profiting from Boesky and his fellow arbitrageurs; Boesky was moving chunks of stock sufficiently large to keep other corporate carnivores at bay (which may have allowed Milken to rationalize the covert partnership); and if Hurwitz succeeded, Drexel would land a whopper of a stipend on the back end—$22 million.

And it looked like the Texan would succeed. The fact that Gene Elam even consented to a meeting with Hurwitz and his Drexel muscle—while they were ostensibly still playing the friendly-takeover game—belied a company shod in quaking boots. PL's panicked attempt to court a buyer less odious than Hurwitz had dried up with the last potential suitor not even bothering to make an offer. After the first round of talks derailed, Hurwitz was on the phone to Elam, kissing and making up with such ardor that his lips may have been chapped by the end of the call. Back in San Francisco for a rematch, Elam and Hurwitz faced off again, with the former's Salomon suits and the latter's Drexel suits functioning as the most handsomely compensated messenger boys in existence, shuttling back and forth down the hallways to deliver offers, counteroffers, counter-counteroffers. Hurwitz still wanted to deal. And Elam, although he strained not to tip his hand, knew he had to take what Hurwitz presented.

Behind the closed door of an office that felt like an old Indian sweat lodge, Gene Elam sold off the Pacific Lumber Company for $40 a share. In the end, 82 percent of shareholders approved the deal. Lawsuits, appeals to state agencies, and a lot of general wailing and gnashing of teeth were no match for the Hurwitz Express.

NOR WAS JOHN CAMPBELL, a man who liked to think of himself as the most cultured and erudite person in the room, as well as a good reader of a man's agenda, hidden or otherwise. Born in the Blue Mountains of New South Wales, Australia, Campbell learned two critical lessons early on. From his father, an Australian intelligence officer, he knew the value of being plugged into scuttlebutt. And when the Australian government built a dam to form a catchment area for the Sydney water district, flooding his family's ranch, he learned of government's almost limitless power to do whatever it wanted. True, the family moved to a beach community about twenty-five miles from Sydney, where John was able to get in a good bit of surfing, but the eviction was compulsory nonetheless.

It was only supposed to have been a one-year gig, but in 1969—Pacific Lumber's centennial year—John Campbell settled in Humboldt County. He'd come west from Chicago to matriculate in PL's sales training program. That's what he was going to be, a salesman back in Chicago. The program had trainees learning everything they could ever conceivably be asked about the manufacture of the forest products they were peddling. Campbell learned the familiar ache in his arms and shoulders after picking up and grading timber that hadn't been dried. He learned that if he didn't wear gloves, he'd go home at night with hands turned black from handling the wood and he'd have to scrub with lemons to get them clean. He learned the difference between heartwood and sapwood, worked in the kilns drying the lumber, then the factory where they finished the products, then in shipping to put up orders. He learned to load Northwestern Pacific Railroad boxcars with his company's wares. About the only thing he didn't do was work in the woods. At the end of the year, the company asked him if he'd like to stay on in Scotia and help out with the new mill that was opening to process second-growth redwood. There was plenty of opportunity for a man like him. And Campbell—a native of a country almost the same size as the United States, with plenty of wild, open spaces of its own—was drawn to the timber industry as a residual manifestation of the romantic Old West, a grand enterprise in the tradition of mining and the building of the railroads.

The flannel-shirt-and-steel-toed-boot brigade in and around town might not have warmly received anybody as exotic as an Aussie had Campbell not also been famously gregarious. Even as his star rose at Pacific Lumber and he began to have direct control over more and more employees, every PL worker, without exception, called him simply "John." John married a local girl whose family included PL execs. The Murphys opened their house to them for the reception. He would eventually trade up to a bigger house with a pool, but the commoner's touch was an invaluable and enduring quality of his. By the time Charles Hurwitz began circling the company, John was the top man in Scotia, a good company man and Murphy loyalist. The Murphys and Elam especially needed John now that they were distracted, getting ready to throw hundreds of thousands of dollars at their lawyers in a futile attempt to top Hurwitz's offer for the company.

WHEN CAMPBELL QUIETLY SLIPPED INTO the sack with Hurwitz, some of the old-line front-office boys felt the stiletto of betrayal. There might have been a critical mass of resistance to Hurwitz's move, and Campbell goes turncoat? The worst reaction to the takeover was taking place in pockets of bolshevik resistance down on the mill floor. There was a lawsuit that went nowhere fast, a full-page ad protesting the company-blessed takeover in the Sunday *Eureka Times-Standard*, a petition drive mounted when Campbell was down in San Francisco that yielded four hundred signatures. When Campbell got word the petition was being passed around, he caught a plane home to put a stop to that backward nonsense, but not before, as he would recall, the majority of Scotia's workforce had signed it. What a load of bullshit. Campbell had been chafing to get the company's cut rate more in line with contemporary industry standards rather than the antiquated models that had guided PL. Now the company was poised for serious moneymaking, and the old hands, congenitally, violently opposed to change of any stripe, were locking arms against it. The deal was bad for workers, shareholders, the local economy, the environment. Or so they said. Bullshit. The Woodworkers Union set up shop across the bridge in Rio Dell, plotting the only attempt to unionize the workforce since the late 1940s. Bullshit. The petition drive was nothing but a protest against change, and unionization was simply another change—a calamity. Hurwitz was hanged in effigy over the bridge and pelted with epithets, anti-Semitic and otherwise. Anti-Hurwitz and -Maxxam graffiti was scrawled in the shipping department for Hurwitz to see on his visit to town. Bullshit of the ugliest kind. Hurwitz wanted nothing more than to increase—yesterday—the cash flow of the concern he was acquiring. To do that, the timber neophyte needed Campbell, a man who moved comfortably both in Hurwitz's world and in Humboldt. And when Hurwitz told him he wanted to double production, Campbell patiently explained that there would be some logistical difficulties to be surmounted, but he knew it would soon mean busy days at the mills. Campbell was confident he'd done the right thing.

But they made him suffer for it. It was clear his relationship with the Murphys was collateral damage. He was shunned by his own employees. His wife separated from him and filed for divorce. And when Campbell, like Ulysses S. Grant, occasionally sought consolation in the flowing bowl in one of the area bars or at the Scotia Inn, he did it unbothered by company.

Campbell was, however, bothered by a new species of environmental activist, and damned if he could figure out why they were picking on Pacific Lumber, a famously conservative, avuncular outfit known for taking care of its people and being responsible stewards of the land. A company that had worked with the Save-the-Redwoods League since the 1920s to sell and donate pieces of its own land for public enjoyment, that had held off cutting some of its park-worthy old-growth groves until the money was available to purchase them and lobbied other logging concerns to do the same, that gave scholarships to every employee's kid who wanted to go to college.

Word was PL had more than doubled its cut rate, from 140 million board feet in 1985 to 330 million in 1988. The company said the numbers were more like 178 million before and 298 after. Haggling over the proper figures was just part of the drama. But it was a fact that guys in the mills were sopping up all the overtime they could. The ostensible reason for the cranked-up production was that an inventory had showed the company had a lot more timber than previously thought. Hurwitz, for one, was plenty pleased to learn he'd paid $800 million for an outfit worth just south of $2 billion. But those inclined to darker ruminations were convinced that the man—known around Scotia variously as Uncle Charlie or "that sonofabitch"—was sweating to pay off the debt he'd incurred when he swooped in from Houston and nabbed the company. A single redwood, brought to ground expertly by a seasoned saw jock, could yield as much as $30,000 worth of milled timber, and Takeover Charlie needed that money back in Texas. Some people in Humboldt never met a conspiracy they didn't like.

Surely the heat would die down on its own, and the reek accompanying the way new money was made would dissipate with the coastal winds. Besides, Campbell and others at the company had always been more than happy to sit down and chat over Danishes and coffee with the folks from any environmental group that wanted a hearing. Such a request was not an unreasonable demand, and John Campbell was not an unreasonable man. Groups like the Environmental Protection Information Center (EPIC) might have been staffed by hairy misfits, but they'd been around since the mid-1970s and worked more or less inside the boundaries where civilized people settled their differences. They respected the fact that this was a nation of laws.

But this new species? To Campbell, they were something else. It seemed like they didn't want to work with timber companies at all, but against them—to the point of hounding them out of business. Opposition was their default mode. It had become a freak show—carpetbagging interlopers were rolling in, walking naked in the woods, stringing banners across U.S. 101, getting air time on the *Today* show, blockading active timber harvest sites, *living in trees*, for God's sake. Campbell was baffled by their tactics, their motives, and their aims, so in January of 1987, he took a meeting with one of the young activists loosely organized under the aggressively emphatic moniker Earth First! His name was Greg King, and at first he claimed to be a journalist, which, when Campbell was feeling charitable and expansive, amused him just a little. King may have been a reporter for a Sonoma County alternative paper, but he plainly wouldn't know objectivity if it had bitten him on the ass. And by the time of their meeting, King had quit his job to agitate full-time.

Of course Campbell was as much in favor of free speech as the next man, but these activists had cost his people thousands of hours of lost work, and the company—already under considerable pressure to pump more cash back to Houston—was hurting. Campbell looked at King and asked him if he realized that if the young man kept at it, Campbell was going to be forced to let folks go.

"If I have to lay off people," he asked, "will you accompany me when I go down to the plant to select the people to lay off?"

"You don't understand," King said. "In issues of this magnitude, there has to be some suffering."

So this was it, Campbell thought. A siege. No compromise. And certainly no reasoning with these people. The executive looked as if the activist had just pissed on his pant leg.

"Thank you, Mr. King," Campbell said. "This interview is over."

King would prove to be prescient.

There would be plenty of suffering to go around.

THREE

Dave and
Ed and Judi
and Darryl

"THE FIRST NIGHT WAS CLEAR, AND we lay down in the darkening aisles of the great Sequoia grove. The majestic trunks, beautiful in color and in symmetry, rose round us like the pillars of a mightier cathedral than ever was conceived even by the fervor of the Middle Ages." So wrote President Theodore Roosevelt after accompanying the iconic preservationist and Sierra Club founder John Muir on a trip to Yosemite National Park in May of 1903.

In 1869, five years after the Yosemite Valley had been set aside as a park, John Muir began spending part of each year there. Grazing had already altered the meadows below the sheer cliffs from the way the land had looked since the retreat of the most recent glaciers, but Yosemite—the setting for Ansel Adams's transcendental photographs in later decades—was among the first wild places deemed worthy of rescuing from further exploitation because of its recreational and spiritual value to humans, and as such it's as good a place as any to mark the birthplace of the American conservation movement.

The movement's motives were noble and its means respectable, its captains exemplary models of all that was proper in the society of the day. They ran businesses, held elected and appointed offices, posed for portraits in their Sunday finery before the woods they were protecting for posterity. The Save-the-Redwoods League began in 1918, using established, sensible capitalist transactions as a means to an end: it paid cash money for forest land and kept redwoods away from the mills, and it was not the norm for its officers' wives to put their bodies between loggers and trees, as Laura Mahan had. Roosevelt endorsed the conservation ethic, saying, "I feel most emphatically that we should not turn a tree which was old when the first Egyptian conqueror penetrated to the valley of the Euphrates . . . into shingles." Conservationists *conserved* and were themselves conservative, prudent citizens. So it was for many decades, until the baby boomers grew up and rebelled against their parents as no American generation had before.

Conveniently enough, there was plenty against which to rebel. The American Century saw rivers dammed and redirected to control flooding and make power, to conjure citrus orchards out of hard-baked desert. Ore was extracted from under the ground; mountaintops were blasted off to take the coal within; high-voltage lines buzzed with the juice that connected one Western outpost to the other. Eventually those outposts began to stitch themselves together, in places forming seamless, endless extended suburbs, miles of self-replicating ranch houses, monuments to sprawl that stretched past the horizon. The populace was ravenous and rapidly expanding. Then Rachel Carson smacked it upside the head in 1962 with *Silent Spring,* which depicted a land stewing in man-made toxins. "The 'control of nature' is a phrase conceived in arrogance, born of the Neanderthal age of biology and philosophy, when it was supposed that nature exists for the convenience of man," Carson wrote. The book led to a wave of environmental legislation, including a ban of the pesticide DDT and increased governmental regulation. That very same wave washed away David Chain's job at the Armco plant. (Pasadena, Texas, could have been exhibit A for Carson's warnings.) The antiwar movement helped mobilize enviros, too. The nature lovers and the peaceniks realized they had a common enemy: America the Bully, whether the party on the receiving end of the aggression was a powerless nation or a plundered planet.

The enemy kept busy. In 1966, the Sierra Club mounted a newspaper ad campaign to shoot down a proposal to flood the Grand Canyon. The copy read, "This time it's the Grand Canyon they want to flood. *The Grand Canyon.*" In the summer of 1969, the Cuyahoga River in Cleveland caught fire, shooting columns of flames five stories into the air and making the city the butt of jokes across the country. What's not so well remembered is that the fire was the third time the river had burned since 1936. The first Earth Day came the following spring, in 1970. Trees were planted, speeches made, backs slapped. A troika of significant federal legislation followed in the early 1970s—the Clean Air Act, the Water Pollution Control Act, and the Endangered Species Act. Establishment environmentalists, those who posed for pictures with congressmen and presidents at bill signings, now had a few more tools in their kits. But really, not much changed. Not until 1980, when a burned-out environmental lobbyist stomped into the desert and emerged a warrior.

The Earth First! creation myth usually unspools as follows: Dave Foreman, an air force brat who had a brief, unhappy brush with the Marine Corps, worked for the environmental lobby in Washington. The job left him profoundly disillusioned, brooding over the Earth's fate, convinced of a looming eco-apocalypse if environmentalists limited themselves to rubber-chicken fund-raiser dinners and polite, misguided compromises. To work within the conventions of society was to hasten the extinction of life on the planet. So at the dawn of the Reagan revolution, Dave Foreman and a knot of radicals in the making went into the Pinacate Desert in Mexico and came out with a cause.

They drew partial inspiration and assistance from author Edward Abbey. Abbey was a drinker, a serial philanderer, an all-purpose hellraiser, and a man who wrote about the desert and wild places with a ferocious passion that was infectious, rude, and elegant. (Before he died in 1989 in Oracle, Arizona, Abbey left instructions—very funny instructions, actually—that his burial be accompanied by gunfire.) Foreman got the idea for the locale of the desert pilgrimage from a book of Abbey's and adopted the tactics used by characters in Abbey's credulity-straining comic novel *The Monkey-Wrench Gang*, in which a band of merry pranksters runs around plotting sabotage of industrial society.

The creation myth somewhat resembles the truth, but it would be a mistake to assume that Abbey was the wild-eyed wizard who dreamed up ecotage or monkey-wrenching. In fact, in comparatively mild forms—such as knocking down or torching unsightly highway billboards or dumping sand into the fuel tanks (or dried beans into the radiators) of heavy equipment—it had been going on for years. Dissenting timber workers spiked trees during labor wars early in the 1900s. But it was Abbey—and Foreman, and the other cofounders of the movement—who saw the shock potential of the tactic, a tool for when avenues within the law had been exhausted, a last line of defense. As Abbey wrote, "At some point we must draw a line across the ground of our home and our being, drive a spear into the land, and say to the bulldozers, earthmovers, governments and corporations, 'Thus far and no farther.'"

Our democracy was representative in name only, its agencies wholly owned subsidiaries of the venal industries it had been their mandate to monitor and rein in. The public trust had been violated. The *planet* had been violated. Foreman's new life was an utter renunciation of his old existence working for the Wilderness Society. From now on there would be "No compromise in defense of Mother Earth," not for these guys. They could do the work that was their duty, their ethical calling, and have one hellacious good time doing it. They'd engage in everything from theatrical, high-minded pranks to bold acts of ecotage that gave them a jolt of adrenaline and a shot of pure purpose. They'd grow their beards, get drunk, piss in the campfire, howl at the moon, and, while they were at it, give mighty progress a swift and long-overdue ass-kicking.

In a slight irony, it was John Muir—Roosevelt's camping buddy and Sierra Club founder—who helped plant the seeds that would, generations later, be nourished by the sacrificial blood of revolutionaries. Muir didn't invent the idea, but he helped popularize it: all of life is interconnected. "When we try to pick out anything by itself, we find it hitched to everything in the universe." The idea was central to Muir's thinking and to the inchoate field of ecology. It also implied that the well-intentioned work of groups like the Save-the-Redwoods League was blind folly. "Saving" the occasional, isolated scrap of land was impossible. Living systems, forests in this instance, can't exist as an archipelago amid the clear-cuts and sprawl and outlet malls. Let's say a piece of forest is set aside, not even to develop it as a park, just to leave it as it is. That scrap of land is not saved if the erosion from a logging operation upstream turns the river that connects both pieces of land from Tiffany-crystal clear to chocolate-milk muddy. It is not saved if its acreage is insufficient to provide habitat for roosting birds in numbers adequate to ensure that the birds will reproduce. After three and a half billion years of evolution, one might assume the web of life would be of a considerably dense weave. But when Muir was touting his ideas, the training wheels had barely come off Darwinian theory.

The pure essence of the new radicals' ethos couldn't have been simpler: in every decision—from where to have lunch to whether to have children—the Earth had to be considered before any other factor.

That thinking wasn't likely to incite many riots; Aldo Leopold, regarded as the twentieth century's most influential wilderness advocate, had said as much before: "A thing is right when it tends to preserve the integrity, stability and beauty of the biotic community. It is wrong when it tends otherwise." It was the next ingredient to be folded into the mix that gave the nascent movement its potency and legitimized its embrace of outlaw tactics if other means failed to halt the environmental slaughter.

That was the notion of biocentrism or "deep ecology". The Norwegian philosopher Arnie Naess coined the term in 1972. The interrelatedness of existence of which Muir spoke was a cornerstone of this thinking, but Naess went further in saying that the human species needed to completely overhaul the way it lived, to exist in harmony with nature rather than attempt to subjugate it. Deep ecology categorically rejected anthropocentrism, or human-centeredness, as wrongheaded and ultimately ruinous to all life. The world did not exist for humans to enjoy, exploit, or harness. To believe otherwise, to embrace the notion of human superiority, was to be a species-ist. Coal doesn't exist for you to mine. Rivers don't exist for you to dam. Trees don't exist for you to pose for your vacation pictures in front of or mill into two-by-fours. Deer don't exist for you to shoot when you've got a hankering for venison chili. Rock columns don't exist for Ansel Adams to photograph. It doesn't matter if the entities are sentient or not—they exist, period. And a human being has no more intrinsic value—possibly less—than any other manifestation of life in the physical world, including everything from a cute baby seal to toadstools to viruses. All natural systems are created equal, possessed of inalienable rights. There was one crucial difference: the moss growing on the side of a tree could defend neither itself nor an ideal; a human being could. Humans and the world in which they lived would be better off if shuttled back to the Pleistocene era. Barring that, wild places that had thus far been spared the heavy hand that resulted from the dominant anthropocentric thinking deserved to remain so. It was time for a return to a preindustrial, more tribal way of life. And by the way, the extinction of the human species itself might not be so bad in the grand scheme of things.

This wasn't college-kid anarchy. This was a blueprint for an entirely new world, and it had been laid out at the eleventh hour before a few members of the final human generation in which the apocalypse could still be averted.

Every debutante needs her ball, and the little band of eco-warriors decided to bring one of Abbey's *Monkey-Wrench Gang* scenarios to life and stage a coming-out at Glen Canyon Dam in Arizona, a symbol of all that had been lost and a subject about which Abbey also wrote in his best-loved work, *Desert Solitaire*. The dam sits along the border between Arizona and Utah and, Foreman would later write, drowned "the most awesome and magical canyon on Earth. More than any single entity, Glen Canyon Dam is the symbol of the destruction of wilderness, of the technological ravishment of the West." So they cooked up a plan that would get them noticed, get them in the papers, announce their arrival, and inspire others by example. On March 21, 1981, they unfurled an unwieldy, 300-foot-long stretch of black plastic down the side, creating a "crack" in the construction. Abbey rose and condemned the leaders of the day who had erected a monument to "their crackpot ideology of growth, profit and power—growth for the sake of power, power for the sake of growth." The park service fuzz showed up to shoo them away, and the prank did indeed make headlines. Foreman would later express surprise at how many.

The movement was still young, but it exhibited a more traditional organization than it would eventually claim to have. In later days, it would profess to be decentralized and unhierarchical by design. But at the time, the movement was collecting members—pushing into four digits after the Glen Canyon stunt—and began to publish a newsletter in which Foreman would write, "It's time to be passionate. It's time to be tough. It's time to have the courage of the civil rights workers who went to jail."

The movement also had a name that stated its philosophical aim as declaratively as if it had spray-painted "No compromise in defense of Mother Earth" on the face of the dam that existed to keep refrigerators in Tempe and Mesa and Scottsdale humming. It was Earth First!—the exclamation point the emphatic drawing of the line, of saying: This far and no farther. Earth *first*, dammit.

Those were good days for Earth First! Foreman was charismatic, articulate, indignant, and bluntly funny. Despite EF!'s putative status as a mass, leaderless uprising, Foreman found himself unable to resist the role thrust upon him as the poster boy for the leading edge of a new (albeit plenty scruffy) groundswell of radical environmental chic. He was plainly an intellectual, despite his exploiting every opportunity to shore up his redneck creed. Even when he was a lobbyist, he wore his manure-encrusted cowboy boots as a badge of honor. As a speaker, he changed lives. But Foreman was no field marshal. He put his body on the line. As Susan Zakin wrote in *Coyotes and Town Dogs,* her definitive account of the early days of Earth First!, Foreman was dragged by a truck while protesting a logging site in Oregon. "You dirty communist bastard!" the driver shouted. "Why don't you go back to Russia?"

"But, Les," Foreman said in Zakin's account, "I'm a registered Republican."

"It was," Zakin wryly wrote, "the only documented case of one-upmanship by an environmentalist lying on his back in the mud, a fat rubber tire inches from his face."

Earth First!ers looked to history for justification and found it. What was the Boston Tea Party if not monkey-wrenching, Foreman asked. As far as breaking the law, Gandhi and Martin Luther King Jr. pointed the way: the people were under no obligation to observe a law that advanced the agenda of destruction.

The funny thing about movements is you can't always control

which way they move, and in later years Foreman would watch with creeping consternation as a mutated version of Earth First! rose along California's North Coast. It was fertile soil for such an occurrence, a place of incongruity and contradiction, which operated according to its own surreal, homegrown logic. In the late 1960s, a handful of disaffected hippies experienced a moment of clarity, saw the Haight dystopia for what it was, and started rolling up U.S. 101—the Redwood Highway—via thumb or VW bus, intent on giving more back to the Earth than they took. The place was a magnet for back-to-the-land types. They would atone for the trespasses of their forebears and be living proof that a better, more harmonious existence could be found. Then followed the latest crop of northern California entrepreneurs— dope farmers—drawn to the rugged country that already offered plenty of dense vegetative cover and abandoned logging roads. Especially in the southern part of Humboldt County, pot became almost an alternate currency, and the tiny, moribund town of Garberville saw its doom averted by a quite literal grassroots economic revitalization—Humboldt Gold, the lucrative new cash crop. Despite the local and federal governments throwing manpower at the dope scourge—the federal drug task force even parachuted in National Guard members in training exercises to attack operations in remote locales—Humboldt County became as known for its pot as Georgia was for its peaches. Meanwhile, to the north of Garberville, the number of boarded-up storefronts in the string of working-class logging towns along the highway reflected whether the timber industry was booming or busting. And just north of Eureka was Arcata, home of Humboldt State University; its sports team, the Lumberjacks; and more than its share of free thinkers. Humboldt County was a hippie ecotopia for some, a mere workplace for others. In retail districts, pawnshops full of chain saws blended with food co-ops that sold hummus and organic produce.

* * *

THEN HURWITZ TOOK OVER PACIFIC LUMBER and, with a mogul's hubris, found as much as four million heretofore uninventoried board feet of timber—all of it now capital assets on the chopping block. Takeover Charlie owned more fine redwood than anybody in the world. He was the overlord of an industry. And he'd paid less than half the amount at which the company was now valued.

When Earth First!ers began arriving in force in 1985, drawn by Pacific Lumber's sudden headlong embrace of rape-and-run logging, they didn't look like soldiers willing to put their bodies in front of the saw. They just looked like the latest bunch of freaks rolling in with their sleeping bags, redolent of patchouli. Some of the counterculture trailblazers who'd come before them had assimilated nicely into their communities and were disposed to offer aid and comfort should the need arise.

Meanwhile, Foreman—the antithesis of the stereotypical dippy tree huggers who would later rally around the Earth First! flag—was busy lobbing rhetorical Molotovs that more recent converts found misanthropic at best, borderline racist/sexist/you-name-it-ist at worst. He suggested, for instance, that children starving in Ethiopia shouldn't be saved; the Earth was simply seeking to reestablish its own balance. And to feed starving youth was to script an even greater famine in later years, when those children multiplied. Another activist wrote, with equally cold logic and even worse taste, that AIDS might accomplish the radical enviros' dream of reduced population. Such utterances were a slap in the face of the crowd that was later drawn to Earth First!

Also troubling, not to mention newsworthy, was Foreman's position on violence, or at least the threat of it. He wasn't, he said, constitutionally nonviolent. Although he had reservations about it, he couldn't bring himself to categorically denounce violence. "You corner anything, and it's going to fight," Zakin quoted him as saying.

The flashpoint for the debate over violence as a legitimate tool in ecotage was tree spiking. At its simplest, it involved hammering a long spike or nail into a tree. More elaborate tree spikers used electric drills, or a quieter brace and bit, and dropped ceramic—metal detector–proof—spikes into the hole, then glued bark back over the hole to completely conceal their handiwork. Activists typically mailed anonymous letters to "the proper authorities" advising them that trees had been spiked and that cutting in the area would be hazardous. A letter alone was sometimes enough to scuttle or at minimum delay a timber harvest. The long-term aim was to spike enough trees to serve as a deterrent to harvests by slowing the work and gumming up equipment until the labor was prohibitively expensive. Saw jocks who hit a spike with their chain saws would, if they were lucky, merely have to stop and sharpen or possibly replace their chains. But some monkey-wrenchers only spiked trees high above where the sawyer likely would make his cuts. That tactic spared the faller and aimed instead to take a bite out of the mill blade. When a blade hits a spike, the term "monkey-wrenching" is at its most literal. A wrecked blade can mean days of expensive repairs, idle work crews in the shop, and lost revenue for timber barons.

Spiking may be good defense for trees, but it's potentially lethal to humans, and as such it's a felony. The standard defense of spiking is that the target is corporations, not people, and that the spiker is ethically compelled to do everything possible to minimize the risk of injuring workers.

BUT EVEN A MINIMAL THREAT of injury was too much for Judi Bari, a classic red-diaper baby fated to help lead, for a time, Earth First! from a very different philosophical framework than Foreman's. The offspring of middle-class East Coast socialists, Bari went to the University of Maryland and got swept up in the complementary pursuits of protesting the Vietnam War and smoking pot. She became a Marxist, dropped out of school, and got a job at a Postal Service sorting center, aiming to become union shop steward and organize the workers, which she did. She married a fellow labor organizer, and the two moved to the opposite coast, to Santa Rosa, just down U.S. 101 from Humboldt County. When the marriage burned up, Bari got a job as a carpenter. She also sounded great speaking through a bullhorn. Jello Biafra, the lead singer for the renowned radical punk band the Dead Kennedys, wrote, "Judi may be the most powerful public speaker I have ever seen. Her in-your-face charisma and enthusiasm made the impossible possible, doable and crucial enough to do right now. Her razor-sharp sense of humor cut through icebergs of bullshit on any and all sides." Together with another newcomer and fellow fish out of water, Bari would conjure a new vision of Earth First! that would cause Foreman to loudly distance himself from the movement.

That other newcomer was Darryl Cherney. He was central casting's response to a call for a stock New Yorker, short of stature and rapid of speech. He first saw the redwoods when he was fourteen, on a cross-country vacation with his parents, his sister, and the family's two cats. Being a lifelong Manhattanite whose exposure to vegetation tended to be limited to salad bars, the giants made, as they had on generations of others, a life-altering impression. In 1985, when Cherney was twenty-six, he headed west on his own in his van, aiming to live simply somewhere, sing a few songs, and, if possible, save the world. As Cherney was driving down the Oregon coast in the dead of night, he pulled his van over to pick up a hitchhiker. The man was a Cheyenne named Kingfisher, a member of the Native American Church. Kingfisher asked his ride what he wanted out of life. When Cherney told him, Kingfisher said, "You should go to Garberville."

And Cherney did. He arrived in a town that was a latter-day Casablanca in terms of its shadow dope economy and enviro intrigue, and he walked into a roomful of ponytails in the EPIC office. He told them he wanted to live among the trees. They told him about clear-cuts. In that moment, he discovered both his mission and the staging ground for it. In March of 1986, Cherney hooked up with Greg King—the activist who would prophesy pain in his meeting with John Campbell. King, a descendant of the timber family for whom the nearby King Range was named, helped come up with a plan to protect a nearly 100,000-acre watershed. That vast stand included what would come to be known—to the world if not to Pacific Lumber, which still called it Salmon Creek—as the Headwaters Forest. It was a remote and virtually untouched expanse, the largest chunk of old-growth forest still privately held. The proposal indicated to Foreman that Earth First!ers on the North Coast were tuned to an entirely different frequency: he was pro–property rights, and now some of his allies were gunning for a private landholder.

Desperate times, desperate measures. There were plenty of bad guys along the coast doing bad things, but PL, a company killing its prime asset at terrifying speed, took the cake. The chances of Pacific Lumber rolling over and allowing the seizure of such a sizable chunk of its land to be developed into park land were nil. The odds were, in fact, no better than Cherney's becoming a congressman, but that didn't keep him from mounting a cheeky campaign to get himself sent to Washington anyway. Or maybe it was more about getting Cherney a little attention. The media, Cherney knew, love a good quixotic struggle. As did he.

Judi Bari first met Darryl Cherney during that self-promoting exercise, and Cherney's audacity amused Bari to no end. Judi and Darryl, kindred spirits, were soon an item. Both were Easterners, quick and funny and committed to the cause. But Bari had serious reservations about Earth First! As a class warrior, tree spiking appalled her—the guys on the receiving end of a spike's destructive force were precisely the people the activists should be building bridges to, she believed, not imperiling. And too many of the Earth First!ers seemed little more than blustery macho shitheads who hadn't thought things through. But she was drawn to the subversive humor of the enterprise, the sense of uproarious guerrilla theater. Moreover, the Earth First! threat to the phallocentric capitalist paradigm was credible enough that EF! had been the object of FBI scrutiny almost since its inception. Up and down the coast—across the country, in fact—little EF!-inspired episodes of monkey-wrenching were breaking out. But the big story was along the North Coast, where colorful agitators and covert operators were getting things done. Logging equipment was sabotaged and vandalized; workers were denied access to their job sites. And it wasn't just big companies like Louisiana-Pacific or Pacific Lumber, either—little mom-and-pop contract logging operations had been wrenched, too. Not that any of it could be pinned on Earth First!, the organic, leaderless movement. But none of that unaccountability by design mattered when a sawmill blade did a Rottweiler on a guy's face.

His name was George Alexander. He was twenty-three and worked at the Louisiana-Pacific mill in Cloverdale, south of Humboldt in Mendocino County. He was at work a little before 8:00 A.M. on May 8, 1987, tuning into the screech of the blade, his ever-present companion, and wearing a face shield attached to his hard hat. The head rig saw blade hit a nail. A knife-sharp and suddenly airborne piece of steel more than twice as tall as Alexander became a missile, shattered his face shield, severed his jugular, mashed his jaw, made stalactites and stalagmites of his teeth and meat of his face.

Although it's unlikely that EF! had anything to do with George Alexander's near beheading, the damage was done. The media became intensely critical: tree spiking was a political act carried out by fanatics, and the maiming of an honest workingman was nothing less than an assassination attempt. Judi Bari and others would later say that it was a sheer fluke that the accident happened—the tree was so narrow in diameter, roughly that of a utility pole, that it was cut lengthwise, and the blade hit the nail dead-on. If it had been slicing perpendicular to the spike, the blade would have made a clean cut. The tree was second growth, not old growth, and it was spiked after it was felled. The

MO was all wrong for it to be pinned on Earth First! Still, George Alexander gained the distinction of being the only known casualty of tree spiking. That distinction didn't do him much good when the mill closed and he was laid off with the rest of the crew.

Jacking around with a person's livelihood is a great way to draw a ferocious response anywhere, especially in a place where the manly enterprise of timber felling is the fuel of the economy, and an organized backlash was rumbling into position in Humboldt County just as Bari was plunging into EF! Candy Boak, the wife of a logger, formed a group to track the radicals' activities, making it her mission to thwart Cherney and his ilk. Her reward was anonymous death threats. Pacific Lumber, weary of having to call the sheriff to round up trespassing protesters only to see them processed out of jail in a blink, filed the first hundred in what would be an ongoing series of so-called SLAPP (often described as Strategic Lawsuits Against Public Participation) suits against activists, claiming Earth First!ers and their fellow travelers had committed malicious trespass and attempted to oppress the company. Credible rumors surfaced that FBI spooks had infiltrated Earth First! John Campbell continued to regard the protesters as a force that was trying to drive his company out of business. There was never any question in Campbell's mind about whose actions were driven by "crackpot ideology." And in late 1988 Hurwitz signed off on the way things were going by making Campbell president and CEO of Pacific Lumber Company.

Cherney, a onetime child TV commercial actor and now without question the stone cheerfully residing in Campbell's shoe, was exploiting his myriad talents to their full potential. He was smart. He was funny. He wrote and sang pointedly satirical songs—"Spike a Tree for Jesus" was one of his chestnuts—that brought laughs and shored up morale. He gave a good sound bite and could think and strategize on the fly. But his paramount talent, aside from self-promotion, was the ability to dream up absurd activities that let the protesters congratulate themselves on their collective cleverness even as they kept the pot at a rolling boil. Around the same time as Campbell's ascendancy, Cherney staged a production he called Day of the Living Dead Hurwitzes, a march on Scotia, with coffins representing the region's economy and ecology, and with protesters sporting Takeover Charlie masks. They were received by PL workers and sympathizers, two of them for each of the pranksters.

The hippies were by no means the only ones to detect a stench lingering years after the PL takeover. And Hurwitz tended to do himself few favors, operating in commercial enterprises that seemed designed to attract contentious and costly litigation. After Reagan deregulated the thrift industry in the early 1980s, Maxxam had gone on a savings-and-loan buying binge. When the bust came, taxpayers were left holding the bag for United Savings Association of Texas. After the PL takeover, Hurwitz raided its pension fund to pay off a portion of his ballooning junk bond debt. A congressional investigation into Maxxam's purchase of Pacific Lumber concluded there was "significant evidence" of insider trading in the deal. The company was distracted by batting away lawsuits and fighting an unsuccessful shareholders' bid to buy the company back from Hurwitz. Lawsuits and omnipresent antagonism were now facts of life in Humboldt, no more likely to lift than the clinging fog.

But now the battle was not only heating up, it was spreading. Dozers, loaders, and other equipment were wrenched in Washington and Oregon. Nor was all harmonious within the movement itself. Increasingly, Foreman's muscle-bound ethos was only homeopathically present in what North Coast Earth First! was becoming. A hard-edged movement had become some kind of barefoot California alternative-lifestyle trip. Foreman spent portions of his 1991 book, *Confessions of an Eco-Warrior*, unloading on the "class struggle social justice leftists" who'd hijacked EF! (Bari, rather obviously the object of that characterization and a paragon of bolshevism, would review Foreman's work in a radical weekly and accuse the EF! cofounder of "middle-class bias," saying his heroes included "white-man land-rapers like George Washington, Thomas Jefferson and John Adams . . .") In essence, Foreman was already out of Earth First! and further distracted by feds circling him like vultures.

Then the feds made their move, and every Earth First!er realized that what they were up to was seen as more than just games. One morning in May of 1989, Foreman was awakened by FBI agents bursting into his Tucson home and busting him at gunpoint, which made Greg King's contention that EF! was lousy with moles seem less paranoid than prescient. Foreman was charged with felony conspiracy for plotting to wreck nuclear-plant power lines. Gerry Spence, the buckskin-clad Wyoming lawyer who'd gained a measure of fame and notoriety in the Karen Silkwood case, served as Foreman's counsel. Spence's defense held that the FBI had framed his guy. Midway through the trial, Foreman copped a deal to plead guilty to the felony charge, which would be withdrawn after five years of good behavior.

The feds were occupied on other fronts, too. They were looking into threats against Hurwitz in Houston. The local FBI office in Eureka held field training exercises in which it blew up cars with pipe bombs on Louisiana-Pacific property, then investigated. And at times, the violence was more than make-believe: at a protest of Louisiana-Pacific in Mendocino, a timber worker sucker-punched Greg King. The incident led PL's public relations man in Scotia, Dave Galitz, to issue a cheeky memo that said, "As soon as we find the home of the fine fellow who decked Greg King, he has a dinner invitation at the Galitz residence."

And that was just a dress rehearsal for the skirmish that came later in the summer of 1989, on August 16 when the hippies and a family logging operation mixed it up along the Humboldt-Mendocino border. Called at the request of back-to-landers—who objected to the loggers allegedly working outside their plans, cutting on Sundays and late at night, popping off guns, driving like hell, and generally being really crummy neighbors—the mess came to be known as the Whitehorn riot.

Fuses were getting clipped increasingly shorter, and it didn't take long for the hot talk to give way to force. During the melee, one member of the pro-timber faction emphasized his position by discharging a shotgun into the air. Days later, as Bari and Cherney—with Judi's kids in the backseat—were on their way to a demonstration in Fort Bragg, Bari's Subaru was rear-ended by a logging truck driven by a contract Louisiana-Pacific employee. All were shaken but unhurt and dismissed the incident as an accident. But later Bari and Cherney learned that the logger was among those they'd blockaded the day before.

Bari and Cherney thought attempted murder. The sheriff thought otherwise and took a pass on investigating.

The following spring Bari and Cherney committed the unthinkable: they called for a cease-fire. Granted, their call for beating spikes into plowshares was conditional, but it was one of many reasons why 1990 would come to be regarded as a watershed year in the movement.

The seedbed for the change of heart had been a public-interest law conference in Eugene, at which some twenty EF!ers met with a mill-worker. Judi, ever the labor organizer, had been trying without much success to help the Wobblies (Industrial Workers of the World) get a toehold on the North Coast, and she increasingly realized that, while Takeover Charlie deserved a monkey-wrenching of cosmic proportions, millhands doing already hazardous jobs for all of $7 an hour didn't. Furthermore, tree spiking had vaporized whatever novelty appeal EF! had in the eyes of the media after George Alexander got his face ripped off in Cloverdale. The practice turned forests into minefields—and active timber harvest sites were minefields to begin with. Moreover, in the eyes of families that relied on the timber industry, spiking was nothing short of murderous. The anti-EF! backlash was by now charged, sustained, and not at all limited to the North Coast. A Montana congressman had called EF!ers terrorists. Now everybody from talking heads to working stiffs was tossing around the same term matter-of-factly, as if debate on the question had long since been closed. So Judi wrote Foreman a letter, the branch office telling the home office that it was contemplating a truce. Foreman shot back an impassioned response, enumerating the reasons he opposed such a move.

Bari and Cherney did it anyway. The political math was obvious: by going on the record to say that North Coast Earth First!ers were "renouncing" spiking, they were distancing themselves from Foreman, the federally indicted eco-terrorist. Furthermore, the radicals could position themselves as concerned about workers' safety—far, far more concerned than the corporate fat cats who consulted their actuarial tables to divine how many gruesome workplace accidents were fiscally acceptable before the bottom line took a hit. No matter that the renunciation would be impossible to enforce, it would make waves. After letting other Earth First!ers know what was coming and the reasoning behind it, the offshoot group held a series of press conferences along the coast on April 11 in which they disavowed a tactic that to date they had neither condemned nor condoned. The press release read:

Through the coalitions we have been building with lumber workers we have learned that timber corporations care no more for the lives of their employees than they do for the life of the forest. Their routine maiming and killing of millworkers is coldly calculated into the cost of doing business, just as the destruction of whole ecosystems is coldly calculated into the cost of doing business, just as the destruction of whole ecosystems is considered a reasonable byproduct of lumber production. These companies would think nothing of sending a spiked tree through a mill, and relish the anti–Earth First! publicity that an injury would cause.

In other words: workers unite.

Less than two weeks later, PL boss John Campbell made a strike of his own in the ongoing battle to claim the moral high ground. On the day after Earth Day 1990, he stood to address a group of lunching Rotarians in Eureka and clear up some misperceptions. "We're all environmentalists," he told the group. "We're in total agreement with everything that went on yesterday"—meaning the lawful Earth Day observances.

Yes. But what he and Pacific Lumber Company were opposed to, he went on, were the methods used by certain desperate actors in fanatical furtherance of their misguided cause. And with that, John Campbell produced a shank of redwood impaled by eight inches of iron. Brandishing the evidence, he told the aghast Rotarians that the spiked tree, from the Bell Creek area of the company's lands—lawfully, privately held lands, lest we forget—had hit the head rig saw of Mill B in Scotia the week before. The spike caused heavy damage to the saw and shut down the mill for a considerable time. What's more, Campbell said, this was one of three spiked trees to have come through in recent weeks.

He let that sink in. So certain radical environmentalists had found it necessary to make a very big show of renouncing spiking. This is how they renounce spiking.

Sadly, Campbell was saying, this is the world in which we live. It is simply a matter of time before blood is on the mill floor.

There was, however, a broader strategy at work behind Campbell's performance for the Rotarians. The lefty lawyers down at EPIC had been awfully busy since the takeover, and not without some success. Plainly, EF! and the lawyers were in it together—Earth First! clowning around to keep the heat on while EPIC kept at the company with a kind of Chinese water torture of lawsuits every time Pacific Lumber filed a new timber harvest plan with the California Department of Forestry. It was a war of attrition fought over scraps of ground, and it was wearing both sides down. Well, those EPIC meddlers might be stoned most of the time, but they were shrewd, and damned if they hadn't gone to the workshop and produced a doomsday weapon when the timber industry wasn't looking. With Pacific Lumber filing plans to harvest sections of the Headwaters—the pristine holdout, the living, breathing shrine to the unbroken continuity of life, the lungs of the planet—EPIC and a coalition of bigger, not exactly radical groups such as the Sierra Club had somehow gotten a California ballot initiative qualified for the November 1990 election. It looked, to the timber industry, very much like a noose that it was being invited to cinch around its own neck.

Under the Forests Forever initiative, all clear-cutting would be banned, stricter regulations—including those addressing the maintenance of logging roads and the erosion that accompanies their construction and use—would be imposed, wildlife surveys would be a precondition of all timber harvest plans filed, and a staggering three-quarters of a billion dollars in bonds would be floated to buy old growth.

Beginning with Headwaters, the vast stand of groves south of Eureka.

For Campbell, battling the lawyerly money-wrenching was, in the words of EF!'s "renunciation" press release, just another factor "coldly calculated into the cost of doing business." This, however, was a threat on an unprecedented scale, and the timber barons had no choice but to form an alliance. The court of public opinion was a new theater in an expanding campaign, one that would in the new decade prove to be fertile ground from which dark theories of collusion would blossom. Part of the industry strategy, then, involved making sure that voters clearly saw Forests Forever for what it was: a cleaned-up idea borne of blind hysteria and naked malice toward an ordered society. Yes, your average Sierra Clubber might not smell as loamy as your average Earth First!er, but they're all watermelons, as Campbell was fond of saying. Watermelons. Green on the outside, red on the inside.

And how did Darryl Cherney spend that Earth Day, the day before

Campbell's Rotary Club speech? In a failed effort to drape an Earth First! banner from the Golden Gate Bridge. Cherney's job was to run media, make sure the reporters were on the story. Greg King took a cell phone, planning to conduct interviews atop the span during morning rush hour. Ironworkers grabbed him before things got rolling. Nearby, the California Highway Patrol grabbed Cherney, and the Oakland police seized Earth First! files from his car.

So by the time of the spiking renunciation, Judi and Darryl needed a little goodwill in the public-relations bank, because they were gearing up to stage the biggest show Humboldt County had ever seen. It would explicitly put the environmental movement on the same continuum of social progress as the civil rights movement of the 1960s, "turning Charles Hurwitz into George Wallace and John Campbell into Bull Connor and halting the devastation once and for all," as David Harris memorably put it in *The Last Stand*. It would be called Redwood Summer, patterned after the Mississippi Summer of 1964 in which waves of Northern demonstrators marched into the South to oppose, in numbers impossible to ignore, discrimination on the basis of race. A similar infusion of protesters, storm troopers in defense of the redwoods, could bust things open, get Forests Forever passed, and end the latter-day scourge—discrimination on the basis of species.

Bari and Cherney's nerves were cooked; each virtually needed a second mailbox to hold the overflow of death threats. (As did Hurwitz. During a speech at the University of Texas Business School, he was interrupted by shouting EF!ers who demanded his head. Hurwitz's son, a student at UT, was on hand.) Cherney embraced the charged atmosphere with dramatic fatalism wrapped up in a sound bite. In March he'd told Ed Bradley on *60 Minutes* that if afflicted with a terminal disease, "I would definitely do something like strap dynamite on myself and take out Glen Canyon Dam. Or maybe the Maxxam building in Los Angeles after it's closed up for the night." Cherney's on-air reverie about becoming an eco–suicide bomber was too much even for a lot of Earth First!ers, but it reflected the electric air and the high stakes.

Toward the end of April, with Redwood Summer looming, the Mendocino Environmental Center asked police to look into the most direct threats to Bari yet. One was a photo of her made to appear as if she were seen through a rifle scope. The other was an anonymous letter saying, "Get out and go back to where you come from. We know everything. You won't get a second warning."

The Santa Rosa paper quoted Mendocino County sheriff Tim Shea as saying that the war of words was "escalating every day."

"Let's face it," the sheriff told the paper, "the manipulation of the media is behind a lot of this."

Hurwitz himself drove home the gravity of the situation by doing something as unthinkable as the Earth First! divorce: he went *almost* public, submitting an op-ed piece with his byline to the *Houston Chronicle* that claimed the activities of his company had been "grievously misrepresented." But he was still playing by a businessman's rules. After meetings at the capital in Sacramento—during which Greg King kept busy passing out flyers offering a $5,000 reward for jailing Takeover Charlie—Pacific Lumber announced a two-year moratorium on logging in the Headwaters, contingent upon a wholesale cease and desist on the part of the radicals. If EF! resumed its shenanigans, the deal was off and the hippies would bear the blame. The environmentalists now had the power to save Headwaters, if only they would adhere to the mores of reasoned debate at a polite volume through established channels. It looked like a winning tactical move, but Earth First! delivered its response with the predictable theatrical aplomb at a demonstration in Scotia: Sorry, Charlie. No compromise in defense of Mother Earth.

On May 24, 1990, Bari and Cherney were in Oakland gathering recruits for Redwood Summer. They were on their way to rehearse for a gig—Judi on fiddle, Darryl on guitar, revolution on their minds. At five minutes before noon, a sound too loud for Darryl's ears to hear ripped through the car. It was a crack, then a ringing—"Like a sitar was in my head," he would later say.

Bari was in agony, begging the paramedics to please just let her die.

She knew, even as she was screaming, even as Cherney was saying, "I love you, I love you, you're going to live" that it had to be a pipe bomb. She was right. FBI counterterrorist experts were on the scene in minutes, "as if they had been standing around the corner holding their ears," Bari's lawyer would later write. The Oakland police and the FBI quickly established that the device was an eleven-inch pipe with gunpowder and finishing nails, time-delayed with a wristwatch and detonated by a motion-sensitive device. They almost as quickly established who the suspects were: Bari and Cherney.

Bari spent that afternoon in surgery—and under arrest for felony transport of illegal explosives. Despite not being much of a flight risk because she was under anesthesia and her pelvis was pulverized, the cops sent an officer to guard her. FBI special agent Frank Doyle didn't have much trouble cobbling together a hypothesis. Hippies drive around with bomb. Hippies' car goes boom.

As it happened, Doyle had been the instructor at the FBI bomb school the month before on Louisiana-Pacific land. They blew up three cars. Two of the three bombs were in the cars' passenger compartments, as was the one in Bari's car.

Doyle, a twenty-year veteran of the bureau, insisted that the bomb had been placed behind Bari's seat—where she would have seen it when loading the car—rather than directly underneath it. There was a problem with that hypothesis, however, in the form of a hole in the floor of the car, through which they could see the street below. The hole was directly under Bari's seat, not behind it.

Then there was the matter of the watch, which closed the circuit on the bomb but would not detonate it—the motion sensor would do that. By setting the watch ahead, the bomber or bombers had made sure that the device would not explode while he or she—or they—was building or placing it. Would anybody, even eco-radicals and alleged domestic terrorists, be stupid enough to be zipping around the Bay Area knowingly carrying a ready-to-blow motion-sensitive bomb? Furthermore, the device wasn't designed to destroy property or equipment. The nails were meant to maim and kill. Whatever the source, Bari and Cherney had been blown up by an antipersonnel bomb.

Two weeks later, while still in the hospital, in traction and unsure if she'd be able to walk, Judi Bari gave an interview to the same radical paper for which she'd written a review of Foreman's book and other pieces. She predicted the bombing would energize Redwood Summer and make it even bigger than hoped. She also mentioned that Pacific Lumber had sent her a nice get-well card.

Compared to Bari, Cherney's injuries were slight. The ER staff picked pieces of the blasted white Subaru out of him, after which, incredulous and in pain, he was escorted to the city jail, where he entertained dark similarities between disappeared dissidents in Latin America and his own perilous situation. At the moment of the explosion, he'd first thought they'd been rear-ended again. "Then I heard somebody scream out, 'It's a bomb! It was a bomb!' And then it all made sense, that someone had tried to kill us," Cherney said from jail. The Oakland cops interrogated Cherney for hours in the dead of night, and they didn't seem much interested in hearing who he thought might enjoy seeing him and Bari dead.

In the same year that saw the passage of the Americans with Disabilities Act, the bombing left Bari disabled for the rest of her life. It also left her permanently spooked, even more than she had been before. The cops and the feds pulled nails out of the window trim in her house, attempting to link those nails to the ones in the bomb, but to no avail. Mike Geniella, the reporter on the timber beat for the Santa Rosa paper, received a letter claiming credit for the bomb, describing it in detail and saying it was meant for Bari. The letter was signed "The Lord's Avenger."

Still, the feds exhibited a remarkable resistance to distraction from what looked to Bari and Cherney like a vendetta. Why entertain the notion that the author of some crank letter that described in detail the role the watch played in arming the thing actually had anything to do with the bomb? It was a red herring.

The promised arraignments of Bari and Cherney were repeatedly delayed, dragging into Redwood Summer. Prosecutors then dropped charges against the two organizers. It was clear to Judi and Darryl that if the job couldn't be pinned on them, the feds had no interest in pursuing it further. Nothing could have more deeply galvanized the activists' suspicions about the government's law enforcement arm. They'd been on the receiving end of violence before, and nobody in any official capacity ever went to the trouble of giving more than a cursory check of their complaints. Now somebody had tried to kill them, two peace-loving people who had renounced tree spiking, and the response was identical. And while Judi had been in the hospital, the government had mounted a smear campaign that smelled to her like the good old counterintelligence operations of the J. Edgar Hoover days, in which the FBI hatched black-bag jobs to subvert, sabotage, and neutralize radical homegrown groups. This wasn't Mississippi Summer. To her, this was Alabama in 1963. This was Bombingham. But for all her paranoia, the bombing couldn't completely suppress Bari's sense of humor. She and Cherney would later write a song called "The FBI Stole My Fiddle."

With two of its key planners distracted by efforts to defend themselves and clear their names, Redwood Summer proceeded, but not on the extravagant scale Bari and Cherney had envisioned. Bari was all but out of it altogether, and a good number of the other organizers had rushed to San Francisco to support her and were similarly distracted. That was part of the feds' plot, wasn't it? Plot or no, the big show couldn't seem to get traction. Most of the protesters came from California and looked like the usual suspects. The national media failed to seize on the issue. True, there were marches and lockdowns aplenty, at which the good men of the Humboldt County Sheriff's Department were decked out in their riot gear finery to meet the protesters and perhaps engage in a little impromptu pain-compliance training. But too much of what was going on seemed like purposeless noise, disconnected from the aims of the movement. The line between pointed monkey-wrenching and mindless vandalism blurred. Then there was the day in August when John Campbell got himself a human hood ornament.

Campbell was attending a symposium on redwood conservation when agitators showed up and disrupted it. As Campbell tried to leave, protesters grabbed at him. Once he'd made it into his car, he found he couldn't move for the mob around him. One of them jumped on the hood. Cops peeled people off the car. A cop yelled at Campbell to drive. He did, with the hippie still hanging on. When Campbell stopped, state troopers arrested the protester.

Nor could the shenanigans be relied upon to take place during normal business hours and in normal business places. Campbell's yard, or at least property very close to it, became a popular camping destination for activists taking in the sights of Humboldt County. They beat drums and played bad, earnest protest songs. Listen to a humorless ditty from these people and a man would get down on his knees and thank the Lord for Joan Baez, who was downright lighthearted by comparison. Then somebody dumped a dead deer in Campbell's pool. This was an outrage. All he was trying to do was run a lumber company and take care of 1,400 employees, and now he had to have twenty-four-hour security at his home, where his new wife and children slept. These people had no respect for anyone else's rights.

These people were also squabbling aplenty among themselves. It was during Redwood Summer that Foreman publicly declared his divorce from Earth First! To Foreman, the California fruits and nuts had no interest in returning mankind to its feral roots and instead saw capitalism as the true enemy. In: humanism. Out: biocentrism. Out: Foreman and his bunch of hardcore early adopters.

The summer couldn't end soon enough for a lot of those involved. Protesters had been beaten and shot at, arrested and jailed. The media were not as charmed as expected by the high-spirited merriment. The timber companies, bracing for the possible passage of Forests Forever, had been cutting like crazy while they still could. And as summer dribbled away and the masses of troops evaporated out of the county, some of those who'd poured their souls into Redwood Summer were forced to confront the hard fact that they hadn't accomplished a whole lot, but it had taken a whole lot out of them.

In November, Forests Forever, which would have stopped clearcuts and saved old growth, failed by a hair. A countermeasure the timber barons had backed also went down by a much wider margin. The result was a stalemate lacking even the uneasiest of truces. The plates had shifted. The seismic tension remained.

But a routine fell into place in later years, a seasonal milestone like the Dungeness crab haul in the winter or wild salmon in the late spring. The forest defenders always staged a big rally around September 15, at the end of the nesting season for the threatened, redwood-nesting marbled murrelet, when the logging show could resume in those areas. The timing coincided roughly with the dope harvest, Reggae on the River, and the resumption of classes at Humboldt State—a convergence of attractions that ensured a good draw. John Campbell watched his hair whiten and his waist expand, tried to stanch the flow of lost revenue from the protests and the litigation, which he guessed had cost PL millions. True, the protesters' numbers ebbed and flowed—the fairweather agitators tended to clear out when the rainy season came—but pipsqueak Darryl and his core band of fanatics weren't going anywhere. They continued to make trouble for Pacific Lumber, locking themselves down with Kryptonite bike locks in PL's business office, parading down Scotia's main (and practically only) street in animal costumes. It was unfathomable. These people continued to believe they had some right to dictate what the company did on its own lands—*private lands zoned for use in a lawful timber operation*. These people continued to believe it was wrong to grow trees and harvest them, even if the company planted five saplings for every mature tree it dropped.

Protest had become as much a part of Humboldt as the water, the redwoods, and the mountains, as much a part of the living landscape as the scars on Judi Bari's body.

The place was a stew of acrimony, tension, and not a little paranoia. This was the peculiar place into which David Chain would roam, to see the redwoods that people said were worth dying for.

A Warrior
for Two
Summers

DAVID CHAIN AND STEPHANIE KIRBY WERE driving to California with the windows cranked all the way down, and on the morning they got rolling they felt pure . . . *release*. Stephanie's van was loaded with a little Coleman two-burner cookstove, a sack of rice, dried fruit, oatmeal, and a road atlas with a duct-taped cover. It was finally happening.

The morning sun, pressing even early in the day in the Texas midsummer, was in the rearview. Stephanie's twelve-year-old Dodge Ram van ran well—it didn't have AC, but it did have a new stereo David had lobbied hard to buy—and now that van was lapping up the miles to New Mexico and beyond. The hot wind blew on them as Bob Marley, the prophet himself, worked a groove. Then they put in the Mad

Professor dub. Then flipped over the Mad Professor tape for the improvised Sufi songs of praise and faith from Nusrat Fateh Ali Khan. David Chain had fairly expansive musical taste, which accounted for the desperate necessity of the new stereo rig.

"Man, if we're going all the way out to California, we've got to get a new stereo in here," he'd told Stephanie.

"Are you sure you want to spend $300 on a new stereo?"

"It's *definitely* worth it."

It was amazing some of the things guys had to explain to girls. It's not like they were going to have some long, meaningful conversation with the windows open at seventy miles an hour. Now his face couldn't quite conceal a flicker of smugness. Had he been right or what?

They were going. They'd talked about it for so long, sometimes it seemed that they'd talked it right out of happening. It was the summer of 1997, and David Chain had just begun his twenty-third year in a place that was becoming more confining, more limiting, the longer he stayed. True, he'd gone to Arizona once to see a friend, and as a kid he went on family vacations—Colorado, Louisiana, Missouri, New Mexico. But this was something else. Now he, Stephanie, Stephanie's teenaged brother Justin, and her butter-colored Lab mix, Komali, were going to California. They were stoked.

Stephanie and David had been together, although not as a couple at first, since they met in Austin at a friend's. Stephanie had been letting the wind or her whims move her around Texas—Dallas to party and listen to music, Tyler to be with her dad and stepmom, Austin because everybody cool wound up there eventually.

She'd also spent time in the woods of northern California and at times found herself uncomfortable trying to reenter the urban world. She looked very Nature Girl—dreadlocks, no makeup, hairy legs. She and her friends would go down to the bar district in Austin, and all the girls looked like they'd been vacuum-packed into these tiny dresses, wearing so much makeup they must have had to take it off with a sandblaster. That wasn't Stephanie's scene. Not that there was anything wrong with it if that's what those girls were after, wanting to look pretty and impress people. But Stephanie couldn't help but feel a little like a freak in their midst, walking through the reflected neon and beer-bolstered laughter along Sixth Street.

Except when David was there. They'd be at the Ritz playing pool some nights, David waiting to take a shot, and he'd just give her this look that put her at ease. It was as if he had some sort of secret knowledge that allowed him to move about in both worlds. He knew there were more ways to live one's life than the buttoned-up masses would ever know, and yet he could function in the conventional world. At times, Stephanie wasn't sure she could.

But she was sure David knew her immediately. It was that kind of feeling for both of them, a deep and instant recognition of something fundamental. He could tell this woman what songs he wanted played at his funeral.

It started ordinarily. They were introduced and began chatting. She told him she'd been traveling and spending time in the woods and didn't quite have her social-situation sea legs back yet. David wanted details. Where do you go? Do you camp in parks or national forests or where? What do you do on the road?

She told him she was serious about meditating, she'd do it every night. Out in nature, in the pristine setting, it was really easy for her to lock into the vibe. It felt great, almost like her dreadlocks were antennae and she was a big receiver. The reception was so much better out in the clear air. In a city it wasn't pure at all. There were chaotic vibes all around.

David said he totally understood. And Stephanie felt the filters she had in place to block the chaos drop.

In terms of romance, things moved quickly and yet they didn't. One night they got a bottle of wine, David put it in his backpack and they went up to Mount Bonnell, a park on a high bluff overlooking Lake Austin, the downtown skyline, and the beginnings of the Texas Hill

Country to the west. Legend has it that if a couple climbs the 105 steps, they'll fall in love. And maybe Stephanie and David did that night, although not in the physical sense. David was an expansive conversationalist, one of those rare talkers who also excel at listening. They talked about their families, about religion, about Pasadena. She didn't know that much about Pasadena, but she'd seen the Houston Ship Channel and remembered thinking, *This place needs some serious healing.*

They drank wine and talked, and when they came down those steps the Austin police were waiting for anybody hanging out in the park after hours. The funny thing was, although the cops patted them both down, they didn't bother to look in David's backpack with the wine bottle inside.

It wasn't long before she'd moved into the duplex with David, his sister Sarah, David's lifelong friend Christopher Martin, and their friend Joe. And it wasn't long after that they were planning their trip to California.

For Stephanie, it was a reprise of a trip she'd taken the year before with her previous boyfriend, Josiah Hardagon. They'd been living in Dallas and wanted to get out of the city. They'd gutted the inside of the van—it was blue and gray, not pretty but functional—and made it roadworthy, outfitting it with a bed framed with two-by-fours and crannies to store their stuff. Along the way, things between Josiah and Stephanie came to an end and, after some roaming, Josiah decided to stay on the coast. By then Stephanie and a friend had been offered jobs on an herb farm—it was the harvest season—and although they never found the farm or the farmers after a first encounter, they were lucky enough to fall in with a crowd of like-minded souls: people interested in living simply, aware that everyday decisions such as what they ate and where their clothes were made affected the Earth. These people were living templates of how Stephanie wished to fashion her life, and she remembered them well. You met such interesting people on the road, bums and hippies and kids who knew where the nearest free lunch was.

It all sounded like a lot more adventure than David Chain was having in the shipping department of Innovative Communications at Eighth and Brazos in downtown Austin. They saved a few hundred dollars and planned to leave in April.

"Oh, my God," Sarah said days before they were to take off. "Y'all are about to leave and you've got $300?"

David corrected her. "I've got about that much, too."

Stephanie said it was no big deal. They could stop and work if they had to. She could make jewelry to sell.

The goodbye tour rolled on to Tyler and Coldspring, then Stephanie's aunt died and she was called back home to Tyler. Another delay.

Stephanie's father was an ex-hippie Texas lawyer named Monroe Kirby, and while he was quite fond of David Chain and even allowed him and his beloved daughter to live with him and his wife in Tyler, he was somewhat less approving of the notion of them lighting out for the West Coast for a months-long trip with so little money. If they would fix up the house he'd grown up in fifteen miles or so out of town, he'd pay them. They agreed. For one thing, it would cover the new stereo. They spent every day for weeks outside in the heat, scraping off the old paint, flecks of it sticking to their sweating hands and arms, reglazing the windows, getting the old place in shape.

Nothing in this world will instill in a person an urge to flee quicker than working outside during a Texas summer, and the labor made Stephanie and David more resolved than ever. The stereo may have been an extravagance, but it was also a statement of purpose.

Before they left, Cindy Allsbrooks—ever the fretting mother—gave her son a laminated card to put in his wallet. It said who he was, declared that he was allergic to penicillin, and listed three emergency phone numbers. On the back was a verse from Psalms 91:11: "God will put his Angels in charge of you to protect you wherever you go."

Then they were done. Then they were gone, the road ahead ablaze with potential.

. . .

AFTER THEY'D DIVORCED, Cindy and David Allen Chain had spoken warily of getting back together. One night they negotiated a tentative meeting in a sports bar to talk about it. David Allen Chain didn't show up. But there was a guy named Ron Allsbrooks, who, at twenty-five, was spending a good bit of time and most of his money in bars. Ron and Cindy talked all night, trading miseries—it turned out Ron was busted up over parting with a girlfriend. To his surprise, Ron soon found himself living with, and then, in June of 1989, married to a woman and her three children.

Cindy wanted to buy a house in Pasadena instead of renting, but there were few notions that repelled Ron more. "Pasadena stinks," he said. "Pasadena's trash." Ron's parents had a place on Lake Livingston, and they talked about moving out there. A place in the country meant more than an hour each way to work for Ron, but he was working four days on and four days off and didn't mind the drive. He found a place in Coldspring that was a Houston couple's weekender. It was more than they could afford, but Ron knew Cindy would love it. They closed on the house a month later.

The house was not without its tensions. Ron, himself the product of a stepparented home, could at times reveal a ham-handed grasp of the nuances of child rearing. He also exhibited a proclivity to be a bit outspoken in a home that was already bursting with loud opinions. Vivacious, sharp-witted Sarah, for instance, would eventually declare herself a vegetarian, a lesbian, and a free spirit who saw mainstream American existence as distastefully as Ron had regarded the notion of putting down roots in Pasadena. Ron thought Sarah could be a little aggressive about what she believed and how she lived.

David was just easing into adolescence, beginning to mark his territory and assert his independence, when Ron the interloper appeared on the scene. In David's teenage years, when he'd stay out too late, it was nigh impossible to get his butt out of bed in time for school. He was grounded now and then for breaking curfew and other teen indiscretions. The kid could be a handful sometimes. He and Ron had words. Once, after tensions between them had been building for a couple of days, David, standing by the refrigerator, said something that set Ron off. Ron grabbed the boy by the shoulders and David coldcocked him, breaking a finger in the process.

When David was a sophomore at Pasadena High School, he got to be more than Cindy and her husband could handle. David kept pointedly referring to his father, and Cindy thought a good dose of the elder David Chain might be exactly what the boy needed. She picked up the phone.

"Come and get him," she said.

David said, "I'll be there in five minutes."

The elder David Chain spent his workweeks on the road, supervising crews that painted industrial tanks and towers. Young David, being essentially on his own, had an enviable amount of freedom for a high-school kid, but he also was responsible for getting himself to school.

When he was home, David the elder was good about spending time with his boy. They'd go fishing or shoot pool, sometimes go to concerts with young David and his friends. David the elder was also a firm subscriber to the sink-or-swim school of parenting. When the clutch went out in David's Toyota, his father asked him, "You want to walk or you want to drive?"

"Drive," David said. And his father sat down and drank a few beers while he watched his boy drop the new clutch in all by himself.

David was wry, charismatic, and a peerless bullshitter who made friends with people with whom he sometimes had little in common. One such friend was Laura Somers, the daughter of a local surgeon. The family had a beautiful weekend house out on Lake Livingston, across the water from Cindy and Ron's place in Coldspring. There David learned to water-ski and watched the sun set behind the pines on the far side of the lake.

Chemical diversions were amply available, too; in such a place even the illusion of temporary escape was hard to resist. David smoked pot, although his father told him if he ever got busted for it not to call Daddy—Daddy didn't approve. David and some of his friends called themselves Herb Life. Cindy and Ron were a little more relaxed in their attitudes toward monitoring David's pot intake. They had little use for sanctimonious piety, but when an acid trip left David so wired he couldn't sleep for days, necessitating a medical intervention, they had a family talk. David told them he wouldn't take acid again. Cindy came to sense a shift in their relationship, less stern parent to child, more friend to friend.

David graduated from high school, partied with his friends, hung out at the mall, grooved to the Fugees and Bob Marley, half-heartedly enrolled in community college, and tried on existences, all of which were ill-fitting. Dr. Somers gave him a job filing and running errands— David thought he might like to be a doctor or a chiropractor—on the condition that David keep taking classes at the junior college. Partying sapped his energy and affected his performance at both school and work. He signed papers to join the navy as a means to possibly get through med school, then thought better of the idea practically before he'd finished signing his name. His dad offered to get him hired on with his crew, but David had by then quietly turned away from any-thing resembling the path to working- or middle-class respectability, at least temporarily. From the time he graduated high school, he'd been searching with mounting frustration for something to give him defini-tion. He'd grown up early and hard and was smart enough to know he was on the freeway to loserdom.

That wasn't the only reason he was at war with himself. Residual anger over his parents' divorce stuck to him like tar, made him vulnera-ble to succumbing to the darker side of his personality, a part of himself he didn't like but couldn't always control. Among his friends he was the most loyal and generous of the pack, but sometimes he wasn't much fun to be around. East Texas was his home, but it was eating his soul.

He left. He moved to Austin, den of all things slack, to be with his childhood friend Christopher, who was going to the University of Texas. And that's how he came to meet Stephanie.

He still talked about chiropractic school, still wanted to be a healer, but the pretty brown-haired girl and her Homeric tales from the previous year made it easy for him to hold off on pursuing those plans. They'd go off to California, find a little piece of land, build a cabin, and hoe a garden. Make something from nothing. Live simply. People had been doing it since before Thoreau, and the number of people doing it in Humboldt meant a couple of newcomers like David and Stephanie would be welcome.

Along the way, through Albuquerque, Flagstaff, and Fresno, David, Stephanie, and Justin crashed in motels and camped. They ate a lot of Mexican food in mom-and-pop joints. When they camped, if there wasn't running water nearby, they had a basin they'd use to take sponge baths and wash their dishes. David and Stephanie were both vegetarians (a serious offense in beef-intensive, barbecue-loving Texas), and they bought vegetables from grocers to stir-fry with rice. They ate twice their weight in rice. They drove across the California desert—one town seemed to have nothing but gun shops—but once through the desert, it seemed like blackberries were everywhere. They picked them and David would make blackberry pancakes in the morning over the Coleman stove, and then they'd roll cigarettes and drink their coffee and talk.

Talk of revolution was a staple. They both agreed it was coming. Stephanie was convinced it would be a popular uprising against the government, and that people would have to die. David's vision was more interior. Each person could learn, live differently, and change the world around them.

"It doesn't have to be like that, Steph," he told her. "Do you want people to die? It doesn't have to be that way if there's a revolution of ideas. That's what we need. We can rebuild our thoughts and the outside world will reflect that."

In San Francisco they picked up Stephanie's little sister at the airport—the trip was her big summer excursion, too—and the four of them snaked up the coast in the van. It seemed to take forever for the dense satellite communities attached to San Francisco to give way to the vineyards of the wine country. There had been old trees there once, too, but not in a very long time.

Then the vineyards yielded to trees, and the trees got bigger and more dense. The very air changed. You couldn't even call it by the same name as the stuff that smelled like cancer and made your throat constrict back in Pasadena. The giant trees were like nothing David had seen before. Pictures couldn't convey the scale. There were trees big enough to drive a car through, which you could actually do, but you had to pay a man a couple of bucks first, and you were encouraged to stop by the gift shop afterward.

At times Stephanie worried if she'd built up the place too much, because she was so excited to get back, that David might be disappointed. When they got to Redway, she pointed the van toward Canyons Peak to the general store at Whitethorn and beyond, a considerable distance from civilization and all that was wrong with it. There was a little stream running through the piece of land, and a redwood that had been hollowed out by a lightning strike. It was a huge thing, big enough that there were tales of a family once having lived in it. Stephanie couldn't help but think, *I'm so small compared to this.* They talked about how cool it would be to live in the tree, in daily awe of its age.

Stephanie had told Josiah she was coming back to Humboldt with a friend. There was no leftover stuff between the two of them; they just weren't meant to be together. Josiah was living in a field next to a river in the southern part of the county with his girlfriend, who went by the name Pooh Bear. Josiah's friend Joshua Ponce was there, too. It was a pretty spot of bottomland. Josiah had a job and a garden to tend. By night they'd all sit around the fire, David pulling out his pouch of Drum and rolling cigs. He seemed a little shy to Josiah, or maybe he was a little uneasy in the company of the ex. Talkative as David could be, he also could hold back, which sometimes came across as manly stoicism.

The early fall was coming. People were drifting into Humboldt for the big Reggae on the River fest and the herb harvest. And it was the beginning of the protest season. Pooh Bear took David and Stephanie to an Earth First! gathering in Redway. The organizers, such as there were in Earth First!, told the group that Pacific Lumber was getting ready to cut in a plan that EF! said was patently illegal, and that it had to be stopped that night. They talked about locking down. Time for direct action. Pooh Bear left with the protesters that night to take part in the action. David and Stephanie drove back without her.

It was the first David Chain had heard of the timber companies and the warriors who battled them in the forest. Later, in Arcata, he and Stephanie met a girl named Nicole. She was sharp and gorgeous, and she'd done some political canvassing back in Wisconsin. She camped with them and talked about the forest, about the need to do something with one's energy. That stoked David's restlessness; he really wasn't doing anything but camp and help Joshua and Josiah in the garden. Stephanie could busy her hands making jewelry, but that wasn't for David. The vision of a utopian hippie idyll that had sustained him for months was evaporating. The scenery might be prettier than back home, but the torpor was the same, as if his pockets were filled with lead.

In the early autumn, when Humboldt County enjoyed the best weather of the year, David and Stephanie felt their romance sputtering. She didn't yet understand that any relationship requires a degree of heavy lifting now and then. If she and David were butting heads, didn't that mean he wasn't the one? Living out of the van for so long had left them bickering over inconsequential things, like which road to take or how to spend their precious funds. Mostly they needed to be away from each other. And David could be a little intense—the old, familiar, negative vibes. They divided their property. David took a little cast-iron skillet and a couple of wooden bowls from the van. Josiah lent him his backpack, and David hitched north. He said something about wanting to see Seattle. He needed to be alone. He needed to clear his head.

A couple of weeks passed. Josiah was outside when he saw a figure walking toward him on the roadside. "And he was smiling," Josiah recalled. "He had this lightness in his step. As he got closer, I realized something had changed him. It was evident something good had happened in his life. He'd shoved off that quiet reserve. He was talkative and outgoing." Like Dave Foreman seventeen years earlier, David Chain returned from his journey a warrior. The forest was calling. It was, Josiah said, "so much more than having a job" to him. The frustration and dissatisfaction of not having a meaningful channel for his energy were gone. David Chain clung to his new calling as if it were a life preserver he'd been tossed just before going under for the last time.

On his sojourn, David had spent time with the Earth First!ers at the Swimmers' Delight campground. Folks were gearing up for a big tree sit along Bell Creek in a contested Pacific Lumber harvest area. Mike Avcollie noticed a young guy helping break down the small camp and pack out gear. The guy worked hard and bore a smile. David Chain had by then taken a forest name. He introduced himself to Avcollie as Gypsy. Avcollie, who'd once been arrested for snoozing while protesting at the courthouse in Eureka, introduced himself as Sleeper.

The pragmatic Texan would find a kindred spirit in Avcollie, who had zero use for the squishy mysticism and religiosity that clouded some activists' minds. He was probably the smartest and certainly the most articulate of the bunch. At twenty-seven, he had a degree and had had a job every year of his life since he was sixteen. He'd gotten radicalized in the eleventh grade when he read the leftist historian Howard Zinn's *A People's History of the United States* and thought, *Well, shit, they lied to me.*

"The problem with American history is the dominant culture lets enough nuggets get through that if you pay attention you just might become dangerous," he said later, and that was exactly what had happened to him. He'd long since been "disillusioned with the dominant paradigm" and sought a new way to resist. He'd protested the Gulf War, read his Martin Luther King and Thoreau, and found that they had much more to do with his Earth First! views than a misanthrope like Dave Foreman did. "Dave Foreman is not a man of the people," Avcollie would say. "I am."

To Avcollie's way of thinking, the new crop of protesters were, by and large, suburban middle-class kids. They'd come out of the antinuke and the budding anti-globalization movements. They weren't just born out in the woods to some dreadlocked Earth Mother. Frankly, he found the media stereotype offensive. They'd *thought* about this, they'd seen that what Charles Hurwitz and Maxxam and Pacific Lumber were doing was an acute local symptom of a worldwide pandemic: the overwhelming influence of corporate power. It wasn't just about trees and whether or not they had souls or were more or less valuable than human life. It was about everyday geopolitical issues, about America—6 percent of the world's population, consuming 40 percent of its resources. This was his public and private philosophy, a worldview that made every act a political statement.

That was Avcollie. The system was fundamentally broken down, rotting from the inside, and operating within legal measures wasn't enough. If he did only what was legal, he couldn't sleep at night. Martin Luther King's letter from a Birmingham jail said that when a law is wrong it is one's moral obligation to challenge that law. Right? That logic gnawed at Avcollie's conscience. But it wasn't as if he bounded out of bed every morning looking forward to getting yelled at, spat upon, pepper-sprayed, and possibly beaten up. He did everything within the law first: he read timber harvest plans, wrote letters, and spoke at public hearings. Most of those legal channels were, of course, not effective—there was no actual public participation in government business, just the appearance of it before the California Department of Forestry and its Pacific Lumber paymasters who did whatever they wanted. But when the only remaining options were those outside the law, Avcollie knew he'd exhausted the legitimate avenues and wasn't just doing direct action for the hell of it. And when the PL thugs or the sheriff's deputies snarled at him and asked why didn't he get a job, Avcollie could tell them he had a job, and that he'd taken the day off work to protest and probably get arrested. Resistance might or might not be futile, but it was morally imperative. And when it came to tree sits and lockdowns and other forms of direct action, the logic was clear: if you expressed your message in such a dramatic way that you might die making it, you had a chance of leading the news.

Tree sits, for example. Even with every bit of safety gear available, it's not safe to be living 150, 180, 200 feet up in a redwood tree. But it was an irresistible photo op and one of the most popular techniques to protest cutting. Just getting up the tree was dangerous. Some used climbing spikes, but others eschewed them because they might damage the tree. Climbers wear a harness with carabiners and loop a rope around the tree and themselves. Take two steps, then inch the rope higher. Two more steps, inch the rope higher. Inchworming all the way up the tree. The idea is that even if both feet give way, the rope will pin the climber's torso to the trunk, leaving the climber terrified but not dead. Sometimes climbers begin to feel different when the forest floor gives way as they climb. They become aware of birds and other wildlife. The ground begins to lose definition, resembling a thick blanket, a blanket that once had covered this part of the Pacific Northwest. The majesty of the giants and their function as living habitat is better grasped from 180 feet looking down than from the ground looking up. The sit itself can be anything from a couple of two-by-fours to an elaborate platform with cables connecting to adjacent sits, making a stand of old-growth redwood a peculiar sort of high-rise village. And life in the trees could be an incongruous mix of high-tech and no-tech: While sitters often used cell phones to talk to supporters and the media, their bathroom was a bucket.

The logic of a tree sit should be apparent. Not even the nastiest of the nastics would knowingly cut a tree with a person sitting in it—it'd be nothing short of murder. (Cutting their ropes or taking their food and gear on the ground—those are accepted and not ineffective means of discouragement.)

The 1997 Bell Creek tree sit was the latest manifestation of Mike Avcollie's geopolitical philosophy in action. (The warriors cheekily named the operation "Liberty," as in Liberty Bell.) He and David—Gypsy—and a tight little crew wound up spending the rest of September and a good part of October there, climbing, sitting, and resupplying. Avcollie would later marry one of the crew, a young woman named Calista Young, aka Cricket. There were just half a dozen or so of them out there—the timber harvest plan wasn't yet active, so the crisis wasn't critical. They got to know each other pretty well, to rely on and trust one another. One night they sat in a circle and divulged their real names.

The taking of forest names was another bit of EF! self-mocking, semi-ironic skulduggery. It had a practical purpose of cloaking one's given name, making it more difficult for the sheriffs to track them down and arrest them. But the monikers very frequently showed flashes of humor. One guy at the Bell Creek sit called himself Dijon. There was Avcollie and his criminal catnapping at the courthouse—hence Sleeper. There was a Garlic and a Felony and a Sawyer. And there was a Gypsy. On the night of his inaugural tree sit, Chain told fellow novice activist Stephanie Trager that his friends in Texas had called him that because of his vagabond ways.

A little mischief was necessary to leaven the sustained and pitched battle, which partially explained why, on a Thursday in August, Charles Hurwitz was assaulted with a pie.

Hurwitz, resplendent in his uniform dark suit, was in Scotia for a round of meetings. At the Scotia Inn, protesters gathered to wave banners and sing. One of them—a longhaired man wearing cutoffs—tried to get into the hotel but security blocked him. He eventually talked his way in and, when Hurwitz emerged, plopped an apple pie from Hoby's, the little market across the street, on Hurwitz's head.

The sheriff was standing next to Hurwitz. He collared the perp, who spent eight days in the Humboldt County jail for assault with a deadly dessert.

The hotelier, Chuck Oppitz, gave the guy credit for buying locally.

JUST AS HIS FATHER HAD wanted to be where the action was when he joined the army and went to Vietnam, David "Gypsy" Chain was happiest when things were cooking. He'd wasted years looking for something without having a ghost of a notion of what it might be. Now he knew, and he embraced the work with the zeal of a convert. He wasn't trying to commune with flora. He was saying, I'm here to save *this* tree, right here. It beat wandering around the mall back home with his friends. Joshua had taught him how to climb, and the exercise hardened his arms and torso and gave him a certain confidence, the subtlest of swaggers. He was a team player. But tree climbers were stars, and David was a very good tree climber.

He and the others also had nonviolence training, which invariably involved a role-playing exercise in which Earth First!ers learned how to de-escalate an explosive situation. Gypsy and another activist had to run once when PL security man Carl Anderson—a former employee of the sheriff's department who was said to have once armed himself with a wrist rocket to shoot at protesters—came upon their camp.

Now and again the protesters could actually convince a crew of gyppos—contract loggers, saw jocks for hire—that they were working on a bad plan. But Avcollie said they were also met with threats: "Fuck you, fuck off, and get the fuck out of here or you're going to get hurt."

Late that year, Avcollie and Calista were on the ground at a tree sit trying to dry their gear after a storm when Carl Anderson and a member of the PL muscle squad named Climber Dan caught them before they could inchworm back up the tree. Climber Dan climbed, tore their gear out of the tree. Anderson grabbed Avcollie and threw him to the ground.

Earth First!ers also got legal training so they'd know what to expect when they were arrested. That came in handy when Gypsy and Stephanie Trager shared a first: their first arrest. A handful of them had gone to the Bay Area to protest the Headwaters deal and Dianne Feinstein's support of it. The idea was to climb parallel flagpoles at an office building, and hang the banner between them while two other activists locked down at the bottom. They made the banner at a warehouse in the middle of a booming storm, during which Gypsy casually mentioned that when he died, he expected it would be as sudden and swift as a thunderclap. Later they did recon on the state office building. Then it was showtime. Gypsy climbed the pole that flew the American flag but he wound up dropping the banner. They managed to get it stretched partway across from the other side, but Gypsy was irritated. He was the last one booked out of jail that night.

Just before Gypsy left to go back to Texas for Thanksgiving, he ran into Stephanie Kirby, and she noticed the change in him. He said he was learning how to climb these huge trees, learning about the environment and how messed up it was, reading books, doing more with his life than sitting by the river watching the water run by. He was boning up on the law and government regulations. He had found his purpose, Stephanie said, and it made him even more beautiful.

She happened to be reading a book that illuminated the change for her. It was a book on meditation, and there was a chapter called "The Path of Service," which talked about the very thing she was seeing in her former lover. As she would recall: "It talks about this quality, this power when a person does not fear death. It's the only power that can conquer the other power in this world, which is the power of not being afraid to kill . . . And it was talking about when you come into that feeling of not being afraid to die, you tap into this huge power. I think that's what David was going through. He was completely willing to give every bit of himself to a cause. He saw it as his path of service. David was picked for that job. He was so strong. He had some kind of power to change something. Years later, he's still changing me. The more I reflect on it, the more I learn from him."

Stephanie bumped into him one last time in the Laundromat in Garberville, not long before he went back to Texas. He was with a girl, she was with a guy. He told her about his plans. They could hug each other and say they loved each other and there wasn't anything uncomfortable about it, even though now they wouldn't be presenting grandchildren to their hopeful parents. And Stephanie knew he still respected her, even though she couldn't get serious about anything. At the time of their parting, Stephanie's greatest ambition was to work on an herb farm.

Back in Texas, Cindy and Ron saw a different son from the one who had left them that summer. David had told Cindy she didn't have to worry about him, even when he was hitching, and he seemed stronger and surer than ever. But Cindy had more questions about climbing trees. He told her he was working to save the redwoods from destruction, that there was a logging company running roughshod over the environment in the name of profit, that the last of the paternalistic capitalists had left Humboldt County and that he—David Nathan "Gypsy" Chain—and his fellow forest defenders were all that stood in the way of destruction. He showed her pictures of him in trees. He told her he was determined to go back. His dreadlocks had grown and his body had filled out, and he pulsed with his newfound sense of mission. Cindy and Ron talked about helping him buy a piece of land to start an organic farm, but that was more their desire to shoehorn David into a comparatively conventional life. His father, David Allen Chain, made it clear he respected his son's commitment but suggested, "There's lots of things that need to be fixed in Texas, too."

Well, they hadn't seen the redwoods. There was no way they could understand.

That December, as David Nathan Chain was back working two crap jobs in Austin to save money to finance his return, a preacher's daughter and occasional model from Arkansas motored into Humboldt County with friends and within days was perched eighteen stories up a 200-foot-tall ancient redwood the defenders had named Luna. Much of the surrounding land, on a vertiginous slope near the tiny settlement of Stafford, had already been clear-cut. A year earlier, on New Year's Eve 1996, Stafford resident Mike O'Neal awoke in his small house to two unfamiliar sounds. The first was more accurately the absence of a sound—for once it wasn't raining. The second was a series of explosions, like somebody was dynamiting up the slope, a sound that built to a cumulative roar. He looked out his daughter's second-floor window and saw a mountain turning to mush, loosening, causing the big trees to topple into each other, like dominos each weighing tens or hundreds of tons, all of them along with the rest of the debris rumbling toward the home that contained his sleeping child. A good chunk of the Pacific Lumber clear-cut—barren, without critical ground cover, and on seismically unstable land—had peeled loose in the seasonal torrent. Now a slide mass the width of a football field and as high as thirty feet was heading for people's houses. O'Neal ran ahead and got people out. When it was over, one house had a pickup run through it. Others were obliterated by mud and vegetation.

"Mountain Mike," as he was known, was a man whose ancestors had traveled the Oregon Trail. His grandparents had been botanists, and Mike himself had worked in sawmills and in the woods. He guessed he'd planted more than a million saplings over the span of his life. He was no tree hugger. He knew a thing or two about forestry, sustainable and otherwise, and he knew the slope had given way because of the clear-cut. Mountain Mike was a soft-spoken man, slow to anger, not opposed to the notion that trees could be harvested and wages made from the enterprise. He never would have dreamed of taking on the company town of Scotia just up the road. But now Mountain Mike's house, which he had built himself out of recycled redwood timber, was full of liquid mountain. Now Mountain Mike was mad. Stafford residents stayed where they could—with relatives or friends, a few in their cars. Mountain Mike and his family spent two months in a motel, then rented a house for another year and a half in nearby Rio Dell.

THE CITY WAS GRINDING AWAY at David again. During the day he was working downtown, in an unair-conditioned warehouse making salsa. His other job was at a Mexican restaurant called Trudy's, along an anonymous stretch of north Austin thick with mailbox stores, furniture outlets, and highway flyovers. That was where David Chain met another girl who swept him away, a diminutive and sweet waitress named Ravyn Erlewine. The first shift they met, Ravyn was training to be a hostess and David was running food. Their eyes locked. He seemed so familiar to her. They got together for coffee a few days later. Erlewine gave him two stones from West Virginia, where she'd been a white-water rafting guide for two years.

David Chain had just turned twenty-four. He was working hard to save money to head back west. He lived to get back, but he could feel Gypsy slipping away. Double shifts at Trudy's weren't getting him any closer to the coast. He didn't have a car. And he was riding the couch circuit, crashing with a circle of friends.

The black moods visited him most reliably when he drank. If you worked at Trudy's, you shut down for the night and started drinking in the bar upstairs. David's frustration at not being where he wanted to be shot out in flashes of anger, emotional outbursts. He talked about how his father was angry, especially when he drank; then David, ever his father's son, would drink and get especially angry. Indulging in vice was now calcifying into habit, and he didn't like it. His relationship with Ravyn was strained by their living in a romantic hothouse similar to the one he'd inhabited the year before with Stephanie Kirby. They crashed together. They went to work together. Between shifts at Trudy's they'd go upstairs and take a nap together. It was too much.

The old David was there, too. Ravyn was charmed by the way he had a tooth that caught on his lip a little, and by his broken pinkie from when he'd slugged Ron. And in Texas, where the ranks of kitchen workers include a good number of Mexicans (some of them undocumented; then as now, INS raids weren't unheard-of), David made a point of hanging out with the help and trying to learn Spanish from them.

He spent so much time evangelizing about the redwoods that some of the Trudy's crew called him the Pied Piper, and they'd stop what they were doing and listen to him. In another life he might have been a motivational speaker, so infectious was his zeal. He'd show friends how to tie knots, tell stories about climbing trees. He couldn't say it too many times: he lived to go back.

Ravyn wanted to go to California with him—she was nearly as sick of Austin as he was. But she was increasingly wary of the moods, the anger. Once, they fought all night long. Finally, they had a talk about his drinking. David was starting to lose people he cared about, including Ravyn. After ten intense weeks together, they were through. Then he seemed to get a grip on the darkness and the drinking that exacerbated it, but Ravyn feared the grasp wasn't strong and refused to take him back. One night at Trudy's he asked her to step onto the patio. He begged her to stick with him. She refused. She was wary, maybe still a little angry. But she held on to a quiet hope that they'd have another chance—David had said he was going out to Humboldt to organize and get things set up for the protest season and he'd be back in three weeks. Their separation would be a pause.

She last saw him around eight o'clock on a slow August night. Ravyn was waiting tables. David came in, went to where the staff kept their stuff, got Ravyn's keys out of her purse, and went out to her car to retrieve some of his things. He came back in and held out his hands like he wanted a hug.

Ravyn glared at him and walked away.

David Allen Chain—a man who liked his beer and his motorcycles American, and his prime rib well-done—drove to Austin to spend the weekend with his son before he left for California again. David said he wouldn't be coming home for Christmas—the trip would be too expensive. A strange feeling came over the father as he was leaving. He gave his son a big hug and said in his gravelly drawl, "You ain't coming home," and left. As he was driving away, he felt a pang and thought that he ought to go back to David's, but he fought the feeling off.

"Fuck, I don't want to do this," David Allen Chain thought, "but he's twenty-four years old and he's a man."

ONE OF DAVID'S FRIENDS at Trudy's was Gabriel Deutsch, who, as the child of parents in the Children of God religious cult, had literally been chased off several continents by the time he was a teenager. Deutsch's grandmother had bought him a new Acura Legend, and that was the vessel in which they made their escape. The action camp was starting September 10 and David, now a veteran of one protest season, had some organizing to do. He talked about Earth First! with zeal and urgency. Deutsch, constitutionally a skeptic and like Mike Avcollie in possession of a ferocious intellect, wasn't down with all of the rhetoric but kept his reservations to himself during the drive.

They drove straight through to California, stopping at a county park in Malibu, riding the roller-coaster in Santa Cruz. They drove up north, then out into the Mattole Valley to see Josiah and Joshua, whom David considered nothing less than brothers. They struck Deutsch as sweet, but it seemed like they were kind of into the Rainbow People thing, an amorphous, egalitarian movement like Earth First! that since the early 1970s had held gatherings in which adherents preached nonviolence, prayed for world peace, and celebrated elements of American Indian spirituality.

At the Earth First! action camp, where about a hundred people were gathered, things got even more intolerably black and white. No compromise meant no compromise. David Chain, now Gypsy again, helped lead training for recruits who'd do backwoods training. All this prep work for "direct action" struck Deutsch as the product of a polarizing orthodoxy, of resistance as a means to no end. And running around in the woods while loggers were working? That sounded to Deutsch like a counterculture version of capture the flag, and just about as productive. Gypsy played up the humor in the conflict—"He was motivated by more than raw angst," Deutsch said—but there was no question where he stood.

The protest climate was different in 1998, in part because Bari had died the previous year, four months after being diagnosed with cancer. (The fringe of the fringe hypothesized she had, *X-Files*-style, been "given" cancer—maybe a COINTELPRO job.) On her deathbed she'd made Darryl Cherney swear that he wouldn't settle the civil rights lawsuit they'd filed against the government in the wake of the bombing investigation. They'd filed suit claiming false arrest, conspiracy, slanderous comments, and illegal search. As that suit gurgled through the bowels of the federal courthouse in Oakland, an angle of the controversy even more contentious and potentially significant in the larger picture appeared to be about to come to a close. The activists called it, simply and acidly, the Deal.

The Deal. Everybody from Senator Feinstein to Secretary of the Interior Bruce Babbitt to Takeover Charlie had been sweating over it for years. Governor Pete Wilson was about to sign it. It would ultimately pay nearly half a billion dollars for 7,500 acres, the cream of the Headwaters and some surrounding lands in Humboldt County, but it would still al-low Pacific Lumber to log adjacent parcels and permit the incidental "takes"—killing—of coho salmon and marbled murrelet.

Campbell honestly believed the Deal would put an end to all the noise and couldn't believe that the parties were still debating it after three years. The protesters had been trying to save the Headwaters for more than a decade. Here was a plan—Campbell called it the "last, best chance"—to do just that and what were the hippies doing? Fight-ing it. They didn't want this thing to be over. They were protest junkies whose lives would be without definition if they had nothing to oppose. At best, a lot of these kids were just one heartfelt commitment from being homeless people. Not only that, the anarchists were just plain *rude*. As Campbell would write in a guest editorial in the Eureka paper: "They have put their own followers' lives at risk in a reckless campaign that their own instructional materials say is intended simply to create chaos. And when the federal government last month sent its top wildlife scientists to take public testimony on the Headwaters plan, these ac-tivists rose and pointedly turned their backs on the process, making a mockery of serious environmental review."

What else could the company offer? The salmon would be pro-tected, and so would the steelhead trout. As for the marbled murrelet, both the state and the feds had agreed that the company's plan to log only in previously harvested parcels would have almost zero effect on the birds' nesting habitat. In terms of wildlife, the Deal was far more restrictive than the Endangered Species Act. And if the activists suc-ceeded in scotching the Deal? Well, sadly, Pacific Lumber's hands were tied. It would have no choice but to sue the government, which could have the unfortunate effect of ultimately costing taxpayers far more than the sum now on the table.

Despite the company's spin, opposition to the Deal was far from limited to barefoot, Dumpster-diving kids in Humboldt County. Main-stream enviros were furious, convinced that the Deal was an abject sellout, galvanizing proof that the purported watchdog agencies were ineffectual lapdogs of the industry they were in charge of monitoring, a greenmail ransom paid to a man who threatened to level the old growths if his demands weren't met. (Never mind that Pacific Lumber, under the old regime, also had a long-term plan to turn the saw jocks loose in the Headwaters, too.) It was the product of ceaseless negotiations; it was proof that consensus was impossible, compromise unacceptable.

By then, the Deal was about more than a grove of redwoods and Douglas fir. It was also about the bust of Hurwitz's savings and loan, the fifth largest such bust in history, and charges of a government vendetta. Nothing so complex could be completely clean, but the fact remained that Headwaters was still the largest contiguous stand of old growth remaining in private hands, the jewel that Greg King and Darryl Cherney had dreamed of saving for the ages. The state and federal governments would pay Maxxam some $480 million for Headwaters and more for adjoining parcels—a sum that amounted to more than half what Hurwitz had paid for the whole company. And besides saving Headwaters, the Deal also included a pledge from Pacific Lumber to behave more responsibly and submit to an unprecedented level of government oversight. After years of public meetings and private threats, the parties had put together a set of regulations for PL to follow that was practically as thick as the San Francisco yellow pages. It would guide the company into a new era of exemplary land stewardship. The Habitat Conservation Plan, as it was called, was either a model for forest management in the twenty-first century or a license to kill, depending on whom you believed. Either way, it looked like the Deal was likely a go. Pacific Lumber was even playing nice, placing a moratorium on logging old growth for the time being.

Still, a good number of the North Coast enviros were enraged. Under the terms of the Deal, PL would still be allowed to log some seven hundred acres in what was called the Hole in the Headwaters. The idea that PL could punch a doughnut hole out of the area was exactly what environmentalists had been talking about for decades: unless vast swaths are saved, endangered and protected species are going to be killed no matter what restrictions are placed on the company's behavior. The hole served as a buffer for the south fork of the Elk, known as one of the finest coho spawning beds in the state. Coho populations had been in a freefall for years in North Coast waterways and the consensus among biologists was that development such as logging was largely to blame. Logging and the construction of logging roads, no matter how carefully engineered, silted up the streams, and the removal of vegetative cover warmed the water temperature.

Critics were holding out for a so-called "debt-for-nature" swap, in which all the disputed land—and possibly much more—would be protected in exchange for forgiving some $800 million in claims the Federal Deposit Insurance Corporation and the federal Office of Thrift Supervision had filed against Maxxam for the failure of the thrift. Maxxam would have none of that. The company disputed the government's claims and charged the Clinton administration with keeping the heat on Hurwitz in an attempt to force him into accepting the terms of the Deal.

Meanwhile, the activists kept up the full-contact action in the woods. That spring, Avcollie had another run-in with Climber Dan, who hadn't cooled off much over the winter. At an attempted blockade, Climber Dan threw a gallon jug of water at Avcollie, hitting him in the head. Then Climber Dan poured the water on Avcollie's head. Then came the familiar tirade: "Get the fuck out of here, you piece of shit, you stupid motherfucker. I've had enough of your dumb-ass shit." When a crew encountered protesters and went to call the sheriff, they returned with ominous news: "We called the sheriffs and the sheriffs aren't coming out here. They say they have a real crime to deal with. They said we can do whatever the fuck we want to you."

The pattern was the same elsewhere. A truck drove up to where Avcollie was squatting. The driver put the grille about an inch from his face and laid on the horn for about five minutes. One guy put his knee on Avcollie's neck and held his face in the ground, then gave him a couple of good kicks when he let him up with the warning, "Don't get up here again or you'll really fucking get hurt."

Another logger stopped and apologized to Avcollie.

Violence or the threat of it wasn't the only way crews handled hippies, and it certainly wasn't company policy to allow workingmen to blow off a little steam by thumping Earth First!ers. Some tried to coax them out of tree sits, calling, "Hey, hippie, you want pizza?"

The hippie to whom those queries were directed was Felony, aka Jennifer Walts. One morning the guy wasn't in such a good mood.

"You think you're up there changing something and you're not doing jack shit," he said. "You should get down and get yourself an education."

"I *have* an education," Felony shouted back. "I have a bachelor's in history from HSU."

"Yeah?" the guy shouted back, surprised. "Me, too."

The tree sitters could never tell how the PL workers would greet them—sometimes a diatribe, sometimes grudging concern from guys who had kids of roughly the protesters' age. Julia Butterfly Hill—who would not come down from Luna for two years and would land a book deal and a new career as a speaker—received regular cell phone calls from John Campbell telling her that her latte was getting cold. Some woods crews even hollered up to make sure tree sitters had enough food and water.

But the climate was increasingly sulfurous as the Deal lurched toward completion, and all sides assumed the worst of their opponents. In 1997, a pack of hippies opposed to the Deal marched into the Eureka office of Congressman Frank Riggs, threw sawdust all over the floor, dragged in a gigantic stump, trashed the place, locked their forearms and wrists into ninety-degree pipe lockboxes called black bears, and waited for the sheriffs to come. And come they did, with pepper spray and a video camera purportedly to record the events for training and insurance purposes. It was a spectacular public-relations blunder for the department. The video got out during discovery for the civil trial stemming from the incident and it was widely disseminated. Deputies were shown dabbing spray directly on the eyes of protesters who weren't resisting and couldn't if they had wanted to. It was believed to be the first time pepper spray had been used on passive detainees.

It looked a lot like torture. Young women screamed in pain. The sheriffs appeared to be thugs called to do Pacific Lumber's dirty work. And ever more, when there was the least little bit of news about the Deal or protesters or developments in the pepper-spray case, that video clip could be relied upon to turn up on the TV again. The noise got bad enough that Riggs, himself a former sheriff's deputy, felt compelled to rise on the floor of the House to defend the actions of the sheriff's department and the Eureka police. His office had been trespassed upon, Riggs said, and two employees terrorized. The Earth First!ers were not peaceful protesters but "wanton lawbreakers," who were only dosed after being told that they were resisting arrest. And it had been impossible to cut them out with power tools because the authorities were afraid a spark might set the sawdust on fire.

Whether one believed Riggs was standing up for an orderly society or simply functioning as a stooge of the timber industry (he consistently got low approval ratings from environmental groups rating members of Congress), the introduction of chemical warfare in the conflict was startling. The duration and intensity of the siege defied even the cockeyed logic that Humboldt County had operated under for so long. If the forest was about to be saved (at least in the popular consciousness outside Humboldt, although people inside knew better), why were these self-appointed enviro-commandos still at it?

There was one possible explanation, a conspiracy theory so seductive that a good number of locals had fallen for it like crush-stricken schoolgirls. Pacific Lumber *wanted* the Earth First!ers around because they were irresistible to the media. As long as the media were focused on the story, the public pressure would be on the government to save the precious redwood forest from that old sidewinder Hurwitz, and Takeover Charlie would have himself an almost half-billion-dollar check for a few thousand lousy acres that, truth be told, weren't park quality, weren't all that great to look at, and couldn't feasibly be developed as an inviting spot for a family picnic.

Gypsy Chain had left Texas headed for his second summer in the woods and hit a firefight. He was in the middle of the biggest and longest environmental battle in the country.

One of the major battlefields for the conflict that summer was in Pacific Lumber's holdings in the remote Mattole, a seismically active area buffeted by coastal winds and thick with old-growth Douglas fir. Protesters were blockading and cat and mousing in an effort to slow logging in the valley until they could get a hearing on their request for a restraining order to stop the timber harvest plan—if the hearing came after the trees were down, of course, the case would be moot. The issue, once again, was the coho salmon. The threatened fish were in Sulfur Creek, and the activists contended Pacific Lumber didn't have the necessary permit to "take" the fish.

Things got heavier. Seven activists were arrested at a blockade. Protesters were on the receiving end of death threats from loggers and security. Loggers knowingly felled trees into other trees that protesters had climbed. A logger tried to cut down a tree a woman had climbed. Kids were punched and had their gear cut.

Jay Moller, an attorney in nearby Redway, collected the protesters' declarations of abuse and more. Three activists complained that they'd faced deadly force. The sheriff's deputy who took the report told them that they had no right to complain because they'd been trespassing.

A judge granted a temporary restraining order on August 15.

* * *

DESPITE THE MORATORIUM ON LOGGING old growth and the imminent Deal, Pacific Lumber couldn't seem to stop sawing itself in the foot. It was on track to rack up another one hundred violations, as it had in each of the previous two years, for everything from erosion on down to offenses such as assaulting the biomass with a discarded gum wrapper. A lot of the violations were what they called fix-it tickets, as in: Fix it before I come back next time and we'll forget about it. But three hundred violations of the Forest Practices Act in three years was staggering.

The Earth First!ers were going to have to choose carefully where to focus their efforts in the traditional protest season. From their perspective, it was a question of whether they would have direct action in the woods to protest PL's numberless illegal harvest plans, or have direct action in town to get the media to report the Deal for the sham that it was.

Avcollie had spent a good part of the year working hard and saving in order to take a couple of weeks off for protest season. Other people did the same, arranged their lives so that they could say they did more than vote, to take part in civil disobedience. He saw Gypsy's sly face the first day of action camp and was glad to see him. It was Avcollie's third year and Gypsy's second, and it seemed like everybody at the camp was an old hand.

"What's the deal, is everybody a trainer here?" Gypsy asked Avcollie. "Is there anybody who does actions?" Avcollie felt a spark and excitement coming from Gypsy. Avcollie and Calista were doing the nonviolence training, which everybody always thought was boring. They'd do role-playing, talk about how hard it is to get your arms in a lockbox, discuss how to talk to an aggressive cop or logger. Gypsy was getting to do the backwoods stuff, which everybody always thought was fun and cool. Here's how you get supplies up a tree sit. Here's how you walk in the woods.

It was shaping up to be the best training camp ever. In addition to those who'd taken part in years past, a new crop was rolling in because the Deal was very much in the news. The energy was palpable. This year, they were going to get some things done.

Gypsy renewed his friendship with Felony. To her, it felt like they were in the process of becoming a couple. They were united in a mutual dislike of one another's forest names. Felony was so named because she wanted a reminder that what they were doing had potentially serious legal consequences.

" 'Gypsy' is really counterproductive, like we come in and wreak havoc and then leave," she told him.

Whatever. He called her Jennifer.

He wasn't a wanderer, wasn't some blissed-out hippie—he was more of a stand-your-ground kind of Texan. "You know that gray area where the extreme left wing and the extreme right wing come together in that don't-tread-on-me area? He was right there," she said.

He'd introduced himself to her in the pitch black of night at a tree sit. He held glow worms to his face so she could see what he looked like. Like other girls, she was charmed, but also a little standoffish when, after the end of the 1997 season, she didn't hear from him for nearly a year.

On the night of September 16, the group was at the Williams Grove campground near the town of Myers Flat, a hamlet that got by selling beer and gas and redwood knickknacks to campers and motorists cruising the Avenue of the Giants. The Earth First!ers were, through the excruciatingly democratic consensus process by which they did everything, attempting to decide whether the CDF was going to follow up on their concerns or whether an action in the morning was necessary to buy time. A good number of them thought it would be okay if they focused their efforts elsewhere, but Felony and Avcollie were cynical when it came to weighing the odds of the regulators doing their jobs.

"Yeah, right," Felony said as the debate raged. "They're going to stop the plan at 6:30 in the morning." By the time dinner was finished and they had the most tentative of plans, those who thought they'd go on the action, should there be one, headed back to Grizzly so they could get an early start.

By midnight it had started to drizzle. Felony, Gypsy, and two others got into her little convertible—the top wouldn't go up—to make the forty-five-minute drive to Grizzly. As they approached a roadhouse, Gypsy floated an idea: "You want to stop and get a shot of whiskey?"

The other two guys took a pass, but Gypsy and Felony went in. Felony drank some coffee to try to stay awake and Gypsy did, too. They'd both slept so badly the night before. When they went outside the other two guys were asleep in the car. Felony drove the narrow, curving two-lane with fat redwood trunks growing right up to the edge of the pavement. She noticed she was almost out of gas, actually hoping the convertible would conk out so she could just sleep a little. Gypsy was chatty, riding a coffee jag. He talked and talked, told her, "I'm setting my roots here. I'm done with Texas. I don't want to go back there."

They traded stories of heartbreak and false promises. Before long, Gypsy's chatter had exhausted Felony and she turned on the radio to shut him up. "You're right, I should stop talking so much," Gypsy said.

It was maybe 1:30 or 2:00 by the time they got to Grizzly. Felony climbed into the tent of fellow activist Mountain Goat, and Gypsy followed her in, climbing over her and lying against the tent wall. "I can't believe how tired I am," he said. "I hope we don't go tomorrow." When Felony coughed, Gypsy told her she shouldn't go because she sounded like she was getting sick. Felony took that chivalrous gesture with relief. The idea of getting up in four hours didn't sound like fun. Felony threw her arm over Gypsy and put her head on his chest.

By the time she awoke, the crew was already gone.

Later, she saw a stunned Farmer come walking down the road, saying over and over, "His brains fell out. I saw his brains. I think he's dead."

Felony thought Farmer had to be wrong. She ran up the hill as fast as she could. She ran down to the base of the tree that'd been felled. She shrieked, "You fucking loggers, you killed my boyfriend."

One of the protesters came over to where Ammons's spotter, Reback, and the yarder crew were sitting, told them thanks for the help, that none of this had been part of the plan. Reback didn't want to hear it. The woods were not some half-assed hippie playground. This was no place to be fucking around.

"You need to stay over there," Reback said. "We're not too happy with you guys right now."

As Felony was making a spectacle of herself, the rest of the Earth First!ers were tuning into comments from the PL crew and the sheriff's deputies arriving. One of them said not to bother calling an ambulance. If Felony's memory is correct, a deputy told her there would be no investigation because "as far as we're concerned it was an accident."

In the first hours after Gypsy was killed, that was also the official word from the Earth First! office up in Arcata. Josh Brown got the call and mobilized the PR machine, issuing a press release that an activist had accidentally been killed protesting an illegal timber cut. Pacific Lumber issued a preliminary release of its own saying that one of the trespassers had been killed when a falling tree collided with and brought down another tree in a sort of domino effect.

Big A knew better than that—he'd dropped the tree close to perfect—but Big A was by then at Redwood Memorial Hospital waiting to give a urine sample for a drug test. He was visibly agitated. The technician asked him why he was in such a hurry.

"I just killed somebody," he said. "I'd like to get this over and done with so I can go home."

Big A lived in a ramshackle motor home by the ball field—the scoreboard noted it was donated by Pacific Lumber—and over a one-lane bridge in Fortuna. He had one of those THIS FAMILY SUPPORTED BY TIMBER DOLLARS signs that could be seen all over, especially around

Scotia and Fortuna. He had a covered workshop attached to the house and a yardful of ratted-out pickups, drive shafts, and random car parts. Friends were showing up out of concern and Reback, who'd known the guy since he was three years old, took a shower and drove over. Big A didn't know half the people he worked with, but it seemed like all of them were there at his house. He would have just as soon they weren't there, but you can't stop people when they mean well. Reback and Big A drank a few beers out of the fridge Big A had in the shop. It was always stocked with Keystone and off-brand soda. The soda was for Ammons's teenaged son, who drank so much of it Ammons always bought the cheapest he could find. After a while Reback said, "Let's go get something to eat," and they headed over to La Costa for some Mexican food.

Reback heard somebody ask Big A, "Why didn't you kill them all?"

Gypsy
Mountain

 GRIEF POURED LIKE A RAIN of hammers on Cindy and
Ron Allsbrooks's house.

Bridgett's children were there. Sarah was just then navigating
through more than three hours of country roads from Austin. Ron got
the message as soon as he arrived at the chemical plant to pull his
graveyard shift: Call home immediately. He drove those sixty-five miles
back to Coldspring knowing that he'd lost not only a son but Cindy as
well. He had a feeling, even before he got home, that their marriage
was finished.

Cindy was trying to get her mind around the concept that her son
was dead, and the natural response was paradoxically to deny—*This.
Can. Not. Be.*—and to seek details and confirmation. She got on the

phone to the emergency room, thinking that Nathan was just hurt but being worked on. They'd take care of her boy. But the woman at the ER gave her the number for the coroner's office. She called it. The coroner, Frank Yager, would write in an investigation report that Allsbrooks told him "she had been called by the legal section of 'Earth First' and they told her that their son had been killed during a logging protest." Yager told her he had a John Doe, that the body had no ID. Allsbrooks described Nathan's three tattoos. The coroner said he'd have to call her back in ten minutes.

She passed the excruciating minutes telling Bridgett, "There's no way, there's got to be a mistake."

The coroner didn't call back. Allsbrooks couldn't take it anymore and called him.

"Yes, ma'am," he said. "That's your son."

Earlier in the day, Juan Freeman, a grandly mustachioed sheriff's detective, had been dispatched to Grizzly Creek to investigate the case. As he arrived, he heard chatter on the radio that witnesses were being released from the scene. He got on the horn and asked that they be held, but it didn't do any good. None of the protesters would speak to him. Their story was they were too upset. So when Freeman spoke with Allsbrooks around 11:00 P.M. Texas time, the detective in charge of the investigation didn't have a lot of answers and seemed to Allsbrooks almost stingy with the ones he did have. Then Freeman started asking *her* questions, pumping *her* for information, which felt odd. Wasn't he supposed to be the one who knew what was going on? Allsbrooks wanted to get off the phone. She looked at the receiver with slightly raised eyebrows. She asked him where the nearest airport was and he told her Arcata-Eureka.

She and the rest of the family sat up until three or four in the morning, rolling variations of a question over and over, trying to fathom a death that was as freakish as it was tragic: "What just happened?"

The next day, September 18, she got a call from a Humboldt minister who'd been trying to make peace between the warring parties. He told her that he had prayed with the kids and prayed with the logger, and that the logger had prayed, too, and had asked for forgiveness.

"I'm so glad y'all prayed. I'm so sorry for everybody involved," she said. Then she went back into her shock state. It looked like an accident, Freeman had told her. A bizarre accident.

Then came the videotape and the entrance of the redwood rabbi.

Off Highway 36 toward Grizzly Creek are the old Grange Hall, Pacific Lumber's mill at Carlotta, and a handful of boarded-up combination gas station–liquor stores. Before Grizzly there was a cedar house in which a Jewish mystic and her family lived. Her name was Naomi Steinberg, and she was a student rabbi. To her, understanding the ecology of the land was an inherent part of her job, an intertwining of topography and spirituality. Her husband had been teaching the children of millworkers and PL executives for almost twenty years in Scotia. His first job was working at Murphy Elementary School, named for the family that ran the company that owned the town. It was a great environment for him. On back-to-school nights, the place would be packed with parents, welcoming and hardworking, plotting something fruitful, perhaps better than they'd had, for their kids. Naomi Steinberg's plan when they'd moved to the North Coast was to plant a good garden, meditate while it was growing, and can lots of vegetables when they were ready. She knew nothing of high finance or deep ecology.

Then the takeover came. A neighbor of Steinberg's who worked for PL was thinking of running for county supervisor because of the way the company was behaving—a little judicious government oversight seemed to be in order. The neighbor pressed Steinberg into helping with the campaign and, after an election with enough suspicious irregularities to be worthy of a banana republic, it was no surprise the prospective reformer lost. "It was," Steinberg would later say, "a tremendously sobering experience."

From there, Steinberg got involved in the lawsuit to fight Hurwitz's raid of the PL pension fund. She published *Takeback: A Newsletter of the PL Rescue Fund*, which existed largely for the sake of anti-takeover forces to keep abreast of the flurry of malevolent activity and the good citizens' efforts to stand up, most of the time in various courthouses, for what was right. Eureka lawyer Bill Bertain, born in Scotia into a longtime timber family, had sued to invalidate Hurwitz's takeover. There was still a stench over the way Takeover Charlie had gone for the $55 million PL pensioners' fund and terminated the plan in favor of one offered by Executive Life Insurance Company, a subsidiary of a company that was a major buyer of the junk bonds Hurwitz had used in the takeover. And Hurwitz was blatantly using the sale of redwood to annex more companies and expand his financial empire. In a leveraged buyout, Maxxam had gone after Kaiser Aluminum—which, like Pacific Lumber, was undervalued and slow on the uptake—and won.

Steinberg was by then an activist through and through, but she tried to keep her involvement quiet for the sake of her husband's job. She met a Jewish meditation master who drew out her diverse interests—nature, justice, spirituality, the imperative to lead a moral life. She started volunteering at a congregation in southern Humboldt County, and when she went to lead high holy days as a student rabbi in 1995, she couldn't keep her environmental views to herself. She arrived at Yom Kippur services with a draft of a letter to Charles Hurwitz, imploring him as a fellow Jew to repent for the wrong he'd done. So began an annual tradition of writing Takeover Charlie a letter every Yom Kippur.

A pivotal moment in her activist life came when she was asked to speak at the September 15, 1996, rally outside the Grange Hall, to six thousand people standing in the rain. As Steinberg spoke, she felt blind, uncontrollable rage—as if, she said, it was coming out of the ground itself and pouring through her. Somebody later said she sounded like the prophet Jeremiah. Her voice descended to a guttural growl she'd never heard when she said, "Mr. Hurwitz, shame on you." A mass of 1,033 people stepped over a line to trespass on Pacific Lumber property, but the sheriffs ran out of citations and were only able to arrest one thousand. The line to get arrested was so long that the protesters let Steinberg take a cut so she wouldn't have to wait. It was the largest act of civil disobedience in the history of the American environmental movement, organizers claimed.

The large and well-organized environmental community in the Bay Area was by now aware of the Humboldt situation, and star-spotting became a semiregular pastime. Bonnie Raitt showed up, climbed the steep trail, and then ascended Luna and presented Julia Butterfly Hill with Raitt's Bay Area Music Award. Woody Harrelson did the same, and although he wasn't toting a Bammy, he did spend the night in the tree. Jello Biafra from the Dead Kennedys. Mickey Hart from the Grateful Dead. And the celebs weren't immune from arrest. Raitt would feel a particularly acute connection to the cause, later dedicating a concert to David Chain's memory. She also would persist in her willingness to face arrest.

Things in 1998 were different. The seasonal approach to direct action pretty much ceased. Before, tree sits tended to last no more than a few weeks, with people rotating in and out of the trees constantly. But now Luna was turning tenacious Julia Butterfly Hill into a rock star and tree sitting itself into a way of life for adventurous types. Sits on Bell Creek and Bear Creek were rolling. It seemed like a few people were coming to view tree sits not as temporary measures designed to slow or stop cutting but as a way to avoid calls from credit card companies looking to collect on delinquent accounts. The Deal was still contentious, and the possibility of salvage logging—in which dead, fire-prone trees are harvested—might further threaten Headwaters. The civil case the pepper-spray victims had brought against the county had ended in a hung jury in San Francisco. Protesters were by then a chronic presence in the woods, and the tension level between both activists and loggers spiraled up.

Above Grizzly Creek, they'd set up a sit in a tree the activists called Aradia, which they believed to be the oldest tree on the mountain. Gypsy was one of the first people to climb that tree.

Then Gypsy was killed. Naomi Steinberg drove to where some of the Earth First!ers were camped. She'd been preparing to give comfort in her role as a student rabbi, but she wound up sobbing over the campfire for hours. Years of anxiety for the nonviolent protesters—exposed to the elements, working high aloft trees, vulnerable to loggers with bad tempers and chain saws—poured out of her as the rage had when she'd spoken at the rally.

The next day, a Friday, criminal defense attorney Jay Moller called and asked Steinberg if he could use her home to meet with the Earth First! witnesses, who had still refused to speak with the sheriff's department. Steinberg said of course. Moller had done pro bono work for Earth First! and other environmental concerns in the area for years. Now he was stepping up to represent the protesters in the criminal investigation. Ayr Eisenberg and others who had been on the mountain when Gypsy died were adamant that the witnesses should not talk to each other about what had happened because if they did and word got out that they had, it'd appear that the EF!ers were trying to get their stories straight. Moller had admonished them similarly, and when he interviewed them at Steinberg's, he did so individually. For once, consensus would not be the Earth First! way.

What Moller heard told him Big A should be charged. Steinberg spent the day talking to Allsbrooks on the phone, comforting the activists, and listening to Big A's tirade as activists dubbed copies of the heretofore undisclosed videotape on her VCR.

In the first wave of sketchy bulletins after Gypsy's death, the irony was cheap, easy, and irresistible: Tree hugger killed by falling tree. It sounded like an *Esquire* Dubious Achievement Award, and media around the world gave fleeting attention to the story. A protester had been killed in an apparent accident. The proper authorities promised a full and impartial investigation. Both Earth First! and Pacific Lumber were battling on the public-relations front with sketchy information and hastily hatched theories.

Then EF! flashed the smoking gun. The videotape would make the story a sensation.

The two-person Earth First! video crew of Mike McCurdy and Zoe Zalia had captured a frightening eruption of rage, adrenal fear, and confusion. McCurdy was by no means a protest newbie. He'd sat in Luna. He'd tried to engage a logger near Stafford who was cutting an old-growth tree and the guy just kept on sawing, with McCurdy close enough that the sawdust flew in his face. At the Bear Creek tree sit, the sheriffs and the loggers arrived together, and the tree McCurdy was sitting in was rammed with a bulldozer. Climber Dan had cut McCurdy's stuff out of a tree and cut his rope so he couldn't come down. He'd been told of loggers felling trees at protesters out in the Mattole, an area so remote that if a tree hugger went missing, nobody might know about it for a long time.

But that morning on the mountain was a whole new level of surreality. From the protesters' perspective, this guy was a homicidal maniac from the get-go. Big A was threatening to kill them, so McCurdy and Zalia scrambled uphill. They had the foresight to put in a fresh tape after the first confrontation in case the camcorder was seized, then the two of them got separated and McCurdy came down the mountain alone.

Visually, the tape didn't show much, and the camcorder wasn't even on in the critical moments. Earlier, Zalia stood on a fresh-cut stump; the camcorder panned to show a clear-cut. During the recorded showdown, the brush was so dense it was hard to make visual sense of the confrontation, but the audio made Big A's fury quite clear. McCurdy hid behind a tree and, breathing hard, whispered with a trembling voice that they'd come across a seriously pissed-off logger.

"Get outta here! Otherwise I'll fuckin', I'll make sure I got a tree comin' this way!"

"All right, well, let's not talk about that. You know we're not gonna—"

"Cocksucker!"

The Earth First! media machine kicked into overdrive. Message: the videotape showed the logger threatening to fell trees in the direction of the nonviolent protesters who simply were on hand to tell the logger that he might be breaking the law and at minimum was working a bad plan. A protester was then killed. Simple. Tragic. Proof positive Pacific Lumber regarded the protesters, who were there doing the California Department of Forestry's job, as subhuman hippies. The subhuman hippies, meanwhile, were ripping audio and video copies as fast as they could to hand out to reporters and producers. A transcript hit the Internet, along with digital audio files.

The tape radically strengthened the EF! case, and it made for dramatic broadcast news.

THE DAY BEFORE, JOSH BROWN had been sitting in the little EF! office in Arcata writing a press release about the previous day's lockdown above Grizzly Creek. Somebody had to do media and he was good at it. The phone rang. If Josh was absorbing what he heard correctly, Farmer had come down the mountain telling Felony that Gypsy's brains were falling out. Felony had called Julia Butterfly Hill up in Luna; Hill had called her friend Robert Parker who was now calling the EF! office with the news. Brown and Angela Wartes, who was also in the office, started calling everyone they could think of: all the emergency responders, the CDF, even the Pacific Lumber spokeswoman, Mary Bullwinkel, in Scotia. Somehow they got Sarah Chain's work number in Austin, and Wartes took a deep breath and made the call.

The media queries began to roll in. Brown told them what little he knew: Looks like an accident. Logger didn't know they were still there. Wasn't a direct hit. Domino effect.

Then the survivors drifted in and the story changed radically. The true horror of what Big A had threatened to do and then had done was apparent. "Dude, that's as fucked up as it gets," a friend told Brown. Brown sat down with Ayr and Sleeper and they transcribed the videotape for what was to be a bombshell for the following morning: Look, this guy was a raging lunatic. And we've got the tape to prove it.

The protesters had said they were too upset to talk immediately after Gypsy's killing, but it looked to suspicious observers as if they were holding something back. Then sixteen-year-old Farmer, aka Jeremy Jensen, wrote and released a statement that confirmed the suspicions of seasoned woodsmen. Farmer's statement said a Douglas fir had killed his companion, a mistake at least one other activist duplicated. Goddam stupid hippies didn't know what they were talking about. Couldn't tell a redwood if it hit them in the head.

Never mind that the tape only showed the first encounter, that portions of it were inaudible, and that by the time of the fatal encounter McCurdy was out of the area. Had there been no tape, it would have been the Earth First!ers' word against the loggers'. With the tape, the protesters had powerful evidence of the violence to which they were continually subjected—violence that the culture within Pacific Lumber tacitly condoned. Violence that had left one of the forest defenders on a slab at the county morgue.

The Earth First!ers at the action camp knew they'd have to blockade the gate the following morning or Pacific Lumber would be back to continue logging and destroy the scene of the homicide. Forty or fifty of them got there at 4:30 A.M., and within ten minutes the first logging truck pulled in, saw them, backed out, and drove away. A water truck had already beat them to the scene and gone up the road—to spray and keep the dust down—and there was a fine Earth First! moment when they quarreled about whether or not to let the guy and the truck go out or hold him there, because if he were allowed to leave, he'd just go water other roads and logging there would proceed as well. It was a classic, pointless debate. The guy in the water truck looked a little scared before they cut him loose.

Then the sheriffs came. After the pepper-spray fiasco, the sheriffs knew that EF! was quite capable of turning being arrested to its own advantage, much as the civil rights protesters had, so nobody got arrested this time. This was a big deal. They'd never blocked a road and completely shut down a logging plan. This was a mass occupation in the making, an action both exhilarating and gravely serious.

The Gypsy Mountain Free State was up and rolling.

They cut Gypsy open. On the night his fellow warriors had declared a free state in honor of his sacrifice, forensic pathologist Mark Super conducted the autopsy, with Yager assisting. They noted the clothing: brown hiking boots, a brown T-shirt that had been partially cut away, an olive long-john shirt tied around his waist, a deer antler tied to his belt, scattered bloodstains. They noted that the head was flattened because of severe skull fractures. They noted numerous broken bones. They weighed the brain and found that less than half of it, only 620 grams, remained within "the cranial vault." The principal findings: "Comminuted [pulverized] 'egg shell' fractures of calvarium and basilar skull."

David Nathan "Gypsy" Chain, twenty-four, of Coldspring, Texas, had died of blunt-force head trauma and thoracic injuries. He'd died in a flash, just as he'd predicted when he and Stephanie Trager and some friends had been on their hands and knees painting banners in the middle of that pounding thunderstorm outside the warehouse. "That's how I'm going to go out," Gypsy had said. "In a flash."

Back home in New York, Trager thought about that when her father read her the item in the paper about an activist being killed in the woods. She also thought back to that first night she and Gypsy spent in the tree sit the year before. Gypsy had told her that he felt like he was much more meaningfully occupied than he would be if he were back home. "I'd be wasting my time there," he'd said. "Me and my friends just hang around." She also thought about how he told her he didn't believe he was fated to live a long life.

While the autopsy proceeded, Freeman was conducting an examination of his own, interviewing the Earth First! witnesses, with Jay Moller along to look after them. The sheriff's office had already issued an initial press release saying the killing appeared to be an accident, which would later fuel suspicions of a sham investigation. Pacific Lumber had 1,600 workers and plunked some $170 million into the local economy. You didn't have to be an eco-radical to believe the whole county—lock, stock, and governmental barrel—was in the pocket of its largest private employer.

The EF! network was abuzz with the news that one of their own had been martyred, and people were coming up from all over the West to see what they could do and show their support. Their brother's blood had paid for the land, and they descended on the place. On the afternoon Gypsy was killed, investigators said their access to the death scene was being hampered by activists, while the activists accused the sheriffs of carelessly dithering—What's the rush? It's just a dead hippie who's hugged his last tree—while daylight bled away into the Pacific.

Over the weekend the activists' numbers grew. The mood was part vigil, part siege, part Lollapalooza. A sleepy-looking guy named Walleye with dreadlocks the color of sand said he'd given up his recording studio and rapping career to come defend the forest because, "The Mother comes first. The Goddess comes first." And so he'd come, to live among the trees that some of the activists said had souls and spoke to them.

Aside from the radically amorphous, anything-goes, animist spirituality to which some but not all of them subscribed, practical concerns had to be dealt with, too. They put up a tarp and a ramshackle rampart along the highway barricade to protect them from the beer bottles—and the occasional gunshot—coming from pickups barreling around the bend in the highway. They called that border of the free state the front door, and a lot of people, freaked out at being so close to the enemy, went up the hill to comparative safety, and were reluctant to come down. They painted banners. They played drums given to them by Indian elders, lounged on the ground, smoked dope, and waved at one another with hands attached to wrists dangling chains. Whenever the sheriffs came, they were ready to lock down as soon as the alert sounded. They hauled in an old junked car and blocked the logging road (these were called "batmobiles" in EF! parlance) and two people were ready to lock down into it. All the way up the mountain the road had been blocked with logs and other debris, making a stiff hike or an all-terrain-vehicle ride the only ways to access the site. Up on the landing the vibe was borderline convivial, with Earth First!ers who hadn't seen each other in ages. Was it the last time they'd gotten arrested in Sacramento? Or was it at the protest of the Nike store in Eugene? A shoeless girl held an infant close to her against the approaching late-afternoon chill.

Over by the landing the activists had named Monstertown, past another barricade and a rubber death-head mask, a man called Jumping Stick was sitting next to a loader above where Gypsy was killed. He, along with all the others, was waiting for the sheriffs to come. Waiting to go to jail. Listening for Gypsy in the trees.

Earth First! was, in a spasm of rather awkward logic, simultaneously demanding a complete criminal investigation and preventing it. The professed reason for occupying the mountain—apart from the fact that it was now a holy place, not to mention that it was a fine backdrop for TV remotes—was to keep PL from going to the scene and destroying the evidence that would conclusively prove Big A had murder in his heart. Portions of an Earth First! press release from the Monday following Chain's death suggested a paranoia that had been validated by violence:

Confrontation looms this morning as Earth First! enters its fourth day of blockading the logging road leading up to the site where "Gypsy" David Chain was killed by a tree now believed to be intentionally felled in his and other protesters' direction last Thursday, Sept. 17 . . . Approximately 50 people are occupying the road, located on Hwy. 36, 17 miles E. of Hwy. 101 in order to prevent the crime scene from being destroyed by Pacific Lumber . . .

Sheriffs called the killing of Chain an accident even before they had interviewed a single witness. Earth First! is insisting that a manslaughter investigation take place immediately before the downed trees are removed. Seven witnesses report that the logger changed the trajectory of the trees he was falling in order to aim them toward old growth logging protesters . . .

The release then raised the possibility that Gypsy's killing might be what the Earth First!ers had for so long failed to win—a Deal breaker, despite the fact that Governor Pete Wilson had signed the bill authorizing California's part of the purchase just two days after the activist was killed:

With $500 million dollars about to line the pockets of the MAXXAM Corporation, it is not surprising that the Humboldt Sheriff's Deputies and the Department of Forestry are reluctant to prosecute Pacific Lumber. Contrary to news reports, the Headwaters deal is far from complete. The money will not be released until Pacific Lumber is issued a Habitat Conservation Plan (HCP). If the company commits a serious crime on its land, the HCP can be denied . . . Pacific Lumber has committed both violations of the Endangered Species Act and committed manslaughter, according to Earth First! Additionally, if the logger is tried, Earth First! expects it will be revealed that he was only following an institutionalized policy of falling trees and committing other acts of violence toward protesters.

Fresh troops brought donated food and water in produce boxes, cell phones, and two-way radios. It was like resupplying the world's biggest tree sit.

It went on for three weeks. The wait was making them frazzled. Things were falling apart. Helicopters were buzzing overhead. People the Earth First!ers believed to be plainclothes cops were pulling up trying to snare them, asking where to buy pot. The front door was still there, but it wasn't occupied much. The front door was the front line, and nobody wanted to be there. The night before they got raided, they'd had a feeling they might get popped the next morning and started packing their gear out. Josh Brown slept next to the junk car that night. He woke and thought, "Ah, they're not here." The next thing he heard was people yelling, "Raid!" Fifty or sixty sheriffs and California Highway Patrolmen were retaking the mountain, pepper spray in hand. One girl refused to unlock herself after the sheriffs doused her eyes three times. Another attempt to block the mountain road the following day resulted in more pepper spray and six more arrests. One of them was Ayr Eisenberg. It was, Darryl Cherney said, a pathetic end to a historic occupation.

When the PL crews reclaimed the place, they found some hippie had taken a dump and smeared it around the gauge panels and antenna on a piece of heavy equipment. Josh Brown apologized and said in the paper that if they found out who did it, they'd ask them to leave. Darryl Cherney later wrote a song about the incident. He called it "The Process of Elimination."

AT THE TIME THE OCCUPATION was rolling, David Allen Chain was back in Pasadena, assigned the grim task of casket-shopping for his son.

They buried Gypsy on a Thursday, a week after his breath had left him. He had wanted to be cremated, but his father couldn't handle it. He had wanted his organs donated, too, but the autopsy had prevented that. Before the service, at which David Nathan Chain's face was covered with a sort of veil, David Allen Chain forced himself to look. Cindy Allsbrooks couldn't.

Ravyn Erlewine, the girlfriend with whom he had parted less than amicably before his westward sojourn, was staying at a hotel in Pasadena. She had worked very late the night before Gypsy was killed, and didn't go to bed until around 4 A.M. When she woke in the late morning, after tossing and turning and getting frustrated that she couldn't sleep longer, she opened her eyes and saw David Chain at the foot of her bed, wearing the white painter's shorts he always wore and an orange T-shirt. He was looking at her without much expression on his face. She thought, *We'll talk soon*. She was sufficiently weirded out by the dream or vision or whatever it was that when she went to work that day, she told a friend about it. Later in the shift, Gabriel Deutsch called Trudy's from California to report that David Chain had been killed. The manager put her arm around Ravyn and said, "We need to go outside." Ravyn thought she was in trouble. The manager said, "David has been killed."

Ravyn's mind seized. "Who is David?" She felt numb, cold, and most definitely didn't want to hear any more than the bare details she'd been given. She got a ride home.

Before they'd broken up, she and David—both Geminis—had felt like twins. Ravyn had never felt that way about anybody before. David was going through an old scrapbook of hers and found a tracing-paper original of her mother's batik. It was of two faces sharing one eye. David saw that and knew it was them. They were each going to get tattoos of that design. But they dragged their feet—body art is something of an extravagance when you're trying to save for a big trip—and then came the breakup. The day before the funeral, Ravyn got the tattoo on her shoulder blade. She had known David Chain all of ten weeks, and now a remembrance of him was a permanent part of her. She took the paper design to Pasadena to be buried with David. Sister Sarah Chain and another ex-girlfriend of David's would, without discussing it, get tattoos in his memory. All three of them were between their shoulder blades. The similarity of the three designs was subject to interpretation, but it was a striking coincidence nonetheless.

There for the funeral, Erlewine went through a duffel bag of David's stuff that Gabriel had brought back with him. Inside were necklaces, a pipe, and a letter—unsigned and apparently unfinished. It was dated August 12.

Ravyn, my love,
I'm writing to clear my mind.
I don't know if this is something I'll ever give you or not, but often I have an easier time putting my thoughts on paper. I know nothing of what's to come, and I've stopped trying to guess. You know how I feel about you, maybe not to the full extent, but you know. I definitely see how you could be so unsure after the way I've treated our friendship. I never meant to cause you any pain. I was very selfish . . . in my behavior. You are the most incredible person I know, and I squandered your affection and trust. That may be the biggest sin I've ever committed. I'm not going to worry about our fate too much if I can help it. When I break it all down in my head I know that what will be will be. I also know that I can deal with the pain or joy of the outcome. Everything I've learned about positive thinking and energy refuses to let me put my thoughts toward what I would consider a tragedy in my life. I am instead focusing my energy on what I really, really want and need. I've started to make really big steps in the right directions. I'm feeling good about what lies ahead. I'm ready to accept whatever you decide without an argument. I know I won't get angry about it for sure. I love you unconditionally and if you feel I'm not healthy for you then I trust your judgment . . .

More than three hundred people from all stages of David Chain's life turned out at the Grand View Funeral Home in Pasadena for the service. The overflow mourners spilled into the lobby. The family was there, of course, as were friends from childhood and young adulthood in Austin. His Earth First! friends Sleeper and Dijon and Felony took a Greyhound across the country to be on hand. Naomi Steinberg delivered a eulogy that attempted to explain why the man most of them knew as Dave or Nathan or Gypsy died. She told them a story about fish.

She told them that ten years ago, she'd taken her children to the spot where Grizzly Creek connects with the river to watch the salmon run. The salmon used to be so dense in the waterways that old-timers said they could practically walk on them, that they made the river "look like a shining stream of silver," Steinberg said. When she took her children, however, they saw only a handful of fish.

"But it was still wonderful," she said, "to watch the female swish her tail in the gravel to make a nest for her eggs, and then the males would dart in, competing for the privilege of fertilizing them, in the beautiful, ancient dance of life.

"A few years ago we went back to Grizzly Creek and saw to our sorrow that because of erosion caused by logging on the steep slopes above, the channel was filled with mud and debris. The creek water was a mere trickle and no longer met the river. My children got down on their hands and knees trying to dig out the mud so the creek could flow unimpeded. We saw no salmon that year. I hear that in the great storms last year some came back, but I know those gravel spawning beds are buried under silt. And with the shade trees overhead stripped away, the water temperature rises too high and the hatchlings will perish. And so the beautiful dance of the salmon will come to an end.

"I am telling you this because Grizzly Creek is the very place David was working to protect when he was killed. This brave young man understood what so many have failed to grasp—that the delicate balance of nature is more important than the corporate balance sheet."

She told them that in her religious tradition one said a prayer every morning thanking God for the gift of life. And that when she had heard that a young man had died defending her backyard, she had made a vow that every morning for the rest of her life before thanking God for her life, she would thank David Chain for his.

"May he long be remembered as one of the true heroes of our time."

More grief was unleashed at the graveyard just down the road from the junior college David had attended. They buried him under a canopy that was too small to shade all the people gathered. Steinberg filled a paper cup with soil from the grave. In the Jewish tradition, mourners don't leave until the casket is lowered into the ground and literally or symbolically covered in dirt. It appeared to Steinberg that the cemetery crew thought the knot of people was overstaying its welcome.

Sarah Chain looked at the casket and asked, "Is it all right if I touch it?"

"Of course you can touch it," Steinberg said. "It's your brother. It's your brother's casket."

Cindy Allsbrooks stood at the hole where her son would be lowered into the ground, wondering if she had the strength to draw another breath, shed another tear.

After the burial, the mourners shared the overabundance of food typical at a wake and traded stories at Cindy's sister Karen's house, endeavoring to stitch together a remembrance of an incomplete life. Somebody had written a song. Others told funny stories. Erlewine asked Ron to step outside with her. She told him David felt as if he and his stepfather had mended their relationship toward the end. That did it for Ron. He fell apart.

Gabriel Deutsch gave Erlewine the orange T-shirt, the one from her dream, if that's what it had been.

Cindy and Ron Allsbrooks had more than an emotional burden to bear. They'd had to finance part of the burial and monument costs.

NAOMI STEINBERG HAD ONE MORE errand. As soon as she'd learned she was going to Houston she called Hurwitz's temple, Beth Israel, the oldest congregation in Texas, to seek an audience with Hur-

witz's rabbi to see if she might accomplish what the Yom Kippur letters and ads in the Houston Jewish newspaper hadn't. After David
Chain's funeral, Steinberg got a call that the rabbi had forty-five minutes for her, just before Friday night services. She ascended the stairs
of the magnificent building—it was bigger than the airport back in
Humboldt County, she thought—and saw HURWITZ BUILDING etched
in stone on the new hall. She hesitated at the mezuzah, the case con-
taining a scroll of parchment with a verse from Deuteronomy. Could
she kiss Charles Hurwitz's mezuzah? She felt a momentary wave of revulsion, but then realized it was her mezuzah, too, kissed it, and
walked into the empty, cavernous hall. A janitor directed her to the
rabbi's office.

"You've had a hard week, haven't you?" Rabbi Samuel Egal Karff
asked.

"I've had a hard *decade*," Steinberg said, and she put her head down
on the rabbi's mahogany table and wept as hard as she had at the campfire.

Steinberg said she knew their time was short but wanted to meet
with Charles Hurwitz's rabbi because Hurwitz was "the point at which
our lives connect." She asked that the rabbi ask Hurwitz to see that
David Chain's death site not be disturbed until the investigation could
be completed. She asked him to implore Hurwitz to examine the company's policies and practices to prevent further loss of life. The rabbi—
a longtime activist for homeless people who was also full of facts and
figures about the company run by his congregation's fabulously wealthy
benefactor—said he would intervene on the first request but not on the
second. Besides, Karff asked, hasn't the forest been saved? Hasn't an
agreement been reached?

"We do not have the time for me to sit down with you and critique
this agreement," Steinberg said.

Steinberg joined the rabbi for Shabbat services. She stood in the
front row in the best clothes she'd brought with her to Texas, and she
sang her heart out.

That same afternoon, two thousand miles from Houston, some two hundred protesters gathered near the Eureka waterfront, carrying placards that said KILLED BY GREED—MURDER, INDEED and the like. They marched on the Humboldt County Courthouse, where local lawyer Steve Schectman told them that he—and so far as he knew, only he—was conducting an independent investigation into Chain's death.

The environmental activists, of course, were not alone in being adept at the fine art of applied propaganda. One day the alert went out that a representative from the group Women in Timber would be having a press conference at the Eureka Inn, a stately chalet just off the main drag. The timber interests presented a prim woman in business attire who begged for perspective, saying it would be nice if once, just once, some of the media had been present to make a big deal out of one of the workingmen who had died in the forest.

"There've been hundreds of martyrs out in the woods," said Claudia Lima, the wife of a contract logger. "Hundreds of people have lost their lives."

One among the knot of TV reporters and newspaper scribblers asked her to assess the new reality, in the wake of Gypsy's death. Claudia Lima looked somber, as if a migraine was about to descend upon her.

"This isn't politics now," she said. "This is life and death. I just wish it'd go away, I swear to God."

Lima wasn't the only one at her wit's end, exasperated at the way the media were feasting like a pack of half-starved coyotes on the novelty of a dead tree hugger. "It's very painful to the people who have lost their own relatives in the woods," said Mary Bullwinkel, PL's public-relations point person who was also a former reporter. "They wonder, 'What if this was a timber faller that was killed?' There would be a one-day story—'How sad'—and then it would go away. This was not intentional, period. And I think it's sad that our opponents are using this as a new cause."

* * *

THE MORE CINDY ALLSBROOKS HEARD, the less she understood. People were saying her son was a martyr—"one of the true heroes of our time." Her Nathan? He was the little boy who would not get
out of bed until she made a snake with her arms and tickled him under the covers. He was a boy who, after the Pentecostal services that
the family attended for a time, would stand on a table and preach in
his underwear. This alleged martyr the forest defenders called Gypsy
was not the son she knew. Still, she sensed that he had had a better
grasp of the world as a bigger place than most people, herself included,
and there was no question that she needed to see where he died in order for his death to be explicable to her. Environmental groups offered
to fly her, Ron, Bridgett, and Sarah out for a memorial and shuttle them
around. Two days after she put her son in the ground, she was on a
plane to San Francisco.

She took in the Bonnie Raitt concert, the one dedicated to the
memory of Gypsy Chain. Raitt introduced herself to the family backstage and offered condolences. There was an abundance of environmental literature at the show. One booth was running a video about
Julia Butterfly Hill, who was still up in Luna. Sarah Chain picked up a
flyer that was essentially a primer on deep ecology, "the concept that
nature existed to exist in and of itself." She would later recall: "Just as
humans exist without something more powerful destroying and consuming them to their extinction, nature should be given the same opportunity. This is so much a part of my ideology now, but at the time I
remember being enlightened."

Then there was a memorial service in Berkeley, with Steinberg and
others speaking. The memorial card suggested that contributions in
Chain's memory be sent to North Coast Earth First!'s post office box
in Arcata, with a note indicating that the donation was for the Gypsy
memorial fund.

Then there were the media. As Sarah Chain said days after her brother's death, "It's this huge worldwide story, and I'm his sister. I feel like I don't have time to mourn the loss of my brother. It's such an event right now. It feels too big."

They drove up the coast and when they hit the tall trees, Allsbrooks had to get out and look. The family was so taken with the giants that they were almost late for another memorial service, this one at the Methodist Church at 11th and Q Streets in Arcata. She turned to Gypsy's friends at such gatherings for comfort. She turned to Steve Schectman—the lawyer who had assured the crowd at the courthouse that he was conducting an independent investigation—for justice.

STEVE SCHECTMAN WAS FROM ALBANY PARK, an immigrant neighborhood on the north side of Chicago. "I grew up thinking there were only Orthodox Jews, conservative Jews, and Puerto Ricans," he said. His parents were first-generation Americans, descendants of Yiddish-speaking émigrés from the Ukraine. His father and all his uncles had gone off to fight in World War II. His father had come home, gone to night school on the GI Bill—the first member of the family to go to college—and planned on going into advertising, but anti-Semitism blocked his path. He started a company called Industrial Staples, which made stiff metal fasteners that held pieces of furniture together. At home, Schectman's grandparents lived downstairs. He and his sister were discouraged from speaking Yiddish so as to better assimilate.

Schectman was a good football player but he wasn't big enough to play for a gridiron powerhouse, so in 1970 he went to Drake University in Des Moines, Iowa, which matriculated a considerable number of children from the big city six hours east. He played football for the Bulldogs—the only Jewish kid to make the varsity team—but quit after half a season. As had been the case with his father, guys were coming back from the war to go to school. But he was nineteen and they were older—twenty-six, twenty-seven, some of them—and bigger, bruisers on the field. Getting knocked around was a lot less fun than being a radical, and he was becoming one. He suspected the FBI of surveilling him—or if not him personally, some of the other people in on his subversive collegiate shenanigans. From the time he was young he'd had a thriving sense of outrage, beginning with a fury about his parents' generation's response to the Holocaust—"How could you not oppose this? You were in the army!"—then, as the lies and the body count rose, about Vietnam. He was not by any means a passive person. "If they come knocking for me," he said, "I'm not going quietly."

After Drake, he enrolled in the apprentice law program at the New College in San Francisco—in which aspiring lawyers supplemented class time with hundreds of hours of supervised legal work as interns—and became a well-regarded human-dignity lawyer, albeit one with a rep as a bit of a streetfighter. He was, by the mid-1990s, married with two great kids, and at the top of his game professionally.

He and his family were vacationing at Grizzly Creek Redwoods State Park, and Schectman passed the time reading *The Last Stand*, the book about the Pacific Lumber takeover in which Eureka lawyer Bill Bertain was a prominent character. He decided to call Bertain and have a meeting to see if they might work together.

"I appreciate what you're doing," Schectman told him. "Let me help you out. I'm good at wrongful discharge."

The case to which Schectman referred, involving the firing of an employee over alleged unsafe timber harvesting, dovetailed into the Stafford mudslide action. (One of Pacific Lumber's arguments in the company's attempt to absolve itself from responsibility in the slide was that the slope was known to be among the most unstable areas in the county. But why clear-cut on such an unstable slope?) In July of 1998, after living for too long out of a dumpy motel in Eureka, Schectman moved his family and his practice north. He knew Stafford had the potential for a big payout. Personally, part of the motivation for the move was to give his children a better education than they'd get in the city. Professionally? He was a transplanted big-city lawyer narrowing his practice to a single dominant purpose: draw a bead on Takeover Charlie, one of the richest and most morally corrupt capitalists in America.

Schectman had tried and failed to represent the families of three workers who got caught in a debarker at the hardwood-chip facility in Scotia in September of 1992. Nobody ever figured out exactly what happened. The machine jammed and one or more workers went to clear it. Then, unexpectedly, the rig started up again. Three dead—the sad, preventable continuation, Schectman contended, of "a history of industrial accidents that are related to increased production."

He was driving his Volkswagen van—the family camping vehicle—to San Francisco when a news bulletin came on KCBS that an activist had been killed up north. He started pounding on his cell phone, trying to reach somebody who knew what had happened.

Now, as the Stafford case made its way through the system, he had a victim in another case with the potential to melt a jury: a grieving mother. Schectman introduced himself to Allsbrooks at one of the memorials. By the next month, she had retained him.

Which is why Schectman stood at the base of Gypsy Mountain, before the sheriffs had busted up the free state, saying he "almost certainly" would represent Chain's family in a wrongful death suit everybody knew was as sure to come as the rains. He represented Hurwitz's position on Headwaters thus: "You give me the money, or I swear to God I'm going to cut every fucking tree in the forest."

"Mr. Hurwitz," Schectman said, "is a multinational, international planet-raper."

Schectman's flaming rhetoric was exactly what you'd expect from a litigator aiming to turn public opinion in his favor and show his new client that he was an indefatigable, passionate ally in her fledgling campaign for justice and recompense. But nobody on the outside knew what was coming when Cindy Allsbrooks gave a little talk down in San

Francisco exactly five weeks after Gypsy Chain died. She was set to spill the details of a very interesting meeting she'd had days before. She knew quite a bit more after that meeting, and it still wasn't adding up. With every new piece of information, it was as if an alarm were sounding, blaring ever louder.

Schectman's release alerting the media to her press conference was not subtle: MOTHER OF SLAIN ACTIVIST REVEALS COVER-UP.

The release promised that the mother of the slain activist would disclose the "chilling details" of a conversation she'd had with the sheriff's investigator, Juan Freeman, days earlier.

If any of the reporters who turned out for the news conference the next day were expecting the embodiment of some convenient bayou stereotype, Allsbrooks was a disappointment. From the first syllable out of her mouth there was no question where she was from, but she was dressed for serious business, poised, pointed, eloquent, clearheaded, and fundamentally, righteously angry.

It was a bravura performance.

She said she was very nervous and wouldn't be standing before the assembled media if she didn't think it was vital.

"I now know the indescribable pain of losing a child," she said. "I have an empty ache in my heart which will never go away."

She said the picture being painted of her son as a smelly, ignorant tree hugger was inaccurate. Then she got to the meat of her comments.

"I have lost my son in a forest on a hill in the deep north of California and now I find myself at the tail end of a storm that has been brewing for, as best as I can tell, about thirteen years," she said. "But nothing prepared me for the shock of learning that the Humboldt County Sheriff's Department intends to implicate my son for his own death. I have been told by the department that they will recommend charging my son's friends, the activists who were with him when he was killed, with manslaughter. Mr. A. E. Ammons, the Pacific Lumber employee who cut the tree that killed my son, is not even a suspect."

She paused, sighed, and looked back into the white light of the TV cameras.

She said her meeting with Freeman was a virtual parade of red flags, that Freeman and the rest of the sheriff's department were plainly biased and incapable of doing an impartial probe into her son's death. Alternately referring to prepared notes and speaking extemporaneously, she said she had had no idea that activists like her son were hated in the county. She also made it clear she herself was no eco-radical. She was without agenda except as a mother.

"I am not here to advocate for any environmentalist group, nor am I here to be used by the Humboldt County Sheriff's Department to further their agenda," she said. "I'm here to demand an investigation by an impartial governmental agency because I've learned that Humboldt County is a company town. Apparently, the Humboldt County Sheriff's Department has no agenda except to exonerate the Pacific Lumber Company."

She had visited the site where her son had been killed, she said, and even if she completely discounted what the Earth First! witnesses had already told her, it was plain that there was no way Big A and Reback could not know the protesters were still there. It was ninety feet from the stump to where the tree broke and hit Gypsy, and in that steep, peculiar terrain you could hear a pin drop, she said.

"I went out to that site and I saw what I saw and I know what the truth is," she said. "And all of us who know what the truth is and who live by the truth can tell when somebody's trying to sell us a bill of goods. And when I went to that sheriff's department on Monday, I was being sold a bill of goods. Mr. Freeman requested that I not come with a lawyer, because if I did he would not be able to disclose certain things to me. I thought that was kind of funny. Throughout my entire conversation with Mr. Freeman on Monday, I did not hear one impartial statement. It was, 'Gung ho Pacific Lumber and I'm going after the Earth First!ers.' "

She said she asked Freeman about the rage on display in the videotape.

"He said, 'You know, these kids were out there messing with this man's livelihood. They were trespassing. Anybody would have done the same thing. Mr. Ammons is just a reasonable man much like myself'— and this is verbatim what Mr. Freeman told me—'A.E. is a man with a conscience.'"

When she left the sheriff's office, Cindy Allsbrooks said, she was torn about what to do. "I knew that if I were to stand up and say that the Humboldt County officials have lied to me, that they're covering up what really happened in my son's death, that I would have to sit here in front of these news cameras and tell this to the whole world . . . But you know what? I want all of America to know what's going on over there," she said. "I want people to know what is happening in Humboldt County."

Another heavy sigh.

"The last thing that Detective Freeman told me was that he was going to recommend to the district attorney's office that the Earth First! activists be prosecuted for manslaughter. I want to tell y'all about the Earth First! activists that Mr. Freeman is talking about . . . I met with these witnesses who were with my son when he died. Two of the gentlemen and one of the young ladies took a Greyhound bus to Houston to be at my son's funeral because they were so fearful that the family would not understand what had happened out in the woods that day. They came all that way on a Greyhound bus. The first time I laid eyes on these people was when they walked down the aisle at my son's funeral.

"These young people," she said, "stood for the truth."

Schectman spoke next, asserting that the activists were "nonviolently exercising their rights pursuant to the Constitution" at the time of the killing, and that: "It's hard not to draw some analogy to what happened in the South during the civil rights struggles—not to say that this is a civil rights struggle of the same proportion, but it is to say that we have a system where the local law enforcement is unable to see the truth for the trees."

Big A was cutting recklessly, furiously, endangering not only the protesters whom he knew to still be in the area but himself and Reback as well, Schectman said. The coroner had released the toxicology results of the tests on David Chain's body, and the story in the paper that he had THC—a chemical component in marijuana that can stay in the body for up to a month—confirmed a lot of folks' suspicions: just another dope-smoking hippie. Probably baked when he got thwacked.

But where was the disclosure of Big A's drug test? Freeman had assumed that the test "must have been negative," Schectman said. "It was a case of the fox guarding the henhouse. Pacific Lumber alone did the test, Pacific Lumber alone has the results and this sheriff is relying on those results. The only reason he's relying on it, he said, is because if Mr. Ammons was not fired he must not have done drugs, because Pacific Lumber has a zero-tolerance policy for drug use. Do they have a similar zero-tolerance policy for reckless violence in the woods?"

Fine, a reporter asked, but the Earth First!ers were trespassing. They were breaking the law. Didn't they bear any responsibility for what happened up there?

Cindy Allsbrooks answered.

"Trespassing is not punishable by death."

Culpability

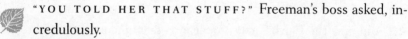"YOU TOLD HER THAT STUFF?" Freeman's boss asked, incredulously.

No, I didn't tell her that, Freeman said. Who the hell ever heard of a cop recommending to the DA what charges to file? You think a lawyer is going to take advice on the law from a cop? Yes, he'd told Allsbrooks he believed that her son's friends were responsible for his death, that they'd led him into the woods without his having any idea what he was getting into, and that they were guilty under the law of involuntary manslaughter. He told her he was going to finish his report and send it up to District Attorney Terry Farmer, who might press charges. He didn't tell Cindy Allsbrooks that he thought it was likely that the activists would be charged, because she didn't need to hear that. This poor, grieving mother from Texas was being used by Earth First! Her Earth First!–sympathetic counsel was a walking, breathing conflict of interest. Freeman had been motivated out of humanitarian concern, against his better judgment, as it turned out. His concern was now buried in politics; Cindy Allsbrooks had gotten up in front of a roomful of reporters and told them that the *Hurwitz* County Sheriff's Department was going to recommend her son's friends be charged with manslaughter.

And the thing was, Freeman could tell his boss the truth while his boss chewed on Freeman's ass, but when the press called to check out the allegation—charge the protesters?—there was nothing he could say but: Can't comment. Investigation's not yet complete.

Privately? Freeman believed Pacific Lumber and Humboldt County would have been a lot better off if they'd never heard of Charles Hurwitz or Earth First!, but his opinion didn't matter in the middle of an investigation. His job was to get answers, scoop up facts, craft a hypothesis based on reason. He'd been trained to study human behavior, and he was adroit at drawing out suspects and witnesses. Courthouse acquaintances used to jokingly wave him off, saying they were afraid to chat with him because they might wind up charged with a crime.

And now the Earth First! propaganda machine and its legal representatives were getting ready to portray Freeman as some kind of Nazi goon, which wasn't who he was at all. Growing up around Los Angeles in the mid-1960s, his was a household in which it was assumed that he would get a good liberal education. But he ran the streets, too, which won him a little trip to the LAPD jail back in the pre-*Miranda* days when the cops could lock up punks for five days if they felt like it. Freeman was pretty sure he didn't want to see the inside of a jail after that little taste. He was discharged from the navy in 1970 and got his psychology degree that same year. He figured he'd be a clinical psychologist.

Instead, he went into the leather-goods business, carving elaborate etchings that would later sell for more than Freeman could afford if he wanted to buy them back. (The word was that this "Juan Freeman" was some obscure neoprimitive artist nobody knew much about.) A series of personal decisions drew him to Humboldt County, and the only reason he stumbled into working at the jail was that it paid better than driving a school bus. He was, he liked to say, just about the only cop who'd previously been a businessman, an artist, and a psychologist.

And when he made detective, his moxie and acting ability helped him peer into the heads of witnesses and suspects. If he could make them believe he understood them, they'd open up and he'd get to the truth.

Freeman knew this case was going to be a "shit sandwich," as he recalled, from the second he got to the mountain and discovered Earth First! protesters were involved. He was sitting in his office working on other cases when the call came in: Logging accident. Fatality involved. The sad fact is, guys get killed all the time in the woods. To the extent that any death investigation is routine, this one didn't look to be terribly unusual.

But then it turned out the circus was in town. "This is not going to be good," he said to himself. He'd known these people and their schemes for years. When all but a couple of them said they wanted to consult with their attorney before they talked to him, it raised his suspicions. But it was a free country. Nobody had to talk to the police if they didn't want to.

It just made his job a little harder at the outset. And Freeman was well aware that if his investigation ended with the revelation of anything less than a dark conspiracy on the part of A. E. Ammons, Pacific Lumber, and possibly Takeover Charlie his own bad self to kill this kid, the Earth First!ers were going to be marching on the courthouse. Again. But he couldn't worry about that. The day after he caught the case, Freeman went to see A. E. Ammons.

. . .

HE LOVED TO FELL TIMBER, loved being outside. Out there in the woods he'd hunt and fish and just spend time when he wasn't working, bringing the big boys down. A. E. Ammons was always an outdoorsman. It didn't matter if he was on the clock or not.

It was impossible to describe, the feeling a guy got when he did it right. He told people he'd just as soon fell timber as have sex, and he loved sex. Every tree was a challenge. How big it was, how it leaned, what was beneath it to cushion its fall, which way the wind was blowing, on which side the big limbs were. You had to study them. You could have two trees side by side and they'd be different. Even in the winter, he loved it. People would ask, "How can you work in the winter? You're soaking wet, you're cold." But once you got going, your mind was on the job, not the weather. Especially with redwood, old growth or not. They were worth more than anything else out there. You'd take a look around, figure out how it needed to come down, and go to work: put the cuts in, put down the saw, and beat it on over. There was nothing else like it, certainly nothing indoors. Working indoors wasn't for him. He'd tried to work in the mill once and didn't even last a day, didn't bother to go back for his check. One winter he worked in a factory and it nearly killed him.

His mother had adopted him when he was six weeks old. His second stepfather was a war veteran with a history of mental problems who'd committed suicide one morning. His mother and uncle and other assorted family members had moved to Eureka after that. Within a day or two of their arrival, the boy was working. The man he came to regard as his real father worked for Pacific Lumber, and the boy himself was raised to live a working life. He remembers stacking boards when he was six years old for the old man. The family lived in an apartment he recalled as no bigger than a pickup. Whenever he needed school clothes, he knew he needed to work for them, and the work made him proud. They hadn't had anything when they'd come to California, and they were now building something. Even a boy could see the potential in the woods.

"I grew up to be hard," Ammons said, and it wasn't the easiest life. You took your pleasures where you could. After his second divorce, he bought a 1957 Chevy with $750 in coins. One day his neighbor came over and said, "Goddammit, we need to dig a pit." And the two of them drank half a gallon of gin and dug a pit and had a big old barbecue the following weekend. Things like that kept your mind off wondering whether the work was going to dry up.

In the timber industry you learned to live with getting laid off—back before "laid off" was a nice way to say "fired"—and he'd tend bar wherever he could in the slack times. He must've poured drinks in half the bars in the county, places where they had real American beer, not that fancy shit they were serving in the brew pubs with the salads and the shiny taps and the big windows that let the light in. And then when the timber companies went back on line, he'd return to the woods. It was part of life. He had pickups to pay for, and parts at the NAPA store in town, and child support. Later, his adolescent boy, Justin, decided he didn't see eye to eye with his mother and moved in with his father—just as David Chain had moved in with his.

A.E. started working for Pacific Lumber around the time of the Hurwitz takeover. He set chokers, moved up to being a landing man, then a deck scaler. Eventually he went back to felling timber. The bosses liked him because he wasn't picky—he didn't have to make $500 in a day. He'd cut whatever needed to be cut. All he wanted was to get out there and do a good job.

He had a habit of giving people nicknames, and he called Hurwitz Uncle Charlie. One time when Hurwitz came to Humboldt and wanted to see a logging show going at full throttle, they hauled him out into the woods and showed him one of the best timber fallers in the business.

They showed him A. E. Ammons.

Other guys were openly hostile toward the hippies, but it wasn't much of a concern to Ammons. He was lucky. As a kind of cleanup man working pieces of land nobody else cared for, he hadn't come across them much. There'd be a lockdown at the gate now and then. One time A.E. got out of the truck and started yelling at them that they didn't know what the hell they were talking about and that they were keeping him from putting food on the table. And one gal said, "You know what? This man's right. We ought to listen to him."

But mostly what he knew about those ying-yangs—his preferred term—he'd heard from other workers. Guys had had their saws and gas stolen, their equipment sabotaged, trenches big enough to swallow a pickup dug in logging roads and covered up with brush. A.E. was an old-time hunter, and he could spot tracks in the bush and tell when his stuff had been messed with, moved but never stolen. If they wanted his tools, he figured, they could have them.

A timber harvest site is a minefield even if you know what you're doing and have the right gear. And here were the hippies, some of them so ignorant they couldn't tell a redwood from a fir, some of them not even wearing shoes. And they had it all ass-backward to Ammons's way of thinking. Years before, when the timber was bigger and of better quality, a guy could make a halfway decent living in the woods. When he went to work for Pacific Lumber, they could put down a million board feet in a day. Now if they did that much in a month it was a mir-acle. His best year with PL he cleared maybe $60,000, but then he had up to $25,000 in expenses. He had to maintain his truck to get to work, his saws, and his equipment. Just a chain-saw motor alone, that was $1,200 right there. You've got to buy a bar; that's $100. A chain was $40 or $50. And now because of the ying-yangs, he was making a lot less. Saving the old trees meant fallers were reduced to chopping toothpicks that had hundreds of years to live. Meanwhile, the trees in what they called Headwaters were big and old and on their way out. The things were going to rot and fall over and go to waste. What those protesters didn't understand was that all the guys out in the woods were environmentalists. They weren't there to plunder the land. They were trying to do a competent job and get paid a fair wage for it, that was all. Ammons had some doubts about Uncle Charlie's impact on the local economy in the long term, but if you took on debt, you paid it, right? The real problem wasn't Uncle Charlie, it was the activists.

And now he'd killed one of them.

The situation was self-explanatory. They'd come up to him and he'd chased them off a couple or three times. He didn't hear anything and went back to felling trees. Yeah, he shouldn't have tweaked, should've gotten on the radio right away and had security come on out. But he'd spent more than enough time with those ying-yangs the day before, and the workday was still in progress. Yes, he'd threatened to send trees in the protesters' direction, but "There was no intent to kill," he would say later. "If I were that good to hit a man on the move with a tree, I'd be the best timber faller in the fuckin' world. I mean, we have layouts built with Cats on flat ground, and if you hit 50 percent you're doing good. So if you can hit a moving object, that makes you fuckin' good."

He didn't want there to be any doubt about how it had happened or why. That's why he wanted to go for his drug test right away—he didn't want anybody saying he'd stalled on purpose.

And now he had this sheriff's detective at his place and Ammons was telling his story. He didn't even think about needing a lawyer. He had nothing to hide. Ammons poured out the story, alternating between self-righteous fury and tears.

"I got a mouth that gets me in trouble all the time," he told Freeman, and that had been the case the day before Chain was killed, when he alternately threatened and charmed Carey Jordan. "I've been that way all my life and I'll never change, probably. But the girl, I fell in love with her. She's a sweetheart. She asked me, if she was in a tree, would I fall it? And I said, 'Yes, I would.' She said, 'You'd kill me?' I go, 'No, you'd be killing yourself because of the simple fact you'd had ample time to get out of the damn tree. You didn't belong here in the first damn place.' And I says, 'You're really upsetting a bunch of people, I mean you're fucking with my life. You're fucking with my family. It's hard to make a living, you know, and I gotta work every day to live.'

"I mean, you see how I live," Ammons told Freeman. "I live really, really simple. I don't got shit. And if I don't work every day, I got even less shit. I mean, right there she thought I was a murderer. You know, but I wouldn't fall a tree with them in it. But I sure like to tell them that. You know?"

There was plenty of blame to go around, Ammons said: "You guys, me and my company. I shouldn't have been there. I should have made up my mind not to do it. You guys should have never let those people go the day before, you know, so they were back there yesterday. And my company should have made sure they weren't there in the first fuckin' place."

Freeman asked if Ammons didn't think the protesters had some responsibility.

"Oh, yeah! As far as I'm concerned they did it to themselves."

"Yeah."

"They killed that kid. I killed him. But they did it. They did it."

"By sending him out there?"

"Yes. Most definitely. I'm the one that felled the fuckin' tree that hit him, but they're the ones that persist in comin' back and comin' back and comin' back and comin' back. So he committed suicide as far as I'm concerned . . . They sent him on a death mission."

He told Freeman it was a wonder that similar incidents hadn't happened already. He said the protesters were "goofy. They could take a sane man and make an animal out of him if you fuck with him enough."

From now on, Ammons said, "I will get a limb and I will beat one of them within an inch of their life. I won't fall any trees. They'll wish I was fallin' trees. But I won't fall another tree . . . not when there's any people."

As Ammons cried, Freeman said, "I don't think anybody's gonna blame you."

Back in Eureka that night, mother duck Jay Moller led his row of Earth First! ducklings into Freeman's office to be interviewed at last. Freeman knew exactly what they were doing—presenting an unconflicting narrative. The story was canned.

THE FOLLOWING MONDAY, Ammons volunteered to clear things up further. He told Freeman over the phone about the order in which he'd cut the trees, about how he never left a tree hanging because it was a hazard to him and anybody else walking around out there, and that when you're messing with really rotten wood, there's no guarantees of where the thing is going to go.

He asked Freeman if anybody had been up to determine whether the tree that killed the kid was the tree that he had felled and not part of another. He said he was probably the only person who could determine that and volunteered to go to the site. "I would dearly love to go do that," Ammons said, "and make it definite."

"Okay, we'll try to figure out a time to do that—"

"We can do it after work, before work, I'll take a day off work, I don't care what it is."

Freeman told Ammons to take it easy. Ammons said he was trying, and that these days it was hard to trust anybody.

"There are people that don't trust the police no matter what," Freeman said.

"Well, I know you guys gotta cover your ass, I need to cover my ass . . ."

"Well, we're all being manipulated by the Earth First! group, there's no question about that. But that's the way it goes. We've got to do the best we can to do a complete investigation here."

"I have no problem with a complete investigation."

Jay Moller had a problem with Freeman's idea of a complete and dispassionate investigation, and wrote him in mid-October to tell him so. Freeman had written Darryl Cherney, by now regarded as the godfather of North Coast Earth First!, asking for a copy of the Earth First! direct-action manual and inquiring about what sort of training David Chain may have had.

"As far as Darryl knows, there are no records about any training and he is unfamiliar whether there is any training for the so-called 'cat-and-mouse' tactic," Moller wrote.

> While Jordan and perhaps another victim-witness had heard of the phrase, none of the victim/witnesses suggested they were engaging in that tactic at the time of David Chain's death. This is simply part of PL's disinformation campaign to blame the victim and it certainly appears as if you are not only taking the bait, but leading the charge. It's as if the KKK were in charge of investigating the killing of a black man during a sit-in in the Deep South, and inquiring whether he had received training in how to sit down . . . To inquire whether David Chain and the other victim/witnesses had some kind of training is about as relevant as inquiring whether a rape victim had self-defense training or whether she wore provocative clothing. Neither rape victims nor victims of angry loggers generally are prepared to be assaulted, and their degree of preparation or training is irrelevant to the real issue: whether the logger exercised due care before falling the tree in the direction of the activists. For you to suggest that Mr. Ammons is not a suspect shows that it is you who has prejudged the case.

This kind of baloney made Freeman wish that he were out on a cross-country trip in his street rod, with his wife and their obstreperous and well-traveled Chihuahua. But Moller wasn't finished yet. He signed off by suggesting that Freeman "should consider removing yourself from the investigation in favor of someone who doesn't have an axe to grind."

After the press conference in San Francisco, Moller had more to worry about.

He couldn't believe Schectman and Allsbrooks's spin at the press conference. He wrote an e-mail to Schectman—in all capital letters—the following day, saying he was "dismayed that you would go public with Detective Freeman's absurd, vile threat to recommend charging the activists with manslaughter."

He was similarly dismayed that Schectman hadn't consulted with him before going public. "In fact, your failure to consult with me is inexcusable," he wrote, "in light of the fact that I have been helping the victim/witnesses on the criminal part of this case. I feel responsible for the victim/witnesses' safety from the forces of darkness and evil and the power of the state."

Schectman's preemptive shot would only give credence to the notion that the protesters, not Ammons, should be charged, Moller argued. And Schectman's putting his presumed client in front of the cameras to make her case would only make it tougher for Moller to defend the activists should they be charged. Moller also suggested that Schectman "redirect your focus" to emphasize that District Attorney Terry Farmer, not Juan Freeman, would be the one to decide what charges were filed and against whom.

Had Moller known the more complete version of the meeting between Cindy Allsbrooks and Freeman, he might have better understood Schectman's motivation in going public with the news even if he didn't agree with it. Schectman had suggested a press conference. Cindy wanted to see Freeman before making a decision on going public. She emerged from the meeting with her mind made up.

It had started badly. Freeman told her not to bring a lawyer. When she came in the company of a young man, Freeman asked if he was a lawyer. The guy said yes. Freeman asked him to get a coffee and wait.

Freeman's suspicions were aroused. He was willing to share information with her but not with Schectman or some other Earth First! attorney. He asked Allsbrooks if she was wearing a wire. Allsbrooks couldn't believe it.

If Allsbrooks found Freeman's remarks outrageous and confrontational, Freeman had a reason for his posture. As A. E. Ammons had said on the phone with him the Monday after David Chain was killed, all parties involved were in ass-covering mode. By this point, Freeman was aware of the possibility that both the sheriff's department and Pacific Lumber might be on the receiving end of a nasty civil action regardless of the criminal investigation's conclusions.

The lawyers were also shielding the protesters. Schectman had accompanied Moller with Mike Avcollie on a second interview at the Humboldt County Sheriff's Department detective bureau on the afternoon of October 9. Not long after that interview began, Schectman told Freeman that if the DA were to offer immunity for Avcollie and other people on the mountain, they might be better disposed to cooperate.

Freeman said nobody was a suspect until he was finished with the investigation, and that he was "not in a position to make any kind of an offer of immunity, anyway."

"Which means, of course, we as lawyers would have to advise our clients that if you're not, if you can't give them immunity, if you can't say they're not suspects then they have Fifth Amendment rights." Moller also said that from the videotape it was clear that the only possible suspect in the case was Ammons.

"That's a rush to judgment you have made," Freeman said.

Freeman tried to ask Avcollie questions about Earth First! training. Moller put the brakes on the line of questioning before Avcollie could answer and Schectman asked how inquiring about that would further a death investigation.

"Well, because I'm trying to find out everything I can about everything that went on," Freeman said. "That's what you guys want me to do."

"No, we want you to do an investigation—" Schectman said.

"Focused on the logger," Freeman said. "That's what you guys want me to do."

The strategy was this: give the protesters immunity from prosecution from trespassing and, as Moller put it, "we could have a choir." But immunity would also mean the activists couldn't be charged with involuntary manslaughter stemming from the trespass.

Freeman said he couldn't make that offer.

Moller said he'd told the protesters they were theoretically exposed to prosecution and that after hearing that they still wanted to tell their story. They wanted to get the facts out.

It went on like that for a while. There would be no interview of Avcollie.

By the time Freeman met with Allsbrooks, the detective wasn't the only one behaving differently. Before she'd simply been the grieving mother. Now, it seemed to Freeman, she was on the offensive. He told Allsbrooks her son had been "led astray" by his Earth First! comrades and they were doing the same thing to her. He mentioned Schectman's conflict of interest and that it was rumored Ted Turner had contacted her and was interested in her story. He said that she was making a mistake getting in bed with Earth First! and that she'd be better off thinking for herself. Earth First!'s goal was nothing less than to shut down logging in Humboldt County entirely and flush the local economy and its working people down the toilet.

"A. E. Ammons is a man much like myself," Freeman told her.

"Oh, so it's okay to fall trees toward activists when you know they're in the forest? That's okay? You're a man like that?"

Then he showed her the legal definition of involuntary manslaughter—unlawful killing without premeditation or evil intent while committing a non-felony—and floated the possibility of culpability on the part of the activists. He said they were guilty, that what they'd been doing met the standard, that her son's friends were responsible for his death.

Allsbrooks looked horrified.

"I'm sorry," Freeman said. "I felt you have a right to know what's going on. If you don't want to accept it, that's fine."

If Allsbrooks was hearing it right, this guy was saying he was going to recommend to the DA that her son's friends—not the enraged logger—be charged with killing him. "Are you crazy?" she demanded.

She lost it and left. She was more than horrified. She was sickened, furious. She'd come to California dizzy with sorrow, still groping for answers, and the cop assigned to investigate her son's death asks her if she's being courted by Ted Turner? She couldn't stand to spend one more minute in Juan Freeman's presence.

The next morning, she visited the mountain where her son was killed. The way the sound carried was unreal. Schectman was at the base of the fatal tree, Cindy was ninety feet away from where the trunk broke and she could still hear every twig Schectman stepped on. *Oh, my God, I can hear everything*, she thought. *There's no way they could not have known these kids were here.*

She phoned home to consult with Ron and her family. She told Schectman, "We're going to have a press conference."

Soon they were on a plane to San Francisco. If there was going to be justice, it could only be exacted in federal court. Practically speaking, federal court was the appropriate venue because none of the plaintiffs resided in the same state as any of the defendants. Humboldt County was within the jurisdiction of the federal court with its base in Oakland, across the bay. And, of course, it didn't hurt that San Francisco was a big media market.

At the time, it appeared Cindy Allsbrooks could not look to the California Department of Forestry and Fire Protection to do her any favors. In the days after her son was killed, CDF slapped Pacific Lumber with the most minor of violations in the case of David Chain. CDF had given the company verbal approval to make minor deviations to the timber harvest plan, but Pacific Lumber hadn't filed the necessary paperwork. It wasn't nearly enough to stop logging on Gypsy Mountain.

The following month, however, CDF looked at the pile of accumulated violations—three hundred in three years—and realized, even putting aside the inflamed passions following Chain's death, it was without a choice. In an unprecedented application of bureaucratic muscle, the California Department of Forestry yanked Pacific Lumber's logging license—already a conditional license—for six months, and ordered the company to cease all logging operations within twenty-four hours. The company was on probation for repeated violations of the Forest Practices Act, and it still seemed to brazenly disregard an agreement between it and CDF that demanded the company straighten up. Pacific Lumber might be the eight-hundred-pound gorilla of the local economy, but it could no longer throw its weight around, as it had three years ago when a local judge had accused the company of "crude application of political power." Superior Court Judge John Buffington had blocked the cutting of a two-hundred-acre grove. Pacific Lumber promptly blamed him publicly for the closure of one of its sawmills.

Now, after years of doing the company's bidding, the bureaucrats had come through with a roundhouse uppercut. For some environmentalists, the suspension was a compound blessing. In addition to putting the hurt on the company and temporarily arresting the destruction of the forest, maybe PL losing its license would be just the thing to scotch the Deal. If the company couldn't reliably follow existing regulations, how, pray, could it be expected to rise to the standards demanded by that Byzantine guidebook, the Habitat Conservation Plan?

The politicians hoped otherwise. The politicians—among them Governor Pete Wilson and Secretary of the Interior Bruce Babbitt—were hoping to cool things down. They were still selling the Deal as a best-case scenario that would save both jobs and the environment, and end the conflict forever. Chain's death was exactly what Babbitt didn't need.

"The underlying issues are very complex," Babbitt said one night on a United Airlines flight, after eating his dinner and drinking his single-serving bottle of wine. "I've been dealing with them personally for a couple of years now in the Headwaters negotiations. Hopefully, we can find some common ground. But I've got to tell you, right now, I don't know where that common ground is."

Far below Cabinet level, meanwhile, Freeman toiled on what he knew would be an explosive report. The final product did not disappoint. It led with the statement that an activist had been "killed while trespassing" on Pacific Lumber property. The report went on to say:

> It was apparent that the victim was not struck by the tree itself as the trunk came to rest within several feet of the victim, but not on top of the victim. It appeared to me that the tree fell somewhat along side and at an angle to the victim. The part of the main trunk where the pieces broke off was above the victim's location.
>
> It was also apparent that the timber faller would not have been able to see the victim from where he was working on the tree. There was thick brush and the victim was in a draw or old skid road out of the line of sight of the timber faller.

He noted that he knew at the scene he'd have to retain a forester to make complete sense of the scene. He detailed highlights of his interviews. He said Avcollie had told him that the activists did not walk into Ammons's fall line, that he started felling trees at them after he chased them. Then he detailed portions of his interview with Mc-Curdy, whom he noted was "arrested previously for activist activities and is currently on probation, and was one of the plaintiffs in the pepper spray federal trial in San Francisco which resulted in a hung jury."

It said that a couple of activists had told PL workers that it was an accident.

It said that in a follow-up interview with A. E. Ammons, "A.E. advised me that he has retained counsel and that I should contact his attorney," Bill Bragg.

It detailed the conversation among Moller, Schectman, and Freeman, when Freeman tried to interview Avcollie the second time.

It said that on October 28 he'd had a conference call with A. E. Ammons and Ammons's counsel. Freeman asked Ammons if he had been wearing ear protection on the day in question. A.E. had said he wasn't "because earplugs make echoes in his ear due to an obscure condition he has in his ears."

ON THE FOURTH FLOOR of the Humboldt County Courthouse, in a corner office overlooking downtown Eureka and the bay, the heat was on District Attorney Terry Farmer, who would decide whether anyone would be charged with any crime in connection with David Chain's death. He'd shepherded plenty of prosecutions stemming from the timber wars, and his hide was thick enough to withstand the blast—organized waves of phone calls and e-mails from around the world demanding justice, or at least the environmentalists' version of it. "I've been called an SOB by experts," he said. "I've gotten past the point where it affects my job." He liked to paraphrase *The Godfather*: It's not personal, it's just business. Making tough and sometimes unpopular calls came with the job, and Farmer would not be swayed by hype or hysteria.

The thing was, Farmer was a child of the Bay Area and was a college student in the 1960s. You want to talk revolution? He'd seen it. He understood that there is a stage in life when young people are passionate and committed and idealistic. But compared to what happened in the 1960s, these people were lightweights. And now, because of his job, had he become part of the corporate capitalist conspiracy that was in desperate need of being exposed, a part of the oppressive power structure that was in need of being overthrown? In moments of levity, the irony amused him.

The investigation was not going to be a rush to judgment, despite the biases of those who claimed to know the truth based on the radical enviro party line. Sometimes, he knew, the party line was just flat-out not true.

To those such as Moller to whom the facts were in sharp focus, Farmer's duty was obvious—a vigorous prosecution of Ammons. But that wasn't going to happen with Freeman investigating. Freeman's bias, Moller wrote Farmer, was "reminiscent of how the people in power protected the KKK's violence in the '60s in the South." Ammons should be charged with the second-degree murder of David Chain and, what's more, "five counts of attempted murder; assault with a deadly weapon and making terrorists threats toward the other victims." But, of course—this being Humboldt and Moller being a realist—he continued: "We still believe that the only substantial chance of conviction is for his gross negligence, that is for involuntary manslaughter. But that weighty matter is for you to decide."

Farmer had asked his deputy, Andrew Isaac, to get the facts of the Chain case and recommend a course of action. Not even Jay Moller had anything but respect for Isaac, a fastidious investigator who dressed better than you'd expect of a small-town prosecutor and wasn't above checking out people before even casual business meetings. In his line of work, he said, you can't afford to take anybody at face value.

Isaac had a brush with the extradition of Bernard Goetz in the early 1980s when, while Isaac was an assistant attorney general for the state of New Hampshire, the subway shooter wandered into the Concord police station on New Year's Eve and said he wanted to turn himself in. Isaac later worked in private practice, handling civil rights complaints, including police harassment. Out of deference to his wife, a Californian who never came to enjoy the pleasures of a New Hampshire winter, in May of 1997 he moved to Humboldt County, where he prosecuted cases against Pacific Lumber for timber violations and against trespassers on Pacific Lumber land. Farmer tapped Isaac for the Chain case because he had some timber experience and because he didn't have any trials or major investigations looming.

Under the law, Isaac knew, both the logger and the protesters might be criminally liable—Ammons if it could be proved his actions were intentionally criminal or grossly negligent, the activists under the "misdemeanor manslaughter" rule which stated that a misdemeanor-caused death, trespassing in this case, could be a felony.

Isaac visited the death site with Freeman and concluded there was no way Ammons could have seen the protesters, nor they him. He reviewed witness statements, toxicology and autopsy reports (noting that David Chain was a "chronic user of marijuana" but not high at the time of his death), the report from a forestry expert, and Earth First!'s videotape. The videotape was so dark and jerky as to be almost visually worthless, but the audio contradicted the statements of at least three of the protesters that they were in near constant communication with Ammons as he felled trees at them. Activist McCurdy narrated in a furtive whisper. At one point McCurdy intoned that loggers were felling trees with activists in the area, but he did nothing to announce his presence.

Witness statements were muddled and sometimes contradictory on critical issues such as who was yelling and when, the number of trees felled and in what direction, and the time between the retreat to the snack spot and the felling of the fatal redwood—Avcollie claimed it was fifteen minutes, while Reback, Ammons's spotter, said it was an hour.

Cumulatively the evidence told Isaac no jury would convict Ammons of criminal liability in the death of David Chain. If his claim that he didn't know the protesters were still in the area was true, there was no intent to kill. And there was a lack of evidence of gross negligence, hence no involuntary manslaughter. If the standard to be used was that Ammons should have known protesters were there, then all involved should be subject to prosecution.

Isaac also believed that the chances of convicting the Earth First!ers were slim. After Chain had expressed his reservations about confronting Ammons one final time, Carey Jordan and Erik Eisenberg had persuaded the group to leave their spot of relative safety and approach again. David Chain didn't respond to Jordan's frantic pleas to move in the moments before the tree crashed to the ground.

Isaac wrote in his report to Farmer:

In the end, the culpability of the parties is inextricably linked. If the loggers' acts during the morning demonstrated reckless disregard for the safety of others, then the activists were on notice of same. Thus, Eisenberg and Jordan, in particular, could be found to have recklessly and illegally led Chain into a dangerous situation. If the logger was cutting responsibly, Eisenberg and Jordan would have had less reason to appreciate danger. Therefore, perhaps jurors would feel that Chain's own moral beliefs and a momentary lapse in judgment or nerve led most directly to his death. Or maybe he tripped. There is no way to know beyond a reasonable doubt.

Somebody's kid had finally died as a result of thirteen years of wacky politics and activism, and as Terry Farmer took a few days to consider his deputy's report he wondered about the innocents in the woods. Was some unseen hand guiding the actions of these kids, trolling for a martyr? It was clear that David Chain was fatally unaware of the physical danger he was putting himself in on that day.

It was also clear to Farmer that this was not a prosecutable case. There were legitimate questions of civil liability, and a civil action was the means by which the case would likely—and appropriately—be decided. Everybody knew a lawsuit was inevitable. But that didn't mean Farmer wouldn't be vilified as the tool of a murderous corporate powerhouse.

In his statement announcing his decision not to file charges Farmer closed in a tone both despairing and subtly exasperated, beseeching combatants on both sides to stand down.

The death of David Chain was a tragedy that need not have occurred. It is the culmination of at least 10 years of conflict between two forces, each of which wraps itself in the self-appointed mantle of righteousness and claims the moral high ground. Each pushes the limit of the law and then demands that the criminal justice system resolve the conflict, presumably in its favor. The criminal legal system cannot do this. It should not try to do this. Our criminal justice process depends on consensus, a community's shared values as expressed in its laws and the community's administration of those laws. When that consensus breaks down, our system can't work. Sometimes people die.

Let us learn from this. Until there is a return to civility and a shared commitment to resolve disputes through lawful means, we can expect another David Chain. One death is too many.

SEVEN

The
Suit

A RETURN TO CIVILITY WAS NOT what Steve Schectman had in mind. From his Eureka office, a gorgeous, creaky Victorian home with old-growth redwood trim, Schectman was in position to finally achieve one of his professional goals: take a big bite out of Hurwitz. The model for the action was the civil case against O. J. Simpson. The previous year, a jury in Santa Monica had found Simpson liable for wrongful death and awarded the estates of Ron Goldman and Nicole Brown Simpson $12.5 million each in punitive damages. Goldman's parents had received $8.5 million in compensatory damages. Goldman was not unlike David Chain, struck down without cause in his young manhood.

Cindy Allsbrooks was also studying the Simpson civil case but for another reason. Even with Schectman's zeal, she knew from the beginning that this job was going to require the marshaling of more legalistic firepower than a little North Coast outfit could provide. She needed a firm with marquee value, a national profile, notoriety. She approached Daniel Petrocelli, who had represented the Goldmans. Petrocelli said he couldn't help her. Allsbrooks's sister Kathy suggested Gerry Spence.

Spence had for years been perhaps the most high-profile American attorney in private practice, representing corporate whistleblower Karen Silkwood, Imelda Marcos, and, of course, Dave Foreman, the crusty Earth First! co-founder. In 1986, in a mock trial that aired on the Showtime cable channel, he presented a posthumous defense of Lee Harvey Oswald. (He lost that one.) Allsbrooks didn't know much about Spence, but Kathy had read all his books and was convinced he could exact a pound of Hurwitz's flesh.

Allsbrooks's request for an audience with Spence landed in the lap of a young associate named Jerry Bosch. Nothing happened for a while. It seemed like Spence was going to reject her case as Petrocelli had. Allsbrooks wrote Spence directly and sent her appeal to Bosch, asking him to hand-deliver her plea to the top man. Bosch did that at a Christmas party, and on New Year's Eve—the second anniversary of the Stafford slide—the phone rang in Coldspring. The firm of Spence, Moriarty and Schuster wished to meet with Mr. Schectman and Ms. Allsbrooks in Jackson, Wyoming. It was, to Allsbrooks, an answered prayer.

Jerry Bosch had gone to the University of Pittsburgh Law School and spent more than five years doing corporate mergers and acquisitions when he got on his Harley, rode west, and landed on Gerry Spence's doormat, intent on doing what Spence did—defend real people who'd been screwed by corporations—or quit the law altogether. The job awakened a dormant passion, and the Chain case hit him at just the right time. Like David Chain, Jerry Bosch had found a calling that buttressed the bedrock of what he believed in after a period of dis-

illusionment and casting about. Corporate greed, Maxxam, Hurwitz—
that was everything that was wrong with American society. With the
Chain case, Bosch could be a hog-riding, ponytailed, crusading lawyer.
And Bosch had a sleeveful of aces: not only was he a recovering corporate attorney but he'd also worked a California wrongful-death case
that eventually hit for $3.5 million. He was familiar with the screwy
wrongful-death statutes in the state. The awarding of wrongful-death
punitive damages there hinged on the infliction of an injury or damage
to one's person or property before death.

If punitive damages were allowed, Bosch figured, this had the potential to be big, although it was never more about money than justice.
In the Simpson civil case, the jury found that a tort had been committed against Nicole Brown Simpson because her dress had been ruined—by blood—before she died, allowing for a monster judgment.
But in this case the core of the action was a wrongful death on behalf
of the estate of David Nathan Chain, not an environmental action on
behalf of Earth First! The Spence firm's involvement with Dave Foreman so many years earlier might have established a level of understanding, but Foreman's Earth First! had been far more militant. David
Chain had been committed to nonviolent resistance, and he had perished violently.

And the death had been in large part because of corporate arrogance—hubris, really. Bosch had been around plenty of corporations,
both in his mergers and acquisitions work and at Spence. But these Pacific Lumber guys were so arrogant it amazed even him. The attitude
was, "We run this part of the world; don't touch us," Bosch said. "We
tolerate these activists because they make us more money." Moreover,
the relationship between the company and the sheriff's department
was beyond congenial—it was conjugal. You didn't need to go any further than Freeman's interview with Ammons to see that was glaringly
clear. It was a revolving door between the company and the sheriff's
department; business seemed to get done on winks and nods. The

ethically gangrenous sheriff's office had all but formally abrogated its mandate to serve the public. Bosch tried and failed to find a way to implicate or sue the county, but the immunity laws were like a suit of armor.

Later, when Bosch struck out on his own, the Chain case would continue to be a labor of love and the subject of numerous all-nighters for him. It was that important.

Bosch met Schectman and Allsbrooks at the airport in Jackson, then took them to breakfast the following morning and told Allsbrooks not to be nervous. She walked into the office and saw the stairs leading down to the law library. She got a tour of Spence's office and that of his partner Ed Moriarty. They were private offices with fireplaces, for crying out loud, complete with fancy artwork. Allsbrooks was by now well aware of who Spence was and, even though he wasn't in the office, she was slightly awestruck and feeling a bit out of her league. Bosch led her and Schectman into a conference room, which started filling up with lawyers.

Schectman spent the next couple of hours laying out the case.

Finally, one of the lawyers asked, "Why did you come to us?"

Allsbrooks told them about Nathan's first trip to California, about the wisdom in his eyes and the peace in his heart upon his return, and about his resolve to go back and pick up the fight. She told them of bizarre meetings with cops assigned to investigate her son's death turning into investigations of her motives and affiliations. She told them she had to put a dream team of lawyers together if she was going after corporate titans.

She said she believed God had guided her to them.

She didn't have an idea which way the lawyers were leaning until Moriarty's assistant, Jeanella Mathis, said, "I'm sitting here the whole time thinking this could have been my son."

The lawyers asked Schectman and Cindy to wait outside.

After about forty-five minutes, they had their answer: an overwhelming commitment from each attorney. Ed Moriarty—a man who fled from publicity as consistently as Spence courted it—told Cindy to go home and burn the DA's report. The Spence firm and Schectman's Pacific Law agreed to work on contingency, splitting 40 percent of the judgment and the glory of beating Takeover Charlie.

RHETT REBACK, AMMONS'S twenty-one-year-old spotter, went back to work the morning after David Chain was killed.

After he'd drunk beer and had Mexican food with A.E., he'd gone home and made his lunch for the next day like he always did, figuring he'd get called into work but hoping he wouldn't. The phone rang as he drank his coffee in the dark. Another chopper needed a spotter, and if Reback didn't come in to work that morning, the chopper wouldn't be able to work either. Reback went.

All that day his knees knocked and the sound of the chain saw made the hair on the back of his neck stand up. *I can't do this*, he thought. But he did it. With Pacific Lumber, you worked when you could because you knew there would be times when you wouldn't. In fact, when the company lost its logging license after Chain was killed, Reback was on unemployment. It was a long six months.

He'd started working for the company right after graduating from Fortuna High. He loved going to get his cork boots and rigging pants and the heavy shirt to keep the brush off of him. This was the path by which a hard worker and good saver could realize the dream: a house with a recliner chair and football on the TV from morning to night on Sundays. That was why he did what he did for money. That was a good life in Humboldt County.

Then that kid got killed and, for all his stoicism and good humor, Reback was haunted in his reflective moments. He didn't sleep for weeks and didn't "take a solid shit" for months. (Upon hearing that, Ammons confirmed that his digestion was similarly disrupted.) His girlfriend had to deal with him thrashing around in bed. It got to where he'd have to decide whether to just go ahead and stay up all night staring into the cool glow of the TV or try to sleep and be afraid of what he might dream.

He was also furious at the Earth First!ers. The company wouldn't let an employee take a step on a worksite without boots, a hard hat, and gloves, and these hippies are running around barefoot. Then one of them gets killed and the survivors get to tell lies on the news. Earth First! was saying the activists had been constantly yelling at A.E. and Rhett, and that the two had to have known they were there. What a load of crap. Reback was right there when A.E. got his saw hung up making the face cut. A.E. shut the saw off, started taking it apart, and sent Reback down to the backpack, about seventy-five yards away, to get another bar and chain. Then, wouldn't you know, by the time Reback got back, A.E. had somehow managed to get the thing out of the cut and was putting his saw back together, meaning Reback had to run to the backpack a second time. And what did Rhett hear that whole time? Not a damn thing. The yarder up the hill, which dragged downed trees into position, was silent. They were probably having lunch or broke down or something. It was dead quiet the whole time—except for him and A.E. yelling, "Up the hill! Up the hill!" But when the thing came down with a force that rattled his chest like a train barreling by? They heard plenty of yelling then.

And *then*, the guys, being decent human beings, did what they could to help. Reback ran all the way down to the backpack one more time to call for help on the radio, but he was too low in the ridge to get a signal out. Back up on the landing, he followed the yarder engineer and the loader operator down to where the victim was to see if they could help. They got the stretcher and the first-aid kit. They had to cut a trail to get down there. The guys ahead of Reback said, "Don't even bother with the stretcher." And what were the hippies doing? Standing around with their hands in their pockets or trying to put branches on the dead guy.

He had no doubt that he and A.E. had done nothing wrong. But then the lawsuit hit at the last minute—fifty-one weeks after the guy got killed. That brought it all back to Reback. And he knew he'd be spending way too much time in the company of lawyers for the foreseeable future. The company had made it clear that it would handle any legal expenses Reback and Ammons might incur. The only thing for which the loggers would not be covered, in the event of a successful lawsuit against them and the company, was punitive damages. Covering punitive damages, as the lawyers explained it, would be like insuring them against a crime—such an act would go outside the scope of their normal work duties. If a lawsuit came, as it surely would, and if it was successful, both Ammons and Reback could be paying off the judgment for the rest of their working lives. For Reback, who was just old enough to buy a six-pack of beer after work, that working life stretched for decades, assuming he didn't get hurt on the job.

Ammons, meanwhile, discovered that when he did go back to work after four or five days, the sound of a chain saw off in the distance spooked him as it had Reback. He found himself working with an almost exaggerated caution, in slow motion.

Ammons had gotten a recommendation from a court-reporter friend for a lawyer. The name was William Bragg.

Bill Bragg liked to bear the image of an aw-shucks, small-town attorney, practicing in an obscure, woodsy corner of the world, when, in fact, he was a partner at one of Eureka's top firms—Roberts, Hill, Bragg, Angell and Perlman—whose office was a somber, tomblike structure downtown. He also happened to be, even in the estimation of his adversaries, just about the best defense attorney in Humboldt County.

It is the job of attorneys in Bragg's position to minister to their new clients' anger and fear in much the same way a physician counsels a patient who's received a diagnosis of grave illness. The attorney explains the legal process, explains that it will be at times excruciating in length and emotionally taxing. He explains that the process is adversarial, but that the attorney is there to protect the client. He explains fees.

With respect to Ammons and Reback, there was no question Pacific Lumber would foot the bill. Since Chain had been killed during the course of Ammons's and Reback's jobs, the company was statutorily required to do so. That was something of a relief, but they still had plenty to be worried about. Anger and fear fed on each other and yielded feelings that a grave injustice had been committed against them. What had they done wrong? Not a thing. That day the hippies themselves had said *they* were sorry, that getting somebody killed wasn't part of anybody's plan, that it had been an undisputed, tragic accident. And then they go on TV and completely change their story and say A.E. and Rhett are murderers.

Bragg—in the position of being his clients' defense lawyer in both prospective criminal and presumed civil matters—sat in his office and spelled the whole thing out to Ammons and Reback. He explained that there was the potential for the two of them to have conflicting interests, or for their interest to conflict with the company's. Most of all, he didn't want them comparing notes and getting their story straight. Rarely are two memories of any event identical, he said. Simply relate the facts as you recall them.

Then he sent them home.

HOME WAS INCREASINGLY NOT a place of comfort for Cindy Allsbrooks. Within six weeks of Nathan's death, Ron seemed to be losing patience with his wife, expecting her to get over it and move on. They used to love to go dancing. People would always stop them and say, "Y'all are such good dancers. Y'all look like you're in love." Now Cindy was either sleeping a lot—a classic barometer of depression—or on the phone with lawyers and activists. He'd cautioned her that "There's people gonna use you for their cause," and now he saw it happening. Cindy attempted to explain that her situation was akin to that of the small group of angry parents who had started Mothers Against Drunk Drivers almost twenty years earlier. She had no choice but to get involved. It was like finally finding a light switch after groping around forever in a dark and unfamiliar room.

Ron comprehended the tragedy of losing a stepson, but he also believed in going to work every day. He had a grasp of how the saw jocks out there in California must have felt. Ron worked in a chemical plant—it stored all kinds of nasty stuff, poisons and acids and oils—and there were probably protesters out in the world who'd be happy to come and block his gate. What if they were there every single day? You bet he'd be angry. You bet he'd be sick and tired of it. You bet he could see how things got out of hand.

As well-meaning as he could be as a stepfather, he could no more easily fathom the fierce, primal bond of a parent—especially of a mother—than he could become pregnant himself. Yes, he had lost Nathan, too, but he would never go through the young man's duffel bag of personal effects and breathe deeply from a pair of his dirty socks just to remember his scent. Such artifacts were worth more than gold to Cindy. As Ron had feared from the beginning, he'd also lost his wife that day. The old Cindy was gone. The new Cindy was trying not to drown, and she was lost to him.

Allsbrooks tried and failed to get the Justice Department to investigate her claims that in Humboldt County the fix was in. A paralegal wrote back that the feds couldn't get involved—strictly a state matter. A few weeks earlier more disturbing news had come by phone: a tree sitter on Gypsy Mountain named Bird had fallen some sixty to eighty feet. This was exactly what Cindy had feared would happen as the Earth First!ers kept up a winter-long vigil on the mountain. Bird had been clipping into a traverse line, missed, and fallen, breaking his tailbone. And he was one of two sitters to fall on the mountain after Gypsy's death. The other, an activist named Recon, suffered a broken back. Did these kids really believe the cause was worth their lives?

At least one of them did. A wannabe forest defender called her at home and said he wanted to be just like Gypsy. "No, you don't," Allsbrooks said. The kid asked, "Then what should I do?" "Get an education," she said.

It was impossible for her to look at her son's picture and see a martyr. She was a mother, in a vortex of despair, and leftist radicals and social progressives were making Nathan a symbol, a cause célèbre, a victim of the American injustice system right up there with Leonard Peltier and Mumia Abu-Jamal. The police state had robbed Peltier and Abu-Jamal of their liberty and Gypsy of his life. Peltier's and Abu-Jamal's supporters were organized and had their own Web sites. That was not Cindy's Nathan. Nor was he another Julia Butterfly Hill, who, in a fit of feverish hyperbole, had already been dubbed the Rosa Parks of the environmental movement.

When Allsbrooks wasn't distracted by work or lawyers or being crossways with Ron, she was examining the artifacts of her dead son's life in a palliative move to cobble together a more complete portrait of the man he'd become in his time away. She knew Nathan loved Bob Marley. She adored the way he'd bob his head when Marley was playing. It was, truth be told, the closest the boy came to dancing. But Allsbrooks knew nothing of Rastafarianism or Marley's place in the world as a spiritual leader if not an out-and-out prophet, as Stephanie Kirby had believed.

They'd played Marley's "High Tide or Low Tide" at Nathan's funeral, but Allsbrooks hadn't tuned in to the words then, and whoever owned the CD had taken it back. The disc was on a Marley boxed set that was out of print, and she'd looked everywhere for at least the song lyrics, to no avail. On a trip to Austin to see Sarah, Allsbrooks finally got a used copy of the disc. And later, while driving to a business meeting, she slid the CD into the player in her pickup:

I said I heard my mother
She was cryin' (I heard her cryin') . . .
And the tears that she shed (the tears that she said)

They still lingers in my head (lingers in my head)
She said, "A child is born in this world,
He needs protection," oh-oh mmm
God, guide and protect us.

It sounded like the phone conversation she and Nathan had had the summer of his first trip. She'd wept and prayed and asked God's protection for her son. Now she felt Nathan sending her the song as a gift.

She sat in her pickup and cried her makeup off.

Her grief could bring her to her knees, and she prayed to Nathan for strength and guidance. *You have to tell me what to do*, she would say to him. And she came to realize that even though her son had been struck down in a moment of violence, he had, at the hour of his death, been on a mission he believed to be critical. He would not want his death to hasten others abandoning the cause. A. E. Ammons might not be charged with manslaughter, but it was clear that Nathan Chain's fight had to become his mother's.

"CHARLES HURWITZ, PLEASE COME OUT with your hands up," Darryl Cherney shouted into the bullhorn. Cherney was in his element, and Judi Bari's ghost must have been amused at the alliance blooming between the proletariat and the environmentalists. In May, the Maxxam–Hurwitz–Earth First! big top proved it always had room for one more sideshow, the venue being the Maxxam shareholders' meeting in Houston. Storming the gates of the annual gathering was not without precedent for environmentalists, but now the forest warriors' numbers had been bolstered by the infusion of fresh troops: steelworkers.

Maxxam had blundered its way into another crisis. The United Steel Workers union had struck against Kaiser Aluminum—a more recent addition to Hurwitz and Maxxam's leveraged-buyout collection—a year after the PL deal was final. Contract talks fell apart over the elimination of bonuses and union workers being replaced by contract employees. Even before the negotiations broke down, Kaiser contracted with a company that recruited nonunion workers and hauled in trailers to house them. And after the walkout, Kaiser made an even bolder move, soliciting Pacific Lumber workers—idle because the California Department of Forestry had yanked PL's license—as scabs, shuttling them up to Spokane and Tacoma.

That was in December of 1998. That same month, a parade of exceptionally strange bedfellows—Earth First!ers; members of the charmingly, anachronistic socialist Industrial Workers of the World, or Wobblies; and members of the steelworkers' union—managed to blockade a shipment coming into Kaiser's Olympia plant. A few out-of-work hands went down to Humboldt County to visit Julia Butterfly Hill and ended up building a pulley system to haul visitors into and down from what was by then the world's biggest celebrity plant. The guys had plenty of time on their hands. They were in the middle of the lengthiest strike in Kaiser's history.

After a long and corrosive standoff with the company, the workers agreed at last to go back on the job without a contract—and saw their capitulation greeted with a lockout. Steelworkers demonstrated in the Bay Area, at Maxxam's corporate headquarters, and at Hurwitz's downtown Houston high-rise home, the four-star hotel and spa called the Houstonian, which included a thirty-foot-wide, hand-carved stone fireplace in the lobby. The neighbors were unamused at the occasional demonstrations. Nestled among discreet pines next to the tony Galleria shopping district, the Houstonian is not often invaded by commoners—with the exception of the staff. (There was, however, an unavoidable and delectable irony to Hurwitz's place of residence. The Houstonian is a member of the Green Hotel Association, maintains its grounds organically, makes a very big deal out of Earth Day each year, and offers free valet parking to clients who carpool with three or more people. The hotel's motto: "Reforest Your Soul.")

Hurwitz, so reclusive that he made Howard Hughes seem a ubiquitous party animal by comparison, was even more scarce in those days, perhaps because whenever he stuck his head out somebody else slapped a lawsuit on it. The Stafford mudslide case was a go and David Chain's parents were making no secret about taking PL to court for wrongful death. Hurwitz also had massive claims against him by the FDIC and the Office of Thrift Supervision for his role in the crash and burn of his busted savings and loan. Hurwitz had maintained that was just political heat to keep him at the table to close the Deal. Meanwhile, even if the Deal did go through, some of the North Coast's litigation-happy enviro-wackos were threatening to mount legal challenges over the proposed Habitat Conservation Plan. They said it would extinguish the very species it purportedly was in place to protect.

That much trouble on so many fronts would be enough to make any man want to stay inside with the shades drawn. But Hurwitz— who, even in the estimation of his own employees, was constitutionally combative, litigious, and silent—was required to present himself at the shareholders' gathering.

The tension built before the meeting, which had been moved from Houston to the Waterwood National golf resort in Huntsville out of security concerns. Cindy and Ron Allsbrooks went to meet their county sheriff, who'd been drafted to assist in assuring order would be preserved at the meeting, to tell him that Maxxam had overhyped fears of disruption. Allsbrooks didn't want the twitchy cops popping a protester who was only fishing in his pocket for a cigarette. When the time for the meeting came, a busload of forest activists arrived in Texas and started making noise. They were greeted by a phalanx of unsmiling East Texas lawmen inside and out, a U.S. marshal's van poised to haul away the unrulies, and metal detectors on the way inside the building. Showdown.

Now the protesters demanded that Hurwitz be arrested for crimes against the planet and workingmen—the Kaiser fiasco proved people were as expendable as trees to him. Cherney, dressed in a suit and a cigar as Hurwitz's conscience, had by then raised the bounty on his jail-hurwitz.com site to $50,000. Burly steelworkers mingled and made noise with forest warriors, their unlikely allies. It was in this surreal setting that Cindy Allsbrooks unwittingly stole the show at an already electric meeting.

Angry steelworkers, about 150 of them, made up more than half of the crowd. They'd pooled what little cash they had to buy Maxxam stock specifically so that they'd be allowed into the meeting and now they had a few questions. They hooted and howled at Hurwitz, especially when—after the Pacific Lumber portion of the meeting—he said Maxxam wasn't guiding Kaiser's hand, and that the workers' complaints were better directed at Kaiser chairman George Haymaker. Hell, Hurwitz only controlled 63 percent of Kaiser's stock, the workers said between snorts. That didn't mean he ran the company or anything. For his part, Haymaker had some good news: without all those pesky union restrictions, the company was leap-frogging in productivity and trimming expenses in all their plants.

The opposition did more than make noise outside. It had mounted a credible, if ultimately doomed, threat to Maxxam. The alliance had pulled together about a million votes—25 percent of voting proxies—to challenge Maxxam's slate of candidates to its board. The coalition favored two former congressmen, Howard Metzenbaum and Abner Mikva.

The insurgency was rooted in capitalist concerns. The Maxxam board, which Hurwitz dominated, had put the company stock in the tank. In 1997 *Business Week* had named Maxxam's one of the ten worst boards in the country, citing CEO domination as the principal reason. From Harvard University to the state of California's public employee pension fund, investors were dumping Maxxam stock for its crummy performance or backing the rebels. The company had posted net losses of some $30 million in the first three quarters of 1998. Pacific Lumber's operating under a conditional license and then losing its license altogether after still more serious violations had hit the parent company. That, in turn, had jeopardized the $480 million Headwaters deal. Hurwitz and Maxxam had accumulated legal fees to the tune of $40 million. And squeezing Kaiser for bigger profits had taken a human toll: by some accounts workplace injuries were up 138 percent at five plants in three states. Weeks later, the Kaiser plant in Gramercy, Louisiana, would blow up, injuring two dozen workers. At one plant alone, serious injuries had gone from an average of four per month to twenty-nine in a single two-week period. On the Internet, investor message boards boiled over with contempt. "Stockholders do care about something besides money," one poster wrote. "Hell has a place for you," said another. Plainly, the challengers argued, this was a company out of control.

Allsbrooks was there to observe. She sat next to Les Scharnberg, who, like Naomi Steinberg, was one of Humboldt County's redwood rabbis. Scharnberg rose to refresh Hurwitz's memory on the Talmud, reminding the CEO that the ancient collection of rabbinic writings forbade Jews from keeping servants' pay from them overnight, let alone for months on end during a walkout. During the allotted question-and-answer time, Jill Ratner, a lawyer for the Bay Area foundation that had helped mount the proxy charge, whispered to Allsbrooks, "Do you want to speak?"

No, she thought. *No way*. As Ratner walked away, Allsbrooks began to hear her son's voice in her head.

You need to step up, Mom.

I can't.

It kept up for twenty minutes, and she eventually had to step outside to the balcony, where she started to cry. *I can't do it*, she kept saying to herself, and to him.

It could be the only opportunity you have to address everyone in the same room.

Schectman saw Allsbrooks rush out to the balcony and followed her. Allsbrooks told him that she couldn't find the courage to do what her son wanted her to do.

"Cindy," Schectman said, "only ask yourself: Can you live with it if you don't do it?"

As she walked back inside, she thought the forum would be over and she'd be off the hook. No such luck. Schectman walked her over to the line of people waiting to speak. She shook as she waited.

The room froze and everyone looked at the woman who held the terrible wisdom that only the parent of a dead child can possess. Although she was petrified, she spoke very plainly: "What would you do, what plan would you implement, to keep another person from harm or death?" she asked. She told Hurwitz she had no malice in her heart. She knew Charles Hurwitz had sons, she said, and she knew he must love them very much.

Hurwitz said he was "very sorry," and passed the substance of the question to Campbell. Campbell jumped around a lot, blaming Earth First!, not the company, for putting people in harm's way. Campbell's stammering obfuscation was so obvious Allsbrooks actually felt bad for the guy and cut him off.

"Thank you," she said. "Think about my question."

Hurwitz's son Shawn sought Allsbrooks out that day. They embraced. She told him how many times she had thought of him, and about Hurwitz as a father. Hurwitz's son seemed very kind. He said his door was always open to her.

She had been so impressed with the seeming sincerity of both Hurwitzes that she almost decided to call off the lawyers and try to work everything out outside a courtroom, with civility and respect, person to person. Almost.

CASE NUMBER C99-4183 LANDED in the clerk's office at the federal courthouse in downtown Oakland on September 10, 1999, one week short of a year since David Nathan Chain was killed on a steep hillside of what activists called Gypsy Mountain. Plaintiffs David Allen Chain and Cindy Allsbrooks sued Pacific Lumber and two subsidiaries as well as John Campbell, A. E. Ammons, and Rhett Reback. The complaint sought unspecified damages, actual and punitive.

There were two arguments. The first was that Pacific Lumber had nurtured a culture of violence just as surely as it had grown saplings. The second was to prove, in Schectman's words, the "nefarious plot" on the part of Takeover Charlie and the company: that it used the protesters to keep the heat on and jack up the price of Headwaters as well as to maintain public and institutional pressure before Hurwitz had a chance to shave the ancient forests bare. Well-intentioned activists hoping to defend a fragile and vanishing ecosystem had instead been unwitting pawns in Hurwitz's scheme, and it had worked. After more than a decade of tortuous haggling, hair-splitting, and deal-making, the Deal had gone through six months earlier, on March 1, 1999—but not before the poker-faced Hurwitz pulled a move so cool that it cornered no less than the leader of the free world.

Two days before the Deal's deadline, the company had walked away from the table, expressing grave concerns about Pacific Lumber's ability to function profitably under the Habitat Conservation Plan. Hurwitz had warned the White House chief of staff that he believed Maxxam's board would reject the plan, and it indeed had. On February 25, a few days before the authorization period for the federal portion of the money was to dry up, Hurwitz got a call from Bill Clinton, who told him he was firmly committed to the Deal and wanted Hurwitz to know he was there to help iron out the last-minute wrinkles. Hurwitz was unimpressed, and told the President why.

Hurwitz's presidential squeeze put the federal government in a sweat and prompted letters promising that, yes, they had gone back and checked their math and, under the freshly revised projections of the Habitat Conservation Plan, it turned out Pacific Lumber would be allowed to cut more timber than had previously been reported. The Deal was signed on the second anniversary of Judi Bari's death. But Pacific Lumber would forever be required to do business according to the numberless rules spelled out in the HCP, and Governor Gray Davis had promised that the regulatory eye would be omniscient and unblinking. The Deal made Pacific Lumber the most regulated timber company in America. But it gave Maxxam something it frequently found itself short of: positive spin. The line went forth: no timber company was doing more for the environment, or inviting such minute scrutiny of its methods, than the Pacific Lumber Company of Scotia, California. Bring on the sweeping reforms. The Headwaters had at last been saved, and Charles Hurwitz was a model environmentalist for the next millennium. Clinton hailed the Deal's completion. Interior Secretary Babbitt said the feat was one for the ages, right up there with the establishment of Sequoia and other national parks. For anybody who'd actually been in Headwaters, that was a joke. Less than ten thousand acres of trees, a lot of them old and rotten, hardly made a national park. The government hadn't a clue what it was getting for all that money. It was a hoodwink of cosmic proportions.

BUT LOOK AT THIS GUY! He's got Bill Clinton over a barrel! You think he's not manipulating Earth First!ers? Look at Julia Butterfly Hill, Schectman said. Do Charles Hurwitz and John Campbell call in their troops to cut her out of her tree? No. Julia Butterfly may not have been well-versed in the complexities of modern silviculture and she certainly didn't know what she was getting into when she ascended the tree known as Luna, but she was sweet and maybe a little sexy, an appealing face to put on an issue that the rest of America regarded as just another story about California freaks waiting for the second coming of the Summer of Love. She wouldn't even come out of Luna after the Deal went down. She issued a press release from her perch detailing why she wasn't coming down. This girl, she was something. Her media acumen had really raised the profile of the issue. She had to be the only tree sitter outfitted with her own day planner to keep track of all her interviews. Campbell doesn't bring Julia Butterfly—or as the timber boss insisted on calling her, "Julia Hill"—down. He doesn't cut her out of her tree. He debates her on CNN.

"They left Julia up there to create an icon," Schectman said. "Perfect media. It's very nefarious."

As Schectman wrote in the lawsuit:

Each time the activists were able to obtain media coverage of the plight of the forest at the hands of the Corporate Defendants, the Corporate Defendants understood they obtained an economic benefit. They understood that as the public grew to appreciate the uniqueness and esthetic value of these Forests—coupled with the activists' assertion that the Defendants would destroy them unless stopped—the value grew. Thus, the activists, without their knowledge, served a valuable economic asset to the Defendants, and, although Defendants may not have liked them, their presence was certainly tolerated, and in fact, in some manner encouraged.

Then, to Schectman's way of thinking, in August of 1998—scant weeks before David Chain is killed—the violence boils over, the result of a shift in strategy. Activists are threatened with all manner of death and dismemberment, chased with axes and chain saws. Trees are felled with tree sitters perilously close by. The activity isn't new, but the sustained intensity is. As a matter of company policy, the gloves are off.

Why? Easy, Schectman said. The Deal was almost a go, Hurwitz didn't need the protesters anymore. So boys, if you want, you can go ahead and harvest one of them—why, one dead hippie is just another incidental take under the Timber Harvest Plan.

Ed Moriarty, who was leading the Spence firm's portion of the case, wasn't sure they could prove a full-blown conspiracy. He said it was like that old saying, "If you're getting run out of town, hire a band and make it a parade." But there was no question that Pacific Lumber knew those kids were there. Nor did Moriarty believe Ammons felled the fatal tree with the intent to kill. But it was highly negligent, especially, as Ammons had said, since he was rattled, getting madder and madder. "He was trying to scare the shit out of them," Moriarty said.

While the involvement of the Spence firm lent the case a certain status it wouldn't have had otherwise, Schectman's emotional involvement was also a plus. He'd lived among the trees and had seen what the company was doing. How could he not be emotionally involved?

"In those trees it's almost a holy experience," Moriarty would later reflect. "And you think of the age of those trees and it reminds me of being in Ireland in some of those cathedrals that are a thousand years old. You get the same feeling, except those cathedrals are dead. These trees are alive."

The complaint also attempted to establish that David Chain's civil rights had been violated because he had been engaged in a political protest and had died as the result of violence committed against him. Ammons believed nothing would happen to him even if he hurt or killed a hippie because the company had fostered a culture in which violence against protesters was tolerated. The company was baldly anti-environmentalist. Carl Anderson had T-shirts made up with the Earth First! logo with a circle around it and a line drawn through it. Then there was the drawing of the marbled murrelet in the center of a bull's-eye out at Yager Camp, PL's site out in the woods. A. E. Ammons was the product of this hostility. He was, Schectman said, "a dog at the end of the leash."

The force of Schectman's passion was clear in the original complaint and subsequent motions, and the prose made the still relatively thin case file read like more than legalistic boilerplate. In an early response to a series of defense motions, Schectman wrote, "The life of

David Nathan Chain was cut from this earth just like the 120-foot-high ancient redwood tree that killed him. This senseless and brutal killing of a 24-year-old man was a result of (1) the actions of Defendants Ammons and Reback on Sept. 17, 1998 and (2) the actions of Defendants Pacific Lumber, Salmon Creek and Scotia Pacific for the past 15-plus years. During this time these companies have done nothing but rape the land and exploit people for monetary gain."

Pacific Lumber, et al., had retained Preuss Walker and Shanagher LLP, which had its offices on the fifteenth floor of a building in San Francisco. Their response was standard. They agreed to the uncontested facts and disputed the ones in contention.

The week after the suit was filed, Allsbrooks again flew to California to meet with Schectman and Bosch, the associate from the Spence firm. Nathan's friend Mike Avcollie was at Schectman's office for a meeting with witnesses, and he couldn't look at Allsbrooks without tearing up. Allsbrooks asked if he wanted to talk. Avcollie said yes. They went out on the steps of the Pacific Law office and Allsbrooks learned what survivor's guilt really is. He and Nathan had wanted to leave the mountain before the final confrontation, but they'd been outvoted, Avcollie said.

"Nathan should be alive," he said.

They sat on the steps and hugged and cried as cars buzzed up and down E Street.

SCHECTMAN WAS GUNNING FOR AT least $10 million in punitive damages against the company, on top of loss of earnings, legal fees, some $13,000 in burial expenses, and the like. If Schectman and the Spence firm took $10 million out of Takeover Charlie's hindquarters, each firm would have exacted justice for their clients. They each would also enjoy a $2 million payday.

In all, the barrage on Pacific Lumber—and, by extension,

Maxxam—came from six different directions. The first was negligence. The second was that David Chain had been exercising his First Amendment right to free speech at the time of his death, and that his civil rights had been violated under California's Civil Rights Act. Third, the complaint argued, was that the company had engaged in "ultrahazardous activity." The fourth alleged wrongful death. The fifth, "joint enterprise liability," addressed the way the company was chopped up. The final component alleged "negligent infliction of emotional distress"— that is, that the plaintiffs had suffered and would continue to suffer injury to mind, body, and soul as a result of the defendants' ghastly conduct.

One of the defendants' main arguments would be to prove David Chain's assumption of risk on the day he was killed. To do that, Moriarty figured, the company would have to allow testimony about how nonviolent activists had been abused by both the Humboldt County Sheriff's Department and Pacific Lumber—led by security chief Carl Anderson. Their witnesses, Moriarty said, are going to prove our case.

But Pacific Lumber gained ground in a February 2000 ruling before Judge Sandra Brown Armstrong. Armstrong was a former cop who favored orderly proceedings in her courtroom. Bosch figured that Armstrong, being a Clinton appointee to the federal bench, would at least be inclined to give his side a fair shake. As the suit snaked through the system, however, it appeared to Bosch and the other plaintiffs' attorneys that it was not so. At that February hearing, Armstrong batted away several of the plaintiffs' key claims. The defense, repeatedly observing that the plaintiffs' complaint was muddled and misleading, had moved to dismiss the civil rights claim, arguing that Chain hadn't been discriminated against. It had also argued that it had long been a standard in California law that punitive damages could not be recovered for wrongful death. Armstrong ruled for the defense, concluding that Chain's civil rights had not been violated, and that the claim of negligent infliction of emotional distress was invalid. She also tossed out the claim for wrongful-death punitive damages. Still in play were the causes of action for negligence, ultrahazardous activity, and the non-punitive elements of the wrongful-death complaint.

Bosch and Schectman weren't unduly alarmed; Armstrong's move wasn't completely unexpected, especially given a lot of California law. It wasn't a tectonic shift. More like a rumble. And a harbinger.

EIGHT

The Dog at the End of the Leash

A COUPLE OF MONTHS EARLIER, on December 18, 1999, Julia Butterfly Hill had descended Luna after 738 days and headed for New York to field softballs on the networks' wake-up news shows. With the corporate media in full swoon, the volume of the whisper campaign among hardcore forest defenders who'd long questioned Hill's motives cranked up to an audible backlash. She'd stopped working with Robert Parker, who had assisted her and taken part in the telephone chain spreading word immediately after Gypsy's death. Now she'd retained the services of an area promoter who helped broker her book deal and fledgling speaking career. As far as the enviros could tell, the Luna sit was not about saving a tree and awakening the masses, it was about getting Julia Butterfly set up in her career. No question, her feat of endurance was epic. Negotiations nearly as tortuous as those that had at long last closed the Deal preceded her descent, and she and her crew had succeeded in buying the tree from Pacific Lumber for $50,000. PL also agreed to a buffer zone and bestowed upon Hill what amounted, for lack of a less anthropomorphic term, to permanent visitation rights.

And it wasn't just that the mainstream newsies were falling all over themselves making hay out of the heroic, brave, and, lest we forget, attractive activist. Look at who her book publisher was, the skeptics clucked. *The Legacy of Luna*, a collection of Hill's treetop writing and drawings that crashed into print just months after Julia's feet became reacquainted with terra firma, was published by HarperCollins. And who controlled HarperCollins? Rupert Murdoch, the potentate of sleazy, right-wing establishment media, proud papa of tabloid TV, owner of the gutter-dwelling *New York Post*. Julia Butterfly Hill had cast her lot with an international capitalist media mogul.

The sniping wounded Hill. Didn't it matter to her alienated former allies that the book was printed with 30 percent post-consumer fibers and paper certified to promote sustainable forestry? Didn't it matter that it was printed with soy ink, and that she was giving away all of her profits? She had suffered in Luna. She could have died up there a thousand times. Now she was just trying to get the word out, as she had been all along, and this was the most ecologically correct mass-market book in the history of the written language. Didn't any of that matter?

In fact, no, it didn't matter to the hardcores. The more widely disseminated the message, the more corrupted the message. And, for that matter, the messenger.

Still, for hooking reporters and producers, you couldn't beat that "Rosa Parks of the environmental movement" line.

History, some believed, would one day record the nationwide shock and revulsion at Gypsy's killing as a watershed moment. As Ken Miller, a local physician and activist had said atop the mountain during the free state, "We always joked that as soon as somebody got killed, we'd win. But we never thought it'd happen."

It was a miracle it hadn't happened before, but to Jamie Romeo and scores of others, Pacific Lumber had clearly gone too far this time. Almost ten years earlier, Romeo had come from West Virginia to go to school at Humboldt State in Arcata and had witnessed the Headwaters campaign from its embryonic stages. She'd seen a cryptic flyer that said, "Come Hike Headwaters" and not much else. A girlfriend of hers already had made the trek, so Romeo asked how one went about hiking Headwaters. "Talk to that guy over there," her girlfriend said. "Talk to Larry Evans."

Evans had been one of the HSU students who'd worked with deep ecologizer Bill Devall and journalist-turned-activist Greg King, who had named the grove Headwaters. Covert forays into the woods were part of the activists' aim to open people's eyes to the wonders of the primordial forest in their midst.

"Show up at my house at midnight," Evans told Romeo. "Don't tell anyone."

That single hike changed Romeo's life. It was as if the trees had been screaming for help, but she hadn't heard them from West Virginia, hadn't heard them from Arcata, hadn't heard them until she was among them, humbled and dwarfed by them. She came out the following night and said, "I'm going to work for this forest for as long as it takes."

Romeo was not alone in having her life altered by a walk in the woods, but if anyone then had suggested to the early activists that the issue would one day be the topic of a telephone call originating from *Air Force One*—Bill Clinton's chat with Hurwitz to keep the Deal alive—the reaction would have been deafening guffaws. That was her freshman year at Humboldt State, when the number of people in the know was so small the movement couldn't even be called a movement.

Nothing was moving. They were just sneaking people into the woods. They'd sit around the quad and scrounge up gas money to take a few people down and show them Headwaters, show them why bad old Pacific Lumber had no business logging in there. It was all about making people aware of a place that had been for most of living memory essentially an uncharted island, the last living vestige of a vast archipelago swept away in a great flood.

It wasn't long after her awakening as an activist that Romeo started collecting written declarations from activists who'd been worked over. It made her feel lucky. The worst that ever happened to Romeo was a tree was felled near her, but she'd seen plenty and heard dozens of stories over the years: saws buzzed in people's faces; trees felled with protesters nearby; activists being beaten, spat upon, and kicked. It was almost as if she was documenting the experiences of political prisoners or dissidents in some Third World country. The documents, which they were collecting for possible use in litigation or potential criminal inquiries, showed a pattern of escalating violence. The Earth First!ers knew who the eco-terrorists were and it wasn't them. Someday, she thought, the material would be useful, and when Gypsy got killed it was apparent that's what they'd been saving it for. The company would try to deny the volatile atmosphere in the woods, but the collected testimonials proved it.

In the early days that atmosphere wasn't as bad, but it was obvious that documentation such as photographs and written statements were critical to taking on the company. There were violations of the Forest Practices Act everywhere. If the act is violated in the forest and no one hears it, does it make a sound? Her first action in Headwaters was to fight a wildlife study "trail" that the company had put in with a bulldozer, needlessly destroying trees and hastening erosion. When the activists went out there they were up to their knees in the mud and mulch. The dozer had cleared everything in its path, ripping chunks out of the bases of giant old-growth trees along the way. The lawsuit against that action didn't go too far, but the next time PL built a wildlife study trail, they did it with a bit more finesse, a lighter touch. They did it with machetes.

By 1992, with Pacific Lumber's voluntary moratorium on logging in most of Headwaters in effect, the company had a keen need to get timber on the ground and headed to the mill. The action shifted to Owl Creek, a smallish patch of old growth not far from the grove that sparked the initial controversy. It was, at the time, the second-largest stand of unprotected old-growth redwood and Douglas fir. But not even in Headwaters had the legal and bureaucratic hairs been split so finely. The company had first filed a plan to log on the site two years earlier. After the predictable courthouse skirmishes, PL got the go-ahead on the condition that it conduct marbled murrelet surveys before, throughout, and beyond the operation. Pacific Lumber logged. The Environmental Protection Information Center sued. PL stopped. That was in June. PL said it had complied with all regulations and then some; the environmental center scrambled for a temporary restraining order and Earth First!ers occupied the site throughout the summer. The standoff stretched into late November.

By Thanksgiving weekend, Romeo and her friends in the woods were cold and tired, and the notion of a warm Thanksgiving dinner closer to civilization sounded appealing.

What followed came to be called, with tongue in cheek, the Thanksgiving Day Massacre.

Pacific Lumber sent its boys into Owl Creek on the holiday and started cutting. Earth First!ers raced back out. The restraining order came four days later; PL was prohibited from even taking out the trees it had already felled until the shouting died down.

The shouting went on for years. In the middle of the battle the marbled murrelet had been added to California's Endangered Species Act and later added to the federal list of protected species. That meant EPIC could sue under the federal Endangered Species Act to put the brakes on any subsequent logging. After the trial, the federal judge hearing the case issued an injunction against Pacific Lumber from logging the timber harvest plan and excoriated the company for running roughshod over a threatened bird. Pacific Lumber sued, demanding to be paid for the land it couldn't log. The government eventually did that, but not until the last month of 2000. By then, the Owl Creek controversy had simmered for thirteen years.

Owl Creek wasn't Romeo's only adventure in the woods. During Redwood Summer in 1990, some fifty or sixty activists had stayed at Romeo's house, crashing everywhere, including on the stairs. They'd gotten their hands on cases and cases of Kryptonite bike locks for a huge lockdown in which activists would put the locks around their necks. Afterward, Romeo and her housemates became semi-famous for using the packages the locks had come in as wallpaper for the kitchen.

Kryptonite bike locks—the choice of radical environmentalists everywhere. They couldn't be cut off with bolt cutters; only a diamond-bit saw would do the trick, and only the sheriff had one of those. The activists would put them around their necks and lock down at the gates before dawn, waiting for the loggers to show up, get pissed, and call the sheriff. Locking down at the gate was safer because there was the opportunity for non-trespassing people to legally witness how the activists were treated. The gloves came off in the backwoods, where observers were often scarce. Once they did a lockdown on equipment out near Headwaters. Romeo and a few others had video cameras to document what went on, since everybody there was at risk of arrest for trespassing. What she saw was unnerving. The loggers showed up, got angry, and produced diamond-bit saws of their own. They were yelling as they cut the locks off the protesters. It looked like a recipe for somebody getting hurt. They stopped using the Kryptonite locks after that. Around that time, somebody from Greenpeace came to Humboldt and showed them how to make black bears, the devices activists used to lock themselves to equipment or other objects. It took years for the cops to figure out how to cut them out of those.

Sometimes a clean getaway, even absent a confrontation, was thrilling. Romeo and some friends had gone into Headwaters and snatched every flag that established the boundaries of a timber harvest plan—so many flags they filled garbage bags. At Owl Creek she emptied a logger's gas can, then ran off with it so he couldn't refill his saw.

Earlier still, around the time that North Coast Earth First! was denouncing tree spiking, Romeo thought it'd be okay to go out to Headwaters and put magic crystals in and around the trees. "Let's spike these with crystals," she'd said. "The saw won't be able to get near it." Bari heard about it and called Romeo to deliver a spirited, two-hour reading of the riot act. If one of the loggers gets hurt because of something they can pin on us, Bari said, they're going to come with shotguns next time.

It wasn't unrelenting ugliness—sometimes their ostensible enemies quietly signaled their support, like the cowed inhabitants of a totalitarian state. The protesters built a blockade with big logs in Headwaters in 1990 or 1991. Carl Anderson—the company security man, who once reportedly toted a high-powered slingshot into the woods—showed up the next morning with a bulldozer operator and had the blockade cleared. Anderson threw a fit—it wasn't surprising; Romeo had seen him lift a protester to his feet by pulling him up by his hair—and then he left. But after Anderson was gone, the most amazing thing happened. The dozer operator put the blockade back and raised his fist in a gesture of support. At least one of them knew Earth First! wasn't the enemy.

Every once in a while, sheriff's deputies who were arresting protesters thanked them for doing what they were doing.

Despite such fleeting, gratifying moments of furtively expressed solidarity, by the time David Chain was killed, Jamie Romeo had close to a solid decade of activism behind her and it had taken something of a toll. She'd quit working at EPIC and was feeling the edges of burnout. Then she heard on the radio that a forest defender had been killed at Grizzly Creek. She headed for the camp at Williams Grove.

She had been with EPIC for five years and hadn't been doing forest actions with Earth First!, but in the hours after Gypsy's death, she reacted as if she'd never rotated off the front lines. The crew at Williams Grove broke up to go get supplies for an action at Grizzly. She grabbed her little dog, Feedback, and headed to Gypsy Mountain, where she stayed, off and on in between classes she was taking at the nearby College of the Redwoods, for the next couple of weeks. At the beginning she stayed at the gate to the logging road, where some of the activists were afraid they'd get raided right away.

"You know what? We can do anything we want. They're not going to touch us now. This is a big deal," Romeo said.

Within days word was going around that Steve Schectman, the freshly transplanted San Francisco lawyer, was likely to be taking the case and—with the Stafford mudslide suit and now a wrongful-death action—he was going to need a lot of help. He eventually offered to take in several activists as apprentices: four years of study and work under Schectman's wing and, like him, they'd be lawyers. It sounded like a good deal to Romeo. She could write and hit deadlines, skills that had served her well at EPIC. She could organize and make a coherent story of a daunting stack of paper. She had experience as an activist and knew Pacific Lumber's tactics, and she had access to an armful of files showing the blueprint of violence. The Chain case had enormous potential, and she wanted to be in on the action.

Romeo, who had thought about law school before, wasn't the only one drawn to do something in the wake of the death. It could have been her they'd killed, or at least a friend of hers. Eventually seven or eight others made apprentice deals with Schectman, working at the outset for basically nothing with the agreement that when the cases hit, the spoils would be shared.

And just look at the judge they'd drawn, Romeo thought. An African American woman would be able to relate to the brutal oppression to which the forest defenders were subjected.

At the outset, when Schectman still had his practice in San Francisco, he worked out of the office of Bill Bertain, the Scotia native who almost a decade and a half earlier had fought the takeover. After a few months of working in those cramped quarters, when Schectman was sure the apprentices wouldn't flake out on him, he rented the three-story house on E Street in Eureka. They all went furniture shopping together and moved into the offices of Pacific Law.

The offices became part legal boiler room, part commune, with apprentices sleeping in the third-floor apartment, on the floor, wherever they happened to collapse at the end of another twelve- or twenty-hour day. Two of them lived and worked in an office that had been a bathroom. They pulled out the tub and put down carpet—home, sweet home. Romeo, who lived in southern Humboldt County, slept on the floor at the office, or crashed with friends or sometimes in the back of her truck.

With both the Stafford and the Chain trials set to start within three weeks of one another, the office was becoming a true 24/7 operation. Romeo reached up to grab a ringing telephone once only to realize it was 4 A.M. A fish-and-game official was calling to leave a message and was surprised to be speaking to a live voice in the middle of the night. One guy would sleep until noon and then work until four or five in the morning. When the pressure was on, they all worked with dark circles under their eyes. But the juice, the *esprit de corps*, was addictive. They'd sit around the conference table downstairs and have long meetings, dividing up the mountain of work—prep work for the depositions, deadlines for key motions and pleadings. Romeo spent a week at Cindy's in Coldspring, going through material, assembling documents, and getting to know the family. School reports, W-2 statements, and other mundane pieces of paper David Chain's life had generated were now part of a case being built to seek redress for his death.

Romeo didn't buy every piece of Schectman's argument, and he suggested to her that he didn't literally believe every word he'd written either. For example, why the contention that the violence out in the Mattole in the weeks before David Chain's death had been a turning point? Simple. It was a way of suggesting a malevolent guiding hand without naming Charles Hurwitz in the suit, which would have landed the suit in the jurisdiction of Humboldt County, Timber Country U.S.A. Anybody who worked environmental litigation in Humboldt County knew that the first thing you did when plotting an action was figure out how to get it out of Humboldt County.

Well, Schectman's yarn made for a tidy narrative construct and maybe a jury would buy it. But there was nothing magical about the summer of 1998. Romeo herself had seen and documented and been on the receiving end of scary stuff earlier than that. Furthermore, Romeo saw Takeover Charlie playing his hand much more shrewdly, by using the presence of the protesters to his own advantage *and* encouraging people to beat the shit out of them because they were slowing his moneymaking operation. It was insidious. But Schectman wouldn't be dissuaded.

"Do you want to win this case?" he'd ask.

Preparing for and watching depositions was bracing. They'd sit in a roomful of documents and pull out anything that had to do with the upcoming deponent, then prepare questions for Schectman. The big front conference room on the first floor of the office was the setting, its main feature a long table. Typically there were charts, blown-up photographs, and other exhibits leaning against the wall. During depositions Schectman was masterful at guiding witnesses into corners and then making them squirm, speaking in a voice that was calm and absent of bluster. During breaks he was like a boxer in his corner, asking the apprentices how he was doing and what questions he should be asking.

DISCOVERY IN THE LAWSUIT ROLLED on as Cindy Allsbrooks kept one eye on the case's development and the other on her own psyche. Those dual concerns frequently intersected and conflicted with one another. One night in early February, Schectman had called her to tell her he'd received the death-scene photographs. Cindy's boy lay at an awkward angle, partly on his stomach and partly on his side, his left hand above his head. The tree had ripped a hole in his skull, exposing the blood and brain matter within, and the crimson contrasted violently with Gypsy's short brown hair and the debris that dusted his body. "Cindy," Schectman said over and over, "I am so sorry."

Allsbrooks made plain her stance on the photos. She hadn't wanted to see her son's face at the funeral home—"That is not my son," she'd thought to herself then, "it is only the shell of a human"—and she certainly didn't want to see photos from the death scene. There could be no comfort in that. "Steve, I never want to see those pictures," she said. "Not in a court or on any other occasion."

In May of 2000, she and Ron attended another Maxxam shareholders' meeting in Houston. In June, she was so exuberant that she had for the first time successfully accomplished a mundane chore—taking her dogs to the veterinarian—that she wrote exultantly about it in her journal.

At times, relative normalcy seemed elusive; the burden of simply getting through a day was heavy. Toward the end of July, Peggy Kathleen Trimm Smith—the sister who had been adamant about Allsbrooks's pursuing Gerry Spence's counsel—died while waiting for a liver transplant. Another death in the family, and yet at times Cindy felt she hadn't ever grieved for anyone until she'd grieved for her son. And, compounding Allsbrooks's misery, her marriage was plainly unsalvageable. That summer she and Ron observed what Cindy bitterly noted was an unhappy tradition—a fight on her birthday—and later agreed they were moving in opposite directions.

Meanwhile, Charles Hurwitz—never one to miss an opportunity for a lawsuit—countersued the government for seeking taxpayer restitution for Maxxam and Hurwitz's role in the savings and loan bust. The Office of Thrift Supervision action was by now fully five years old, and alleged that Hurwitz had propped up the value of United Savings so that it could buy junk bonds from Drexel—which itself had gone belly-up in the interim. The lawsuit sought roughly half the $1.6 billion the failure had cost taxpayers. But now Maxxam accused the Federal Deposit Insurance Corporation of illegally underwriting the OTS litigation. The *San Francisco Examiner* quoted Jill Ratner, who had asked Allsbrooks if she wanted to speak at the previous year's Maxxam shareholders' meeting, as saying that the move meant Maxxam was on the run, that it thought it was going to lose the suit. Maxxam maintained, as it had from the beginning, that the suit was a lawless, politically motivated witch-hunt. (In October 2002 Maxxam and Hurwitz would declare vindication when the company and OTS reached a settlement in which the company made no admission of wrongdoing and dropped the countersuit in exchange for the OTS dropping its action.)

In the fall, Allsbrooks was back in Humboldt County for the anniversary of her son's death, as she had been the year before. She also wanted to meet the son who'd been born to Mike Avcollie and his wife in June. Avcollie and Calista had named the boy Alder Nathan.

Allsbrooks was also on hand to witness a deposition, to lay eyes for the first time on the man who had killed her son.

A. E. Ammons hadn't taken his seat in the conference room of Schectman's office when Allsbrooks walked in. They traded hasty glances. To the aggrieved mother, Ammons seemed on edge. Maybe he was just like that.

Ammons was adamant from the beginning of the ordeal that he hadn't done anything wrong, but it still ate at him every day. He'd probably suffered as much as anybody outside of the family in this deal, he figured. He'd gained weight, couldn't sleep. Even if he'd done it all by the book, he couldn't help what-iffing himself three-quarters to death. At the end of any internal debate he might have, the fact was he had killed the kid. But he also knew if he could just get the facts out in the dispassionate venue of a lawyer's office and then in a courtroom, he could clear everything up.

As the deposition proceeded, Ammons grew relaxed and comfortable as he sat at the conference table in Schectman's office and, over two days, laid out his story.

It was at least partially to Schectman's credit that the deponent seemed so calm and unguarded. At the outset in such situations, the deposing attorney will attempt to put the witness at ease, to telegraph that the witness is smart and interesting and the attorney wants to know all about him and his job. The more at ease the witness is, the more likely he will be to step into the trap of telling the truth.

Schectman had a lot he needed to get out of Ammons and on the record. In addition to the logger's recollections of the confrontations with the activists and a good deal of professional minutiae, some of it potentially incriminating, it was key to establish the casual, anti-enviro hostility, the culture of tolerated violence, that made Ammons, on the videotape, the dog at the end of the leash.

"Did you ever hear about anyone, any employee of Pacific Lumber getting physical in response to any of the activities the Earth First!ers were alleged to have done?" Schectman asked.

"I've heard them but not for a fact."

"I'm not asking if it's true, just if you've heard about it."

"I just heard it, yes."

"What have you heard in that regard?"

"Chased them and wrestled them down and held them for the police department."

"They've chased and wrestled them down?"

"Uh-huh."

"You ever hear anyone say they punched out or physically hit any Earth First!ers?"

"I heard that happened, yeah."

"Ever heard any names associated with that?"

"No."

"Ever hear anything about how Carl Anderson was alleged to have handled some protesters?"

"No."

"And the stuff that you just told me about, that you heard about the Earth First!ers and some of the employees' responses to them, you heard that on the work site, workplace, this kind of . . ."

"Yeah."

"And that was pretty prevalent around the worksite if you tuned your ears . . . Since the time David was killed to present, have you been to any safety meetings where anyone from the company stood up and told people that they couldn't be chasing protesters in the woods?"

"I wouldn't say that we were told that we should chase them, but not to try to—try not to have any contact with them."

"But that's not been clearly stated as far as you can recall?"

"No."

"Since the death of David Nathan Chain, have you been at any meetings at Pacific Lumber where someone in management or super-visory capacity stood up at a meeting and said words to the effect, 'Hey, look guys, if you see some protesters out there and you're cutting trees, put your chain saw down and just stop'?"

"No, I've not been told that."

"And, in fact, you told various supervisory personnel from Pacific Lumber that you kept on cutting on the day of September 17, the day David got killed, even though you knew there were people in the area?"

"I knew they were a safe distance away from me."

"You told them words to that effect?"

"Yes."

"Once you knew the protesters were a safe distance away you kept cutting?"

"Yes."

Schectman later drew Ammons out about the company policies of which he was explicitly aware. Absolutely no weapons on the job site, for example. Ammons said once he inadvertently drove to the job with his deer rifle in the pickup, got spotted, and had to drive home to dump off the gun before going to work. The company handed out green and pink slips and documented violations of policy.

With each delineation of what Ammons and other employees knew about company policies to ensure workplace safety, an omission came into sharper focus. If protest activity had been a chronic presence on PL property for almost fifteen years, where was the explicit policy that said employees must put down their saws when they see protesters, must radio security immediately, and must not do them any harm whatsoever? Where was the policy that said if you so much as threaten to cut a hippie out of a tree, you'll be back to setting chokers so fast it'll make your head spin? Because not one person at that company—from the international, multinational planet-raper back in Houston on down—has any regard for the safety of those dirty, subhuman hippies, Schectman would argue. Furthermore, the company hadn't learned anything as a result of Chain's death.

"Have you ever been to any meetings organized by the company where the discussion took place about what happened on the day David Chain got killed?"

"No."

"There has been no meeting that you know of where they try to use that as a learning example so it won't happen again?"

"None."

"It's never happened?"

"Not to my knowledge."

"Did you ever hear anyone say that they'd been to a meeting where personnel of Pacific Lumber went over what happened the day David Chain got killed so that it could be avoided in the future?"

"No."

"To your knowledge has there been any change in any procedure policies regarding the wood workers since David Chain was killed that related to the policy of the company on how to deal with protesters?"

"No."

Later:

"What did you understand Pacific Lumber's policy to be when you got to work on the 17th of September 1998 as to what you should do if you found protesters in the woods where you were cutting trees?"

"Call and let them know."

"And what was your belief, based upon your observations and experience, would happen if you didn't call?"

"Nothing."

Why? Because, Ammons allowed, the company was much more serious about enforcing its ban on drugs in the workplace than on ensuring the safety of recalcitrant hippie civilians in the woods.

On the second day of the deposition, Schectman asked Ammons in detail about the order in which he had cut the trees, particularly following the penultimate confrontation when the protesters were huddled in their snack spot. Ammons said he cut a number of small, non-merchantable trees to clear the way for the larger ones that he would bring down to be trimmed and scaled. Whatever Ammons said his reasoning was, Schectman would argue at trial that Big A was still furious, that he had chased the protesters into a draw and started felling suckers out of order, effectively making the trees short-range missiles that he could fell quickly to scare the hippies.

Schectman kept hammering at the angle of enforcement of safety rules: "Isn't it true that if the company had told you clearly for years before September 17, 1998, that if you see protesters in the woods and you don't call on the radio, you'd lose your job, that things may have been different?"

Bill Bragg and the Pacific Lumber lawyer objected for the record, then Schectman told Ammons he could answer.

"I can't say that," he said. "I can't state that for a fact, no."

Schectman also produced a report from Pacific Lumber's accident prevention director, Jeff Ringwald, and read an excerpt: " 'Based on our investigation—our interview with your timber faller A. E. Ammons, his spotter helper Rhett Reback, our logging manager Dan McLaughlin—and based on the evidence at the accident site, I have concluded that all company safety procedures and policies were followed as required. This included all training requirements complete with documentation.' Did anyone from Pacific Lumber ever tell you at any point in time that they had concluded that you followed all the safety procedures and policies of the company regarding what you were supposed to do on the day of the 17th?"

Ammons said he didn't remember that.

Throughout the deposition, Ammons's memory fuzzed intermittently. They used photos of the site, documents of statements he'd made. They ran the videotape that the Earth First!ers had shot. Every time they played the video, Allsbrooks had to leave the room.

"I could not be present in the same room with him and hear his words of anger knowing that when they were spoken my son was still breathing and within minutes of those words he was gone forever," Allsbrooks would say later. "The words were some of the most alarming I had ever heard: 'You got me hot enough to fuck.' Where does a statement like that come from in a normal person? Maybe somewhere in the back of my mind I was also letting him off the hook by not having to look at me when listening to the tape played. In retrospect, I should have sat there glaring at him as the tape played. I am too easy on people sometimes, I think, even on the man whose temper cost Nathan his life. But my son is now crossed over to a world where hate cannot exist and I would not dishonor what he stood for by allowing hate in my life."

Schectman was at last finished with Ammons about 1:40 P.M. Schectman told Bragg that Cindy Allsbrooks had requested a private, off-the-record meeting with Ammons—"just as two people face-to-face, if that would be something you would allow. She would certainly appreciate that."

"I'll discuss that with A.E. and leave that totally up to him," Bragg said.

Ammons seemed about to jump out of his chair: "Can I answer it now?"

"Off the record," Bragg advised.

Off the record, A. E. Ammons said yes, he would very much like to meet with Cindy Allsbrooks. He was shown up the creaking stairs to Schectman's personal office, where Allsbrooks had spread out a line of photos of her son in various stages of his truncated life. She was so prepared it was almost like she was about to give a presentation to a business client, but she was also apprehensive. Her job, her motivation for this meeting, was to make A.E. look at the face of the young man whose life he had taken with his chain saw.

Ammons walked in, shut the door, and practically blurted, "I have wanted to talk to you for the last two years. I have wanted to tell you how sorry I am that your son died."

The compassion she felt for this man came as a surprise. She knew that A. E. Ammons hadn't singled out her son for killing. But he had been in a sputtering rage—and even now was so racked with guilt that he could scarcely glance at the snapshots of David Nathan Chain.

Allsbrooks put her arms around him. Ammons responded with more of a clutch than an embrace.

She said she had never hated him, but couldn't understand the threats on the videotape. Ammons's answer was not satisfying.

"Oh, people say a lot of things out of anger," he said. "They just talk." That was A.E. Everybody knew his bark was worse than his bite.

She told him she thought the company would hang him out to dry before it was all over. After she said what needed to be said and she'd done what she had to, she couldn't stand to be in the room with the man.

"Mr. Ammons," she said, "I just wanted you to know that I cannot hate you, and one of the reasons is because my son would not want that. Goodbye."

* * *

AMMONS WASN'T SCHECTMAN'S ONLY WITNESS to offer up goodies for the plaintiffs' case. Security chief Carl Anderson claimed PL president John Campbell wrote a memo after the boss found out about Anderson toting a slingshot into the woods to shoot marbles at a protester in a tree and called him on the carpet about it. (Campbell had no recollection of the meeting.) Anderson had also made T-shirts with the Earth First! logo with a red circle and a slash through it. He admitted to having animosity toward the protesters, and he wasn't alone, he said. He'd heard a sheriff's official tell hippies that they'd be shot if they tried to interfere with Climber Dan Collins's efforts to pull them out of trees. That prompted this exchange between Schectman and Anderson:

"Did you ever form the opinion that it wasn't appropriate to have a sheriff threaten to shoot someone while trying to remove a protester from a tree?"

"No."

"You didn't form an opinion one way or another?"

"I didn't think it would be out of line if that protester did what he had warned him not to do."

Schectman asked if Anderson recognized any of the protesters at Grizzly Creek the day David Chain was killed. "No," Anderson said, "they all look the same."

Anderson also testified to a good deal of nutty hippie behavior: one girl in the Mattole even ran into a layout where a tree was about to go down. He knew these kids were in danger of getting seriously hurt, either by falling out of trees or grabbing chain saws. It was a matter of time.

A June 1992 memo addressing the issue of activists in the woods became the subject of much debate about whether it was or was not the company policy when it came to handling protesters.

Whether it was explicit company policy or not, John Campbell's memo—"Response to Potential Woods Protesters"—ordered workers to notify a supervisor immediately upon encountering protesters and not to engage them in any kind of confrontation. Anderson allowed that he understood Pacific Lumber to be serious about enforcing some policies and not so serious about others. When deposed, Jeff Ringwald— the accident prevention director—said Ammons's behavior on the videotape would not comply with "the '92 policy" because Ammons had inarguably been verbally hostile. When asked, Ringwald said Ammons should have notified a supervisor. Ringwald said he never attempted to find out whether or not Ammons did. The more Ringwald talked, the more apparent it became that Campbell's memo was worthless. Ringwald said the memo didn't factor into his investigation and conclusion that no company policies had been violated in the killing.

"After your discussion with Ammons, you had the impression there was nothing that you could do to make the workplace safer as a result of the lesson learned from this tragedy. Is that fair?" Schectman asked.

"There were no policies or procedures that were violated," Ringwald said. "Obviously we wouldn't want to see this happen again to anyone. This is sad. This is a situation I wish we weren't even faced with."

Campbell, in his deposition, offered a canny alternative interpretation to the events on the videotape as they related to company rules, guidelines, policies—whatever they were. At the time he wrote the memo, Campbell said, the protests were relatively young. He had no idea the conflict would be so protracted, and the company was still trying to figure out how to respond. Over the years, as the hippie shenanigans persisted without relief, it became increasingly difficult to get the sheriff's office to respond to complaints, so loggers would just shut down and walk away. And, Campbell said, Ammons did indeed shut down his saw.

"And that's based on viewing the tape and all the other information you've talked about?" Schectman asked.

"Yes."

"And so you would tell your workers that—"

"Well, the tape shows that he wasn't felling trees while the pro-testers were there."

"Obviously, he kept falling trees afterward, correct?"

"Well, he didn't see them."

"So your information tells you."

"Well, so did the tape, and then they were hiding from him behind the trees."

Schectman also drew Campbell into a discussion about the prob-lems protesters were believed to have caused at the president's home— graffiti, the dead deer in the pool, threatening phone calls, and, most alarmingly, an arson started with oily rags. Schectman asked who did the investigation. Campbell answered that it had been the sheriff's of-fice. Schectman attempted a brazen bit of provocation.

"Did any of the investigators ever ask you if you, for instance, had any extramarital affairs with married women?"

Campbell: "With married what?"

"Yes. Did you ever have an affair with a married woman in the community?"

Pacific Lumber lawyer Charles Preuss jumped in: "I'll object to the form as argumentative and outrageous, quite frankly."

Schectman: "You can answer."

"Did the investigator ask me that?"

"Yes."

"No," Campbell said.

"Did they ask you if you knew of anyone else that may be mad at you for any reasons other than protesters?"

"I think they talked about possibly disgruntled employees."

"Have you ever had any?"

"No."

"Okay. Do you have any disgruntled husbands that at least communicated to you that they felt you were improperly relating to their wives? That never happened?"

"No."

"You sure?"

"Sure."

"Okay. Did you ever have any potential disputes with someone because of what they alleged to be improper conduct of you toward how you treated a member of their family?"

"You mean as an employee?"

"Anybody in the community."

Campbell looked puzzled. "Not that I'm aware of," he said, "but what's this got to do with what we're talking about?"

"Well, you're trying to say, I believe, that all these activities were the result of Earth First! or protesters."

"Uh-huh."

"And usually when an investigation goes on, they try to figure out if there's anyone else that may have a motive. No one ever asked you those questions, whether or not there was anyone else that may have the motive to do some of these things to you?"

"Well, the house was covered with Earth First! stickers."

"Okay. Have you ever heard of COINTELPRO?"

"Pardon?"

It went on like that for a while.

SCHECTMAN HAD BEEN LOOKING FORWARD to this deposition.

"Good morning, Detective Freeman . . ."

"Detective Sergeant."

"Detective *Sergeant* Freeman"—Schectman cleared his throat. "My name is Steven Schectman and I'll be conducting your deposition today, at least on behalf of the plaintiffs."

This was at ten in the morning on November 2, 2000. Freeman's deposition would sprawl over two additional days.

Schectman established the basics: where Freeman worked and for how long. Within minutes he was attempting to establish Freeman's coziness with Pacific Lumber. He asked why, when served with Schectman's subpoena, he had called Pacific Lumber's lawyers instead of Schectman's office. "Any reason you didn't call me?" Schectman asked.

"I did call you," Freeman said. "I called you. I left several messages on your answering machine."

PL's attorney, John Powers, jumped in. As he had already told Schectman, Powers said for the record, the "sum and substance of any contact" Freeman had with Powers's office had to do with the likelihood that coroner's photographs would be available for use at the deposition.

Schectman moved on.

Schectman and Freeman both endeavored to crack the seriousness of the proceedings on occasion. Freeman asked if they could "stop the bus" when he needed a "pit stop." Schectman joked about how unpleasant it must be for Freeman to spend time in the company of lawyers.

But Schectman's intent was serious and multipurpose. Among other things, it seemed to Freeman as if the lawyer were attempting to impugn his credentials as a homicide investigator. Schectman asked at some length for details of Freeman's background and his continuing education. He also asked how many homicides he'd investigated. Around twenty, as Freeman recalled. Freeman noted, with a bit of pride, that he was teaching at the law enforcement academy at the College of the Redwoods down the road. Schectman asked if Freeman knew Carl Anderson when PL's security man had worked at the sheriff's office. Not well, Freeman said. Freeman allowed, when asked, that no, he had only asked one grieving mother if she was wearing a wire and that mother was Cindy Allsbrooks.

Schectman drew this line out a little more, attempting to show that Allsbrooks was, essentially, politically persecuted.

"Is that something you currently teach in your course, that sometimes you want to ask the parents of a deceased person if they have come to talk to you with any kind of a secretive recording device?" Schectman asked.

"No."

After six hours, Schectman wrapped up his first day by asking Freeman if he had an opinion on Charles Hurwitz's business practices as they related to the economic health of Humboldt County.

Powers objected. They recessed for the day.

Freeman left thinking he might need a lawyer after all.

Backstage machinations delayed the start of Freeman's second day by more than three hours. Freeman had called a local attorney who did work for the city and county. The attorney then called Schectman, telling him he probably couldn't get time or authorization to jump in as Freeman's counsel so quickly, and that Freeman's deposition would have to be delayed. Then Schectman got another call from the county, this time affirming that Freeman would be there that afternoon, again alone and without counsel.

Schectman asked Freeman if he had told anyone that Schectman should have been prosecuted for disclosing A. E. Ammons's name. Freeman said he didn't recall saying anything like that. Schectman asked if there was any reason to believe his memory was failing. Bragg and Powers objected.

Schectman kept needling the cop, calling him "Sergeant Inspector Freeman."

Schectman: "Isn't it true that what you were recommending to the district attorney, when you sent it for review, is that you, the investigator, felt the activists should be charged for a form of manslaughter?"

Freeman: "I—I don't know if I put that in writing, but I certainly felt that way."

"You were telling Ms. Allsbrooks the truth when you told her you were going to recommend that the activists accompanying her son on the day of his death be charged with manslaughter, weren't you?"

Bragg: "Well, I'm going to object. That assumes facts not in evidence. He hasn't yet testified that he, in fact, told her that."

"Okay," Schectman said. "You can answer the question."

"I never told her that," Freeman said.

"Would it be fair to say that you told Ms. Chain [*sic*] words to the effect that you felt a case could be made against the activists that accompanied her son on the day of his death for manslaughter?" Schectman asked.

Bragg objected again.

"I told her that they could be criminally liable for that," Freeman said. "But it was a could be, maybe."

Schectman asked why Freeman wrote Darryl Cherney. "Well, because he's a known leader of the Earth First! movement, of which these folks were professed to be," Freeman offered.

Schectman seized on a telling term in Freeman's answer.

"You know John Campbell?"

"I met him once."

"Do you know that he's the CEO of Pacific Lumber?"

"Yes."

"Would it be fair to say he's the 'known leader' of Pacific Lumber?"

"Yes."

November 15. Day three.

Schectman asked Freeman if he had spoken with anyone at the sheriff's department about how the deposition was going. Freeman said he'd spoken with Lieutenant Frank Vulich.

"He asked me how it went," Freeman said, "and I said it was brutal, and I told him how I felt like I was being attacked most of the time but I was doing the best I could to provide the information that was asked for. He said all you can do is the best you can."

Schectman's bilious contempt for Freeman was still fresh long after the deposition concluded. "Whatta piece of shit, huh?" he said a year later as he ran around his office preparing to break camp and relocate to Oakland for the trial. "That guy ought to be in jail."

* * *

TO ALLSBROOKS, THE PRETRIAL SETTLEMENT conference
played out like a miserably cruel skit. She'd flown into Oakland on
Valentine's Day, the day discovery in the case formally closed. Jamie
Romeo and Angela Wartes—the activist who'd called Sarah Chain with
the news of David's death and was by now another of Schectman's
hired hands—picked Allsbrooks up at the airport, took her to dinner,
and dropped her at a dank dungeon of a hotel. Schectman and the
Spence firm were picking up her expenses, and Schectman was per-
petually strapped, always looking for a cheaper hotel, a way to shave a
few bucks off the bills that never seemed to quit spilling out of his
mailbox.

Allsbrooks, her lawyers, the Pacific Lumber lawyers, and a magistrate gathered the next day. From the plaintiffs' perspective, it was a
train wreck of a meeting. The magistrate told Schectman his settlement papers were a joke. Romeo asked the judge to stop logging in the
forest whenever protesters were present. Schectman was mortified. He
was plainly not in control of his own paralegal.

Worse, Romeo kept telling Allsbrooks there was no way they were
going to lose the case. Schectman had a long talk with her about such
intemperate remarks and reminded her of the element of assumed
risk—the activists said they knew they could be facing death running
around in the middle of falling trees. This case, while not as compli-
cated as some, was by no means a ringer. And whether it was or not,
Schectman would not have Romeo making reckless promises to Allsbrooks. At the same time, Schectman knew he couldn't tell his client
that Jamie was full of shit. Allsbrooks had an abiding affection for the
activist-apprentices, who represented a living connection to her son
and the cause for which he had perished.

Pacific Lumber, for its part, was willing to entertain some of the
nonfinancial elements of a potential settlement that Allsbrooks was af-

ter—some kind of memorial, possibly a committee to mediate conflicts between loggers and environmentalists. But that talk didn't get too far because the company was offering an offensive sum—all of $75,000— to settle. Allsbrooks reacted as if she were being offered a steaming turd. *So that's the going price for a twenty-four-year-old tree hugger,* she thought. She left the courthouse visibly angry, refusing to entertain an- other syllable of debate on how much her son's life was worth. Schect- man drove her to a nicer hotel on Fisherman's Wharf, and his client's mood might have lightened had she not then received the news that her aunt back home had passed away. She had to try to catch an early flight home.

She called Bridgett and wept.

Then she called Monroe Kirby, the lawyer father of Stephanie Kirby, David Nathan Chain's girlfriend on his first westward journey. She'd come to lean on Kirby for second legal opinions and perspective. The plain-speaking Kirby was characteristically succinct.

"Fuck 'em all," he said.

The plaintiffs' team was still hoping to recover at least $5 million for loss of consortium and some $13,000 for burial and funeral ex- penses. They had also moved for a continuance on the March 26 trial date—even with the muscle of Moriarty, Bosch, and the rest of the Spence team, Schectman would be fighting on two fronts virtually si- multaneously. The defendants, keeping the heat on, were opposing the motion. Schectman wasn't terribly concerned. A lot of firms over- scheduled. It just happened. The judge might yell and scream, but they'd get their continuance. And even if they didn't, Moriarty had plenty more trial experience than Schectman and would be more than capable of saddling up.

A lot was riding on the other motions Judge Armstrong was con- sidering, however. No matter what she decided, the trial was bound to be a grind—between four and six weeks, depending on how she ruled on limiting certain testimony relating to the history of the protest movement in Humboldt County and beyond. Allsbrooks's lawyers had filed a motion to amend their complaint to more strongly state that an assault had been committed against David Nathan Chain before his death—the physical evidence being that his clothing had been damaged, like Nicole Simpson's had been—in an attempt to bolster the likelihood of securing punitive damages, if not at trial then upon appeal. The key was that under California law, claims for what is commonly called pain and suffering cannot survive death. Schectman and Bosch thought that was plenty evident in the original complaint, but it couldn't hurt to amplify that portion of the case.

Bragg wondered if the attempt to pump up the assault argument after the judge's deadline meant the Spence firm hadn't taken an active enough role in developing the key pleadings, including the punitive elements of the case. Further, the plaintiffs had gone in intending to take Pacific Lumber to trial for a decade and a half of conduct that had attracted protest and that the company had responded with a bogus cover-your-ass policy while tacitly condoning violence, and that Hurwitz had used the protesters to advance his "nefarious"—Schectman's favorite term—plot. That, to Bragg, was why the Spence firm—with all its staff, its notoriety, and its private jet shuttling Ed Moriarty around— had been attracted to the case. If Schectman's theories were allowed, it would justify the involvement of a firm with the stature of Spence's.

And if not, well, it was another random wrongful-death case without the larger and more attention-grabbing themes of corporate malfeasance, conspiracy, and exploitation.

Then Schectman came to Bragg with an offer. "He knew he was in trouble," Bragg said later.

If Bragg would sign off on Schectman's motion to amend his complaint, Schectman would promise not to go after Bragg's clients for punitive damages. It was something of an empty gesture, because there was no earthly way either Ammons or Reback could pay the kind of punitive damages the plaintiffs were looking for even if both of them lived to be one hundred. But it was an appropriate legal maneuver. The plaintiffs would argue that Ammons's and Reback's conduct resulting in David Chain's death had been willful, malicious, and well outside the scope of their work duties—hence the employer wouldn't be liable for punitives. It was, Bragg said, "a sticky wicket." If he rejected the offer and Armstrong ruled in favor of the plaintiffs' amended complaint, his clients would be exposed.

Jamie Romeo and the rest of the gang at Schectman's office, of course, interpreted this development differently. It looked like the Pacific Lumber lawyers could at any moment try to pin the whole deal on Ammons and shake off any suggestion of corporate culpability. Bragg gave Schectman the impression that Ammons might be inclined to testify in a way that placed the blame on the company. Schectman and Bragg could divide and conquer.

Bragg picked up the phone and called the Pacific Lumber attorneys, told them about the deal, and suggested that PL pick up any punitive damages that his clients might incur if the jury found for the plaintiffs.

The PL lawyers vehemently resisted pursuing that option and floated a legitimate question about whether they'd be legally allowed to cover punitives if the loggers' actions were found not to be within the scope of their duties. The PL lawyers were gambling on winning summary judgment anyway—Armstrong would agree there were no factual issues to be tried on any of the claims that might open the window enough for punitive damages to slip in. Any financial hit the company might take, therefore, would be significantly reduced.

The wailing and gnashing of teeth between Bragg and the Pacific Lumber lawyers went back and forth for a couple of days. Finally Bragg called Ammons and Reback and explained the wicket, now firmly stuck. Ammons and Reback said they didn't need the company's protection. Both of them said flatly, for about the three hundredth time, that they hadn't done a damn thing wrong and would say so in front of

God and a jury without fear of the consequences. Thus the wicket was dislodged.

Federal rules of procedure in such matters said that the plaintiffs' motion, a motion for leave to amend, as it was called, "shall be freely given when justice so requires." But the case law also suggested the leave to amend was by no means automatic, especially if the motion did not include any new facts not known to the parties since the beginning of the legal action. Unfortunately for Schectman, that wasn't the case here. And it didn't help that he'd waited almost a year and a half to file the motion. "Plaintiffs do not argue that their proposed amendments are based on any new facts or recently discovered evidence," Armstrong wrote in her order. "Nor do they offer any convincing excuse for their 17-month delay in seeking leave to amend." She wasn't buying the argument that the plaintiffs were merely seeking to "clarify" the assault complaint.

If Armstrong decided not to allow the amended complaint, then punitive damages would be white-knuckling it on the first and third rungs of the original complaint for negligence and ultrahazardous activity, respectively. But Armstrong peeled off those arguments in her ruling, too. The plaintiffs, she said, could not credibly claim that David Nathan Chain's clothing had been damaged before death, as Nicole Simpson's had. If Chain's clothing was damaged, it was by the tree that killed him—and death was agreed to have been instantaneous. Moreover, Armstrong opined, the plaintiffs, short of retaining a medium and conducting a séance, couldn't prove Chain had suffered emotional distress before death.

"Accordingly, because there is no evidence, and no specific allegation, that defendants' alleged negligence or ultrahazardous activity caused Mr. Chain to suffer any loss or injury before his death, those claims did not survive his death and no damages may be awarded based on them," Armstrong wrote. "The court therefore GRANTS defendants' motion for summary judgment on the first and third claims of the complaint."

And with that, Armstrong threw out the possibility of the plaintiffs recovering punitive damages against Pacific Lumber.

A few days later, on February 27, Romeo's birthday, a dozen people were crammed into Schectman's office for a teleconference with Armstrong on the speakerphone. Schectman was asking for a continuance. They were clearly overbooked. Volunteers and apprentices were utterly silent, tiptoeing in and sitting down. After cutting punitive damages out of the case, Armstrong threw Schectman a bone and granted them a delay. Because of conflicts, there wasn't room for the trial on the calendar until October, which was more of a delay than the plaintiffs would have liked. And it also had them going at the same time as the Bari-Cherney civil rights trial against the government, which certainly meant that the federal courthouse in Oakland was going to be a lively place that fall. Still, it was a critical win. At the very least, Schectman wouldn't kill himself working two trials at once in courthouses 270 miles apart. They felt like nothing could stop them now.

NINE

Meltdown

MONTHS EARLIER, OVER THE THANKSGIVING 2000 weekend, an unknown assailant or assailants attacked Stafford's most famous resident. It wouldn't be right to call the event another Thanksgiving massacre—this was more of a surgical strike—but somebody had run a saw with a thirty-six-inch bar through Luna, the majestic unifying symbol for a disparate, diverse, and inherently quarrelsome movement. The tree, Julia Butterfly's home for two years, was about 60 percent sliced through near the base.

Eco-terror? Maybe, but whose side was the perp on? The once-sharp line of demarcation was beginning to bleed a bit. Forest defenders denounced the attack as a cowardly and hateful assault by those who wished them ill. It was plainly evident to them that the damage had been done by a psycho saw jock who knew what he was doing. But others entertained the possibility that the tree—and it was just that and nothing more, a commodity, a product, not a "Luna," not a "her," not possessed of a living spirit—had been cut by one of Hill's former supporters out of jealousy and pure spite. Just like Judi Bari and Darryl Cherney being blown up by their own bomb.

Tree surgeons hiked up to the scene. The principal short-term danger was that Luna might crash in a violent windstorm, of which there were more than a few that time of year. Pacific Lumber's own crews worked through pounding rain and serious wind to brace the big tree. Luna's medical team—which included the president of the Maryland-based American Society of Consulting Arborists—put a series of brackets above and below the saw cuts, then ran cables up the tree and anchored them sufficiently so that Luna wouldn't come down in a stiff and sustained gale. They predicted a good deal of dieback on the crown, which would make Luna a bit more craggy-looking, but they were talking about a thousand-year-old tree, after all. Bottom line? Luna would live. Activists greeted that news with whoops and applause. The violence committed against Luna would not be fatal. She would continue to stand tall and resilient.

Julia Butterfly Hill wrote an anguished poem about the assault and rushed to Stafford where, on the advice of a medicine man, she packed wet clay into Luna's gash. Hill decried the attack and also condemned Pacific Lumber's cutting of old growth in the remote Mattole region, where about half a dozen protesters were arrested that week as exasperated loggers cooled their heels yet again. As ever, the hippies were tenacious and, especially in the Mattole, almost fanatically dedicated. Besides the protesters' playing potentially fatal cat and mouse with the loggers, the weather was cold and wet, and the blockade site was a good twelve-mile hike into the woods. Among the issues, once again, perhaps most contentious was that logging led to erosion, which led in turn to denuded salmon populations. (The salmon PL raised at its hatchery and released in area streams, which environmentalists would applaud when other companies did it, blunted the criticism little.) The six hundred new jobs Charles Hurwitz created over a decade—a welcome development in any local economy—caused the continued pollution of those streams with runoff from clear-cuts. The company accused the protesters themselves of contributing to erosion by plugging culverts and redirecting drainage ditches. EF!ers and Mattole landowners were trying to raise money to buy part of the Mattole and spare the trees from the saw. Pacific Lumber said the place wasn't for sale—the company needed the timber to keep its mills going. The enviros had tried and failed to buy time by petitioning the California Supreme Court.

Meanwhile, Judge Armstrong's latest rulings in *Chain v. Pacific Lumber* were not dissimilar to the damage done to Luna. It wasn't what the plaintiffs wanted to hear. Allsbrooks took in the news from her lawyers. No punitives. Okay. She got a brief tutorial on the peculiarities of the California civil code that made the situation so. Then she issued a ruling of her own: No way are we settling. Punitive damages or not, we are going to trial.

• "The most vilified timber company in California," as the *San Jose Mercury News* had described Pacific Lumber after the company had its license pulled in 1998, was by no means a stranger to courthouse dustups after more than fifteen years of controversy, and it was deft at marshaling the legalistic firepower necessary to defend itself against yet another assault upon its right to do lawful business on its own lands. Armstrong's ruling had been a break in the company's favor.

But Bill Bragg, whose concern was not the corporation but workingmen A. E. Ammons and Rhett Reback, still faced a sizable challenge: it was going to be his job at trial to humanize A. E. Ammons and Rhett Reback as regular guys, the kind of people a jury could relate to, and to disassociate Ammons from the maniac on the videotape. The jury pool for the case would draw from one of the most ethnically diverse metropolitan areas in the country, and the panel would likely include a good number of people who could scarcely afford the $15 to park all day in downtown Oakland with enough left for a coffee from Starbucks across the street from the federal complex. Compelling those people to miss work for a month and a half—and receive the paltry compensation of $30 per day—was going to be a hardship for many of them. But then, maybe they could relate to Ammons and Reback and the way they had adapted their lives to fitfully delivered paychecks, their income fluctuating according to the vagaries of precipitation and litigation. Reback was just a kid, all-American as could be. Even Allsbrooks felt bad for him, playing a role in a ghastly death at such an early age. As for Ammons, true, he could be a bit of a hothead, but as Ammons himself liked to say, everybody knew his bark was worse than his bite. Bragg had no worries about putting him in the box. As for certain company officials and how the jury might regard *them*, well, they might come across as insolent assholes. But that was the corporate attorneys' concern, not Bill Bragg's.

And if Bragg's worries were more than adequate to occupy him, Schectman was nearly drowning in his own. Before Armstrong granted the continuance in the Chain case, Pacific Law hummed around the clock, just like old Mill B in Scotia had in the go-go overtime days right after the takeover. Jamie Romeo didn't take her eyes off prepping for the trial, working ten days in a row and seventy hours a week through January and February. It was, without question, the most intense time of her entire life.

All the apprentices had to do was look away from their work and glance at Schectman to see the pressure was on. His back was driving him nuts and he was getting steroid shots for the condition, which seemed to affect his mood, Romeo thought, and not for the better. He was feuding with Bill Bertain, who'd been in on Stafford from the beginning. He alluded—more than alluded—to serious money problems. The fledgling, noble firm of Pacific Law was burning through capital and nothing was coming in. He'd gotten all the credit cards he could and maxed them out. When the companies called the office looking for their money, Schectman had people tell them he wasn't there. He mentioned there was the threat of losing his home. To the activists-cum-apprentices it made Schectman look all the more committed: he was a hero willing to gamble the house where his children slept, his health, and his credit rating to do the right thing. They were prepared to win Stafford and win it big. They *had* to win Stafford and win it big. Principle alone couldn't sustain the firm for much longer.

On March 5, the day the Stafford trial was scheduled to begin in Humboldt County District Court, Mike O'Neal, the lead plaintiff in the mudslide case, pulled his scrapbook off the bookshelf near his computer and his Catholic psalmbook and made a new entry. "We won!" he wrote. "Four years, two months, five days." Just seconds before midnight the previous Friday, he'd gotten a call that the mighty corporate dragon had agreed to settle. It had been four years, two months, and five days of herding cats, trying to keep his neighbors unified. He'd promised them if they stuck with them, he would deliver. Now he had.

How could he not? Over his life he'd seen the Eel and Klamath Rivers die because of over-siltation. But this wasn't about fish; it was about people, some of whom had lost everything they had, even if around Stafford that typically wasn't much. O'Neal made lots of noise, attracted media attention, worked on bills at the assembly in Sacramento, and retained Schectman, the San Francisco lawyer who heard the noise O'Neal was making and saw an opportunity. Over that span, O'Neal had become something of an international spokesman for the hamlet that Pacific Lumber had nearly taken out. (Some at the company joked that the little collection of sorry domiciles *needed* to be taken out.) He'd spoken to everyone from Fox News to National Public Radio, from *George* magazine to *High Times*. He had pictures of Woody Harrelson helping to sandbag his house. Another picture of

Joan Baez. Another of himself and Bonnie Raitt on top of the ridge that toppled. And of course there were pictures of him and Julia Butterfly together in Luna—so named because the early activists had assembled the tree sit platform by the light of a full moon.

He'd taken quite a stand against Maxxam, O'Neal thought. He never would have dreamed of going after such a powerful company. And they'd had to go all the way to the California Supreme Court to get a biased judge removed from the case. They'd fought and fought. And now he and the community had won. The money? Well, you're talking about people who had never known what it was like to have money. O'Neal drove a 1969 Chevy pickup and would continue to for years after the settlement. The only bittersweet element was the company maintaining to the end that it hadn't done anything improper. That galled him.

But if this was Mike O'Neal's V-Day, Schectman wasn't acting like a triumphant champion of the people. When Romeo arrived midmorning on Monday, she stuck her head in his office. "Is it good?" she asked. "Are we happy?" Schectman said he was writing a press release about the settlement and that the apprentices should assemble in the conference room for a meeting in fifteen minutes.

The apprentices cheered Schectman and asked for details, particularly when they were going to get paid. *Kids ragging me about money*, Schectman thought.

He looked somber and spoke gravely. He said the case had indeed settled, and not for very much money. He said there were going to be some changes around the office, which they'd have to talk about later in the week.

"I'm too upset to talk to you now," he said. "I'll meet with you later in the week."

The bewildered apprentices cleared out and didn't come back until Thursday.

Publicly, Schectman declared the day of the announced settlement a day of reckoning. He called a press conference at the courthouse and said the plaintiffs—some of whose families had been in the employ of Pacific Lumber for generations—were pleased at the $3.3 million settlement. The amounts for the individual plaintiffs would range from a little less than $100,000 to more than twice that. Schectman told reporters Pacific Lumber settled because the company wanted to avoid a trial.

Pacific Lumber's spokeswoman, Mary Bullwinkel, said the company was more than ready to go to trial and that it was Schectman who had come to PL to propose settling three days before the trial commenced.

As usual, the truth was somewhere along the fuzzy line that separated the combatants, and it floated away unreported amid the spin wars. After a series of rulings favorable to the plaintiffs, Schectman had, in fact, asked a PL lawyer, "Do you think we should mediate now?" The plaintiffs' side was by then on a roll, he said, and it was a perfect time to offer the other side a way out. You don't go into mediation from a position of weakness. Once Schectman gave the other side an opening, the game was on. Despite Bertain and Schectman's tussle over how the pot was to be divided, they presented a unified front when they and PL's lawyers sat down at the Red Lion Motel in Eureka to make a deal.

Romeo was the first one into Schectman's office on Thursday.

"It's not working out," he told her. "I want to be a teacher and you don't have any respect for my litigation skills. I can't afford to keep you here." Romeo and the other apprentices came and went as they pleased, turning his war room into a youth hostel. A zoo. They were in the middle of *high-level litigation*. Who needed ten people sitting around a conference room for an eight-hour deposition and expecting to get paid for it? They weren't doing their jobs. They didn't like him. For what they were costing him, he could easily have gotten an attorney—two attorneys—to help him out. And he was going to have to split the attorneys' percentage of whatever Chain hit for with Jerry Bosch and Ed Moriarty.

"This is a real law office," he said. "We live in the real world. I have bills."

Jamie Romeo cried bitter tears.

Schectman said he'd need to see an accounting of Romeo's hours before she got paid. Romeo walked out.

Angela Wartes was next. "You're not going to fucking treat me like you treated her," she said.

In the end, Wartes asked to stay on until the end of May. Schectman said okay.

He unloaded each of them, one by one, negotiating severance terms separately, reminding them that the firm wouldn't see any of the settlement until at least June.

The activists—"young, impetuous, and pissed" in Schectman's estimation—couldn't have been more stunned if the boss had hit them in the head with a mallet. Weren't doing their jobs? They were *living* their jobs. And what about the settlement? Why not push on and nail Pacific Lumber in front of a jury? They'd been thinking they could have gotten $10 million at trial. They didn't know if the $3.3 million settlement amount was good or bad, but even if they didn't see any of it for months, it was more than they had a week ago, right?

Schectman enlightened them on that little matter. Pacific Lumber was calling him a chump for settling, and you know what? Maybe they were right. But he wasn't going to go to trial and make Bill Bertain richer. Schectman had done all the work on the case and Bertain had agreed to a sixty-forty split. Now that the case had settled, Bertain was saying fifty-fifty. Schectman's chunk of the sum wouldn't even cover his expenses. He was losing his ass and the activists were flopping in his office for nothing. They had to go.

In the middle of this, Cindy Allsbrooks happened to call. Schectman went off on her, too. It was bizarre, inappropriate. Allsbrooks felt as if she didn't even know the person she was hearing, let alone why he was yelling at her.

The apprentices gathered in the back room to cry and console one another. Some of them worshiped Schectman. They'd never worked so hard before. What just happened? They'd figured Schectman's cut was supposedly between $660,000 and $850,000. And even with $200,000 in recoverable expenses—and, if Schectman was telling the truth, $300,000 more that he'd never see—*now* Schectman was telling them he was broke?

As the shock wore off, like a dissipating anesthetic, a hypothesis emerged: When he faced two trials, Schectman had no choice but to keep the apprentices around. But with one case settled before trial and the other continued until the fall, they were all suddenly expendable. So he fired them en masse in the Thursday Night Massacre.

So much for Steve Schectman, the principled and noble gamesman who was willing to put everything he had and more up as collateral in the fight. The man the apprentices thought they had known was gone. A few people had murmured about him from the beginning, said he'd burned his bridges in San Francisco, said his hidden agenda was the pursuit of cash, not justice. Maybe the apprentices had been naïve. So was Schectman just a fuckup? Had he had some kind of massive freakout from the steroids, the pain, and the inhuman stress load, from working two trials, one before a hostile judge and the other in the black heart of Hurwitz Country? Or had he been exploiting them all along, planning this, biding his time, waiting for the opportune moment?

One of the more seasoned paralegals, Stephanie Bennett, subscribed to the darker interpretation of events. A former schoolteacher, Bennett was in her forties and had enough experience with the law to see things were not right well before the Stafford settlement. Schectman became more autocratic and dictatorial. He could be charming one day and a monster the next. He picked on people and exploited weaknesses. And in the month before Stafford was to go to trial, things seemed downright dead around the office. They weren't preparing evidence or organizing the case. They weren't working with a mock jury. It was as though the heat was already off. One day there was so little to do that they threw a birthday party for Bennett's dog.

Bennett also had the right clothes and knew how to put on panty hose, so she attended a good number of the pretrial hearings in the Stafford case. Schectman needed her because she was presentable. The others, she sensed, were becoming burdensome.

And then, despite the firm's money troubles, they were remodeling the courtroom in which the case would be tried and splitting the bill with the defendants? It didn't make sense. If Schectman was broke, why was he running out to buy a $500 plant for the courtroom right before the trial? And if he was intending to settle, was this just a bluff? Schectman was a guy who operated on bluster and bravado, and now he seemed sick, dissipated, diminished. He seemed to have lost his nerve.

When the housecleaning came, Schectman asked Bennett to stay. Bennett said she wasn't interested in working for free. She wasn't interested in working for Schectman at all.

Schectman's perspective was understandably different. This sort of pressure was nothing. Yeah, he got a couple of steroid shots. They didn't make him crazy, they helped him walk. His back was messed up from football, horsing around in the water, racing motorcycles. The Chain case had been continued and that had never really been an issue. Even when things where at their worst, he'd de-stress. There was nothing like coming home to the unconditional love of his wife and kids. And then he'd be sitting in the steam room and meditating, feeling the toxins dribbling out of him. Sometimes he'd sit there and imagine he was telling off a judge or go over an opening statement. Sometimes he'd just sit in the dark and tune in to the sound, the *sssss*. Steve Schectman had not freaked out, was not freaking out. Now people were saying Schectman had ruined their lives. Now people were saying he was worse than Takeover Charlie. This turn of events was . . .

disappointing. He'd offered these people the hottest gig in town. *They* had come to *him*. It had been an exchange, knowledge for labor. And now it had spoiled. Sad.

But the activists weren't the only ones shaken by the changes Schectman said were long overdue. Allsbrooks, after getting the blistering telephone treatment from her own lawyer and then hearing what the apprentices had to say, was equally dazed. Some of the apprentices offered to help her find another lawyer if she so chose. Saddened as she was to hear about the apprentices' plight—some of them jobless, homeless, and rudely disillusioned—Allsbrooks said she couldn't do that. She told them that she was sorry and that she had much love for them. But she'd cast her lot with Schectman and felt bound to remain loyal.

Except for a couple of them who stayed, most of the activists moved out of Pacific Law, and the creaky old Victorian grew quiet. Jamie Romeo walked out for the last time two years into the apprenticeship program that she had thought would culminate in her taking the California bar exam.

It was okay. The experience was intense and incredible and she'd never regret it, even if the revolution had sputtered before it could begin. And anyway, she didn't really want to be a lawyer anymore.

TALK OF TURNING GYPSY'S LIFE into a movie had begun not long after his casket and vault were covered with East Texas dirt on a wilting September day. It never went further than most movie talk goes—just talk. Would-be authors had made overtures to Allsbrooks, too, without success. Much as she appreciated the fact that her son's story could be powerfully told, she felt a stronger and more primal maternal pull to prevent her family from further harm. She'd seen their private tragedy make worldwide headlines, and the results had not always been beneficial.

The family and the activists who had been with her son on the day he died had been particularly annoyed at a January 1999 story in *Rolling Stone* magazine, the cover of which named the Beastie Boys as artists of the previous year for the achievement of their *Hello Nasty* CD. The Gypsy piece, teased with the cover line "Death in the Redwoods: Loggers vs. Kids," struck many of those involved as a portrait of people and events they simply didn't recognize. A major source of contention was a single tossed-off sentence, detailing what happened after David Chain left the tent with Jennifer Walts and joined the group on the morning he was killed: "David mumbled good morning, then somebody sparked a pipe packed with Humboldt County weed." Those with more than a journalistic interest inferred that the piece was saying Gypsy had taken a toke or two before he and his comrades decamped up to the site where Pacific Lumber was cutting. This might not have been an issue had that line not reopened a wound first inflicted when Humboldt officials released toxicology results that showed THC was found in Gypsy's system, an indication that he had smoked pot at some point in the previous thirty days. Then there was Andrew Isaac's characterization of Gypsy as a "chronic" pothead.

The fact was, herb was a staple freely shared among many Earth First!ers, and it was even regarded as magic medicine by some. Chain and some other activists also smoked tobacco. Sometimes they blended pot, tobacco, and sage in one hand-rolled cigarette they'd pass around the circle. This was, after all, Humboldt County. There were places in Humboldt where it was far easier to find pot than a Pepsi—and where you were much more likely to draw reproachful comments from gulping the product of an evil multinational corporation than you would for smoking a gift from the Mother. It was entirely possible, maybe even likely, that somebody at the camp at that moment blazed up. But none of the activists who headed to the mountain that morning would later confirm that they had smoked or seen a pipe or seen Gypsy take a hit. In fact, when preparing for direct actions, Earth First!ers were prohibited—as much as anything truly could be in such a movement—from partaking in or packing along drugs or alcohol. It just cemented the stereotype, not to mention giving the cops one more excuse to arrest them.

Chain's companions Carey Jordan and Erik Eisenberg had gone so far as to hand-deliver a letter of objection to *Rolling Stone*'s corporate offices in New York when they visited the city, and they remained unsatisfied at the way they'd been depicted. They and other activists had cooperated with the piece and even posed for photos. The family had talked and shared candid personal snapshots with the magazine. The result, they believed, was wildly inaccurate and showed that the corporate media, including an ostensible counterculture magazine like *Rolling Stone*, couldn't be trusted. Allsbrooks, the most charitable of all the piece's critics, wondered if maybe the writer had done the best job he could in the time he had before his deadline. He had, after all, paid a visit to the free state, hiked up the mountain, and even tracked down A. E. Ammons, who did little to dispel the dog-at-the-end-of-the-leash characterization in parts of the interview that made it into the finished piece.

Then came *The Gypsy Chain*.

Laura Somers, the daughter of Dr. Philip Somers—in whose office David Chain had worked in the interregnum between school and moving to Austin, and behind whose boat he had learned to water-ski—was living in New York and busying herself in the theater scene. She was also suffering from panic attacks so severe that she once wound up in the emergency room. She always thought that she was the brave one, living by her own rules and making her own way. But she needed a change. She needed home. She moved back to Texas and, immediately upon her arrival, learned her friend had been killed while protesting the craven destruction of the forest. The last time she had seen David Chain he'd been in one of his dark moods—full-on jerk mode for no discernible reason. She had blown him off.

Then he'd gone away and really done something, taken action based on something in which he believed. Now he was dead.

Somers conceived of the play initially as an elegiac theatrical work and as a sort of therapy. But once she'd gotten a sense of what Chain had been up to after they'd lost touch with each other, she envisioned a broader and more dramatic story—a fictionalized tale of conflict along the jagged edge of the environmental movement. She traveled to Humboldt County, where she camped with Earth First!ers at a lockdown in the Mattole for a period of days. She was for the most part received favorably as "Gypsy's friend." (Not all the activists greeted her with immediate warmth—some jokingly accused her of being an FBI stooge. Such paranoia had long been a symptom of the EF! mind-set, and had on occasion been proved to be justified.) She scooped up data. Then she went back to Austin and started writing.

It was ambitious guerrilla theater on a frayed shoestring. The group mounted a fund-raising and letter-writing campaign and won grants from IBM and the city of Austin. Woody Harrelson made a donation. And in June they scored a coup: Julia Butterfly Hill, by then arguably more of a star than even Dave Foreman had been in the mid- to late-1980s, would come to Austin and lend her marquee name to a fundraiser. The venue was Antone's, a downtown blues bar of national renown and some notoriety—its proprietor, Clifford Antone, was a guest of the federal government in nearby Bastrop, serving a four-year sentence for drug trafficking and money laundering charges. The date was June 16, the night before David Nathan Chain's birthday. There was a silent auction, a couple of not-very-good noodly local bands, and one very good singer-songwriter.

On August 2, in the dead of a characteristically searing, humid Central Texas summer, *The Gypsy Chain* debuted in a space without benefit of functional air-conditioning. The show was passionate, heartfelt, well-meaning, and, with a run time of three hours and twenty minutes, mercilessly long. Part Loony Toons, part fairy tale, and part polemic, the largely fictionalized work couldn't quite figure out what it was trying to be, largely because the script was collaborative. If some real-life forest defenders believed the trees had souls, in *The Gypsy*

Chain the trees beckoned their would-be savior and bestowed forest names upon him with a whisper. The broad fictionalization had a practical as well as a creative function: Somers didn't want to get sued for slander.

Dozens of people got involved in the production. And "whether they knew Dave or not, many of those people were changed because of the process of creating it, spending five months with the same group of people, meeting Julia Butterfly or other activists, gaining environmental awareness, taking risks for something they believed in," Somers later said.

Even as the thing was rolling, Somers knew she had an unwieldy early draft—the play involved a huge cast, running automobiles, video, rock music, and actors rappelling from the ceiling—and resolved to rewrite as soon as the play's initial run was over.

Reviews acknowledged that, whatever its faults, the production's heart was in the right place.

Nevertheless, Cindy Allsbrooks honored the effort and commitment of her son's friend. On opening night, dressed in black, Allsbrooks sat in the front row, witnessed the martyrdom of the fictional Gypsy, and cried. Afterward, she congratulated Laura Somers. As was Allsbrooks's custom, most everybody involved in the production got a big, Texas-sized hug.

The dislocating experience of seeing one's memories and experiences refashioned into creative fodder was made even more extreme by the actor who played the narrator of the tale. It was the younger of Allsbrooks's two living children, Sarah Joy Chain, and she delivered one of the best performances in the play.

If Steve Schectman and Pacific Law had been overbooked before the Chain trial had been rescheduled, Cindy Allsbrooks's plate was piled high in the summer leading up to the trial with distractions and demands for her attention. She had become, to some in the movement, practically the virgin mother of the Christlike martyr, the fallen comrade, Gypsy Chain. Whether or not she had been used as Ron had warned her, she had in some quarters been reduced to a symbol. She could easily sympathize with the kids in the woods even if—privately—she didn't agree with all their tactics, their confrontations just for the hell of it, protests for protest's sake. She couldn't help but worry about those kids, her son's brothers and sisters. And in the late spring, when twenty people were arrested in the Mattole, it appeared to her and to others that it was just a matter of time before somebody else got hurt or even killed out there. From what Allsbrooks heard, the tension was similar to the weeks before her son had been killed. She prayed that no other mother would have to take the terrible journey she had.

By then, Allsbrooks could be as active or inactive in the battle for the soul of the forest as she wished without worrying about what Ron thought. After struggles that began well before David Chain had been killed, the marriage was nearing its end. In late June, Allsbrooks changed all the bills over to her name, downgraded services, and figured out where she could trim expenses to make the household run on half of what it used to. They'd agreed Allsbrooks would keep the house, where she had her office in an upstairs bedroom—the only room where she allowed herself to smoke. A couple of weeks later, Ron came to haul his stuff off to his new divorced-guy apartment. The chasm that separated them could not be bridged. Both of them cried for what was lost and, by mutual agreement, irretrievable. The unwelcome future Ron had glimpsed as he drove home upon receiving the word of his stepson's death had come to pass. His wife had been lost to him the moment she learned her son had been killed. That Cindy was gone.

THEN THE WAR CAME.

Following the September 11, 2001, terror attacks, with the country shakily attempting to get back to conducting its everyday business in a terrible new world, the semantics of terrorism, of what constituted a terrorist act and what a terrorist looked like, was the subject of exhaustive national discussion. Terrorists—wedded so firmly to their cause that reason and common sense had no place in their worldview—had killed thousands of Americans in a single morning. Earth First!ers had sporadically been tagged as terrorists since the beginning of the movement. Perception, as always, was far more powerful than reality, and for those who viewed damage to the machinery of capitalism as violence upon the owner's person, maybe Earth First! could be viewed, if one squinted hard enough, as a terrorist organization. And although North Coast Earth First! had long before renounced tree spiking and pronounced its unshakable commitment to nonviolent resistance, by 2001 that commitment was eroding. What have we accomplished, dissident voices within the movement asked. Did we save Headwaters? Did we stop Charles Hurwitz from raping the trees that belong to all of us? Has Pacific Lumber committed to sustainable forestry and disavowed the practices that ruin streams and flood the land?

Meanwhile, in the wide world outside Humboldt, more extreme entities were sharpening the edge of the movement the hippies had dulled. The Earth Liberation Front, Animal Liberation Front, and others were committing crimes and making news in much the same way Earth First! had in the old days. And they were willing to cross lines Earth First!ers would not: setting fire to car lots full of air-choking SUVs, firebombing laboratories, liberating animals from captivity. The ELF's rationale: capitalism was destroying all life. The only clear response was to "by any means necessary take the profit motive out of killing." ELF cells operated secretly and independently, without knowledge of one another and without the guidance of a central command. They were obliged to do everything they could to prevent harm to humans, which is why they burned buildings at night. And the ELF also had a degree of technical sophistication, offering free downloads of such publications as "Setting Fires with Electrical Timers: An Earth

Liberation Front Guide" while Earth First!ers in Humboldt County were reduced to photocopying and passing around already dog-eared, thrice-photocopied pages of the Earth First! Direct Action Manual.

The distinction between Earth First! and other "groups" or "organizations" was lost to the mainstream. Law enforcement officials paid visits to timber companies, including Pacific Lumber, showing them how to identify adherents to the various factions based on tattoos and such—much as in the depths of the crack blight cops in the projects trained their colleagues in outlying areas how to identify gang members by their colors and signs. Ladies, gentlemen, meet your new enemy.

"Ninety-nine percent of the people believe Earth First! is as close as you can get to terrorism," said Chuck Oppitz, the proprietor of the Scotia Inn, where Hurwitz had been pied years earlier while defending the American way of business. "Earth First! is just a front for a bunch of shadow organizations," magnets for protest junkies, said Oppitz, whose opinions on these and other matters were as sharp as his cropped silver hair. Right before the World Trade Organization meeting—which turned into the infamous "Battle in Seattle"—they'd had billboards recruiting protesters. To his way of thinking, this was the closest thing these losers had to a real job, running all over the country protesting everything in sight, from the Gap to childhood immunization.

Furthermore, Oppitz believed, Earth First!ers were brainwashed by antimodernist zealots just as radical Islamists were. How could anybody actually believe technology made us worse off? These guys were nostalgic for a time when death—whether by disease, accident, or violence—was much more close at hand.

"I'd call them the Taliban of the environmental movement," Oppitz opined. "I call it a medieval mind-set. They believe the act of cutting a tree is per se bad. Earth First! is the shock troops, the SS of environmentalism. America will not accept terrorism in the forests."

Aside from any G. Gordon Liddy–esque entertainment value Oppitz's sentiments might possess, this was not the only time such views had been unabashedly aired. A congressman had uttered as much. Sleepy-eyed, barefoot forest dwellers might not look like Taliban soldiers wielding Kalishnikovs stolen from their Northern Alliance enemies, but the link had ample rhetorical precedent. And after September 11, it had had potential consequences for the two Earth First!–related trials set to commence at the federal courthouse in Oakland.

In the Bari-Cherney case, there would be talk of bombs and a movement branded with a scarlet "T" by federal agents who, the plaintiffs alleged, engaged in a stampede to judgment against two dope-smoking hippie agitators they believed to be homegrown terrorists. Lawyers in that case sought and received a delay in the trial date. Ground Zero was still on fire; Taliban soldiers were being chased from hole to hole in the ground campaign in Afghanistan. With the first battle of the war on terror at full roar, this was no time to go to trial in the case of two alleged terrorists who were whining about having their civil rights violated.

The latter-day Earth First! in which David Chain found his calling nearly a decade after the Bari-Cherney bombing was no less radical— it was still very much a part of its appeal, after all—but it had by and large proved that those active within it, unlike Dave Foreman, were not "constitutionally nonviolent," even when on the receiving end of serious pain-compliance techniques.

Darryl Cherney had been waiting for eleven years, but he would have to wait a little longer. *Chain v. Pacific Lumber*, on the other hand, would begin on October 15 as planned. It would be the only show in town.

SCHECTMAN WAS JUST BACK from another hearing, more convinced than ever that Armstrong was a hostile judge who had an antipathy toward trying the case in her court, and she punished both parties by dribbling the trial dates on her calendar from mid-October through nearly Thanksgiving. "It's always like this when you're getting fucked," Schectman growled. The calendar on the wall near the kitchen at Pacific Law looked like the cortege of lawyers was going to be out of court more than they'd be in it over the next few weeks. The stop-and-start schedule meant that the trial was going to be more of a hardship on everyone involved, not least the family of the decedent:

OCTOBER 15: Jury assembles and voir dire
OCTOBER 16: Off
OCTOBER 17: Opening statements. One from the plaintiffs, two from the two main defendants
OCTOBER 18: Off
OCTOBER 19: Off
OCTOBER 22: On
OCTOBER 23: Off
OCTOBER 24: On
OCTOBER 25: On
OCTOBER 26: 8:30–Noon
OCTOBER 29: Off
OCTOBER 30: Off

It was a Sunday, although it didn't feel like one to Schectman. He was dressed in Lee dungarees and a blue sweater, and he brewed coffee and fretted over the case's final details. For one thing, those photo blowups from the scene were much too small. Logistics were always a snarl; last-minute worries fell out of the sky. There was the not-so-insignificant matter of getting a physically large case moved from the office to Oakland. Any lawsuit is likely to generate enough paper to appall the average tree hugger, and the nature of *Chain v. Pacific Lumber* and the path it had taken through the system made for considerable bulk: there were depositions and newspaper stories, internal Pacific

Lumber memos and press releases, photos, videotapes and audiotapes, and AV equipment upon which to play them. Getting all the hardware into the courthouse would likely take more time. The security guys posted at the metal detectors at the courthouse entrance were being a good bit more thorough after September 11. All federal facilities had cranked up security, but the federal complex in Oakland featured twin towers, a disquieting echo of two much taller buildings that had, as the world watched aghast, crumbled in lower Manhattan weeks before.

Somebody asked, "What are the chances this thing will settle?"

Schectman hauled out the old lawyer's maxim: "You always do everything you can assuming the trial is a go and just see what happens." But it was worth remembering that Pacific Lumber had never taken a case to a jury trial. Stafford had settled two days before trial. Why, he wondered, hadn't the company done the right thing from the start? Why dig in for a siege as the lawyers' bills pile up if they're going to settle?

"If they would have taken care of their own people—our clients were their workers—if they would have settled up with them for right around a million dollars, without litigation, they would have saved a ton of money, a ton of exposure, and not created someone like me," Schectman said. "And so you have to ask yourself, 'What are they thinking?' I can see why they wouldn't settle this case. But the Stafford case, *it's their own people.*"

He said the Chain case was more likely than not to go to trial, especially "with all this terrorism shit in the media all the time."

And who had gotten rich off all this misery? Pacific Lumber's lawyers. Schectman figured the company had spent $5 or $6 million on lawyers just on the litigation he'd been involved in. And Schectman? He'd been one of the top trial lawyers in San Francisco and now people there would say, "Steve who?" Here he was looking down the barrel at fifty and his credit was so bad that the bank note on the house where he and his family lived was in his parents' name. He'd taken a bath financially and it kept him up nights. In human dignity law, you worked on contingency, representing poor people who'd been screwed by rich people. "I'm an economic litigator," he'd say. "These are all crimes motivated by greed." Pursuing justice for the downtrodden might be the ethical thing to do—and the fact was he was good at it—but it wasn't smart economics. He was in the middle of what appeared to be a lifelong epistolary exchange with the IRS, always paying his taxes in pieces with late penalties. He was at midlife, past the point where one typically starts in earnest planning some sort of exit strategy from full-time work, or making a resolution to spend more time sailing or playing golf. But there was something about injustice that just pissed him off. It was why he'd been incredulous that his parents' generation hadn't done more to stop the Holocaust. It was why he'd delighted in being the token campus radical at the conservative little college in Des Moines. It was why he had gone to law school. It was why he'd moved his practice and his family to Humboldt County. He'd learned to live with precarious finances, and in a sense it was liberating. As Bob Dylan said: When you've got nothing, you've got nothing to lose.

But if they lost at trial now, he and Liz and the kids were going to be living in a trailer park. Even if they won something—and the hypothetical numbers seemed to be tumbling—his checkbook wouldn't recover for years. This judge, she had them by the nuts. Everything she was doing was well within a judge's discretion, but Schectman couldn't buy a break on the motions *in limine*—Latin for "at the threshold"—leading up to the trial. She'd decided Juan Freeman, the investigator so biased against the activists that it was practically in his bone marrow, couldn't testify about his opinions during the investigation. She denied testimony by longtime activists about prior protests. She was allowing just a snippet of the infamous Grizzly Creek video to be played, and was reserving judgment on the transcript of the tape. She'd barred the testimony of an emergency medical technician who Schectman said would testify that Pacific Lumber security chief Carl Anderson had opened David Chain's body bag, looked at the corpse, and said, "Well, there's one that won't be hugging trees anymore." She'd granted the defense motion to bar photos of Chain after death as highly prejudicial. And she threw out the argument that Pacific Lumber had encouraged protesters' presence in exchange for publicity that helped seal the Deal, saying that such conspiracy theories were "pure speculation." She ruled that there would be no testimony about PL using the protesters to keep the heat on and jack up the going rate for Headwaters. She ruled that Pacific Lumber's history of egregious regulatory violations was irrelevant to the case as it now stood—the climate before Gypsy's death was immaterial to the limited questions before the court. Also inadmissible: the T-shirt with the EF! logo with the circle and a line through it that Anderson had peddled, the marbled murrelet on the PL dartboard, and Anderson's "One Shot, One Kill" license-plate frame. If Schectman had tried to introduce the bumper sticker suggesting wiping one's ass with a spotted owl after all the toilet paper was gone, Armstrong probably would have tossed that out, too—even as PL had been wiping its ass on the Forest Practices Act for years. Furthermore, political sentiments among employees other than Ammons and Reback, however colorfully expressed, were irrelevant. Similarly, she would allow no testimony about the culture of antipathy within the company toward environmentalists.

Armstrong had ruled on dozens of questions both weighty and slight. Of them, perhaps a dozen were key. Of those dozen, she ruled for the plaintiffs twice and the defense ten times. The fact that Armstrong had not ruled on all the motions before her was in part because of time constraints when she heard oral arguments. But given the way things were breaking, deferring further arguments until the Friday before the trial could be seen as a modest kindness extended to the plaintiffs' lawyers. Among the questions yet to be decided: a motion to exclude some evidence of unrelated protest activities, some of which purportedly showed mistreatment of activists.

A case that had once been so full of fight was now on the ropes, enduring a hail of blows. The wider narrative, the one that put the

death of David Nathan Chain in a battle that made the taking of casu-
alties all but inevitable, would be the greatest story never told, at least
not before a federal jury in Oakland. It would be a death without con-
text, a tragic, bizarre, and, so far as the jurors were likely to know, isolated incident. The jury questionnaire would quiz prospective members
of the panel on how closely—if at all—they had followed the timber
war, which was now in its sixteenth year.

In the Spence camp, Ed Moriarty viewed himself as a surgeon: get
the patient the best possible outcome the circumstances will allow in
what is never a pleasant situation, do no harm, save a life. Many a law
firm would never have touched the Chain case. The guy was young,
maybe he'd been a little lost for a time; he didn't have any heirs and his
work history did not indicate a looming career in neurosurgery or
hedge-fund management. But principle had prodded him into action,
and as a result his life had been snuffed out. That was what generated
Spence and Moriarty's interest in the first place. As much as Schectman liked to hyperbolically paint David Chain's death as murder, Moriarty—the less brash half of the odd couple—didn't even believe
Ammons really meant to kill Chain. But the fact remained that Big A
had to have known where those kids were, and dropping any tree large
or small in their direction was, pure and simple, an act of high negligence.

And now hope was washing away like ground cover on the hillside
of a clear-cut. Armstrong was clearly pushing them to try mediation one
more time.

As welcome as Armstrong's rulings had been to the defense, Bill
Bragg knew he wasn't dealing with a simple open-and-shut case. Although the plaintiffs' stockpile of weapons had been curtailed, it was
still going to be a challenging trial. His personal and professional sides
were at odds. He'd been through too many trials and knew that no one
emerged unscathed. But professionally? Facing down the intellectual
candlepower of the Spence firm? He was looking forward to it.

Still, there was the question of Armstrong, who could be as rough—or fair, depending on one's perspective—on the defense as she could be with the plaintiffs. After she changed a hearing date by one day the week before, Bragg had to catch a 6 A.M. flight from Humboldt County. He made it to the courthouse at 9:20, twenty minutes after the hearing began, and was chided by the judge. Bragg tried to remind her that he had changed his travel plans at her request. She did not welcome the reminder.

Then there was the time Moriarty got up, walked toward the bench, and said, "If it may please the court . . ."

"It does not please the court," Armstrong snapped. "Sit down."

When Armstrong scheduled the final round of pretrial arguments for October 12, she also strongly urged both sides to try to settle again. Each side, she said, had plenty of reason to be fearful of a jury trial. The award could be nothing. The award could be millions. In a conference call with the lawyers on Tuesday, October 9, she told all parties concerned that she wanted them to concentrate on mediation. She would pick up the motion—originally scheduled to be heard on Friday—the following Monday, the trial's starting day, while the jury pool was filling out its questionnaires. She was also seriously annoyed at the 140 pages of material the plaintiffs had faxed her. "You broke my fax," she said.

The Saturday before the trial—one day before Schectman had sat in his office and predicted that the case was likely to go to trial—Allsbrooks had had a conference call with Schectman and Moriarty and Allsbrooks's daughter Bridgett. The purpose of the call was to weigh Allsbrooks's openness to settlement. She was willing to try, and she was glad to have Bridgett listening in and agreeing with her. Not only did she value Bridgett's perspective, but it meant there was one less family member to whom she'd have to repeat the details of the latest development. Just keeping the family updated was wearying.

Allsbrooks and her sister, Karen, arrived in Oakland on Wednesday the 10th to be on hand for the Friday hearing before the judge two days hence. She had thought watching the lawyers interact might give her some clue as to how the case might proceed, what chances they had before a jury. Now it looked less than likely that a jury would hear a word of the story of her son's life and death. She was conflicted. Had she okayed the mediation because it was the right thing to do? Or was it because she was exhausted?

They filed into a jury room behind a locked door off Armstrong's courtroom on the third floor of the federal building. Schectman, Moriarty, and Moriarty's right hand, Jeanella Mathis, held up the plaintiffs' end. *Nice chairs*, Schectman thought. Federal court, in his estimation, was like visiting the temple of a wealthy congregation. The place didn't look like a police interrogation room where they'd just wiped the blood off the walls before showing the lawyers in to have a seat in a folding chair. On either side of Allsbrooks were David Allen Chain and Karen. They occupied the west side of the table. The defendants—Maxxam's assistant general counsel Joli Pecht, a representative from the insurance company that held the umbrella coverage for PL and two attorneys to safeguard the insurance company's interests, PL's hired guns, and Bill Bragg—sat on the east side. At the head of the table was a retired judge in an American flag necktie who would mediate and take home $7,000 at the end of the day. The money was a bargain compared to the cost of a trial.

In an unusual opening move, PL's lawyers told the plaintiffs they had come to settle. They said the company felt bad that someone had been killed and they wanted the matter concluded. Then Bragg spoke for his clients, Ammons and Reback, alluding to the private meeting Allsbrooks had had with Ammons when he was deposed.

"They wish this had never happened," Bragg told Allsbrooks. "They wish to thank you for talking with them after depositions. They said it felt like the weight of responsibility had been lifted."

Moriarty laid out the nonfinancial elements of the plaintiffs' demands: the creation of a committee to bring together forest activists and loggers, and the erection of a memorial to Gypsy. Moriarty was instrumental in defining the scope of the committee. Schectman, in bad-cop mode, was more interested in the machinations of the company's authority and such, but the committee clearly couldn't be expected to dictate company policy. Together, Schectman and Moriarty were a complementary pair. Schectman's fuel was clear, hundred-proof righteous anger, no matter how steady he held his voice. Moriarty hardly came off as the number-two man at one of the top firms in the country. He looked and acted more like the morning weather man in some secondary television market—older, bespectacled, a little overweight, trustworthy, and above all serene.

After those nonmonetary details were hammered out, it appeared to Bragg that Moriarty was calling the shots. The mediator didn't have much to do with that portion of the negotiations either; he was just there to get them to agree on a number. Then it was a matter of batting numbers back and forth, back and forth. They'd tossed around ballpark figures before. It was going to be a dance to get the defendants to budge from half a million and the plaintiffs to let go of a million or so.

Distractions were few. There was a coffee maker. The California and American flags. The window tracks had screws in the tracks so they couldn't be opened.

For the first eight hours, the mediator was simply a messenger. Then he started sending advice and signals. Eventually he put the defense lawyers in a smaller room. It seemed to get hot in there. The windows wouldn't open in that room either. More screws.

Between 6:30 and 7:30 P.M., Bragg sensed corporate counsel was ready to pull the trigger. They'd closed the gap between offers and counteroffers, and the increments between the two were getting smaller. The insurance guy was hedging, and it appeared that Preuss and Pecht were beginning to lose patience with him, but at that point it was still the insurance company's money—the guy was just protecting his company's interests.

After more than ten hours, progress was glacial and the defense side became apprehensive that Moriarty would get fed up and say, "See you in court." This was the point mediation invariably reached after a grinding day. The ground won was reduced to slivers and the frustration mounted. One remark that might have been regarded as innocuous earlier in the day could make the wheels fall off the deal later on—stalemate. And for the Spence firm, it wasn't about the money—it was redress. It was incredibly risky at this point to not close the deal, to pick up the next day when all involved were rejuvenated, ready for another day's fight.

Bragg played the one card he had.

"I feel I have little impact in the settlement because my clients don't have any money," he told the rest of the defense team. "But I have a large role to play if this goes to trial." He reminded Preuss and Pecht of the possibility of a runaway verdict that would far exceed the amounts they were batting around. Whether the jury would award such a verdict would hinge largely on Bragg's performance at trial. Look at Chuck Preuss, top dog at a high-powered San Francisco firm with two decades of practice in the federal courts, Bragg said.

"And I'm a podunk attorney from a northern California town of 24,000," Bragg said. "You might want to think about that. I sure as hell can't guarantee that when you hop on my back that I'm going to carry you across the finish line."

And with that, he stood up and walked out of the room.

In the end, the two sides decided the life of David Nathan Chain was worth $825,000. After attorneys' fees and more than $100,000 in expenses, David's parents split less than half that. Allsbrooks later said she "wouldn't sell Nathan's baby book for what we got in the settlement."

SO IT WAS THAT AROUND midnight on a Thursday, a woman from Coldspring, Texas, sat amid her whirling thoughts in the dark beside the outdoor pool at the Marriott in downtown Oakland, smoking her American Spirits, drinking wheat beer out of a Styrofoam cup—glassware being forbidden around the pool—and asking her dead son if she'd done the right thing. Cindy Allsbrooks never would have believed a day such as this one would come, not until the conference call the previous Saturday with Moriarty, Schectman, and Bridgett. Damn the torpedoes had been her mind-set and her mantra for so long. She'd arranged to travel to Oakland well in advance of the trial to sit in on the last round of pretrial motions still to be argued before and resolved by Judge Armstrong. Now she wouldn't have the finality of a trial, win or lose. In spite of herself, in the end, she'd settled.

Before, whenever somebody brought up "settlement," Allsbrooks was carried back to that awful pretrial train wreck that had left her depressed for a week.

"So every time somebody brought up settlement I would go back to that day, remembering how that was, and thinking, 'That's not what I'm supposed to do here. I'm supposed to go to trial and fight for my son and all that, and tell the truth, and if I tell the truth we're gonna be victorious.' But the reality came to me today, that no matter how much truth you have it depends on people's mind-set and where we're at, at a certain time. So we had a judge who really didn't want to go to trial over this. I still want to talk to her.

"Also there were things we could not have accomplished in a trial. Number one, a jury never would have given us the nonfinancial things, or they would have, and a jury could have awarded X amount of dollars and there would have been an automatic appeal and then it would have dragged on and I'd always be on the phone with somebody and I'm so sick of legalities, of dealing with this, of dealing with the court system, the legal system. I'm so ready to get on with my life, my girls' lives, my grandkids' lives in a positive way without all this hanging over our heads.

"So I think I went in there today really wanting to settle it. And I think when we got the nonfinancial things out of the way that's when my burden lifted, that's when I felt relieved, that's when I felt we had really accomplished something. But then there also were the lawyers. We went around the table and they were all so very humble and apologetic that this had to even happen. And for one inkling of a second I felt like they really understood what that meant.

"Our chances in a lot of ways were slim because of the jury instructions, because of what the law will allow and punitives had already been thrown out," she said. "It was never going to be a big-money case, but I just did not realize that the nonfinancial things would be as welcomed as they were today."

She had, in other words, largely accomplished what she'd set out to do three years earlier. But she knew some of the activists—including some of those who had been with her son the day he died—would view her as just the latest opponent to cave in the face of Pacific Lumber's mighty legalistic firepower. "No compromise" meant no compromise, and what was mediation if not diplomacy—bargaining with the enemy. Now the forest defenders would not have their day in court. Now the complete sins of Pacific Lumber would not have a public airing.

At the mediation, once she fully saw it was finally coming to an end, Allsbrooks wept. Pecht hugged her. The group walked back to the hotel together, and Allsbrooks's sister told Pecht she was relieved for Cindy that there would be no trial.

That night Allsbrooks, her family, and her lawyers had dinner in the hotel restaurant, Moriarty having changed into his Notre Dame sweatshirt. The party seemed simultaneously weary, enervated, and giddy.

Moriarty reminded Allsbrooks of his advice at their first meeting. She had been terribly upset upon reading the official report on her son's death investigation. "Go home and burn it," Moriarty had told her then.

Allsbrooks told the group about her son, about how he possessed a preternatural wisdom. "Even when he was young," she said, "Nathan was a very old soul."

The next day all the players got a conference room at the hotel, had breakfast together, formalized terms of the settlement, and put the financial terms under seal. In reading through the draft, Allsbrooks noticed a gag order on the nonfinancial terms, too. That would have been a deal-breaker. She told the other side they weren't going to take away her freedom to talk. The lawyers agreed. A press release was drafted. There was a word Pacific Lumber had been using throughout. "I want you to remove the word 'accident,'" Allsbrooks said.

On Saturday morning, they checked out of their hotel, the valets brought the rentals around, and the family drove up to the North Coast, swapping a high-rise Marriott in Oakland for a less swanky Holiday Inn Express in Eureka, next to a used-car lot that played jazz on its outdoor speakers. On Sunday, with little on the agenda but dinner at Schectman's, Allsbrooks thought it would be nice to sit outside someplace and drink beer and eat appetizers. They headed to a seafood restaurant on the marina, where Allsbrooks drank and ate clam strips.

Here, at last, was an opportunity for a psychic bloodletting, a purge. After an afternoon of drinking beer in the sun, Allsbrooks went to Schectman's house, where her lawyer was putting fresh-caught salmon on the grill. When everyone else was eating, Allsbrooks walked around among the trees, smoked, and came to terms with the fact that a portion of her journey was over. She thought, *What do I do now?*

Inside after dinner, guitars and cigars were produced. For a while, Allsbrooks was celebratory, clapping and hooting along. But then the alcohol and her burden overtook her, and she collapsed in Karen's arms. Relief and regret poured out in a torrent of tears, wails choked by sobs, sobs followed by whispered pleas for reassurance that she'd done the right thing. Both of them cried for a very long time.

In the dark of the backseat of their car, as Karen drove back to the hotel, Allsbrooks lay with her head on the lap of David Allen Chain, the father of her children. She asked David to tell her, one more time, the story of the day they brought his namesake home from the hospital. The boy was now a memory that would imperceptibly fade. It was too dark to see the blanket of redwoods in the hills and ridges off the highway, but she knew they were there, just as she knew her son was a ghost among them.

THEY MET THE ACTIVISTS, MAYBE twenty-five of them in all, at the Grizzly Creek campground a few days later. Jamie Romeo was there with her dog, Feedback, both of them veterans of the Gypsy Mountain Free State. Avcollie was there, and Dijon, and Ayr, and Jake Wilson, a peaceful soul who had taken the forest name Shunka since Gypsy had been killed. As expected, a good number of them had felt betrayed upon hearing that there would be no trial. Their friend's killing had been compounded by another injustice, and they cautioned one another to break the news to their compatriots gently.

But they also knew better than to second-guess a grieving mother's motives or judgment, at least to her face, and they were polite and respectful as Allsbrooks sat in a circle beneath the trees at the campground—at the spot where Gypsy had slept the night before he died—and explained what had happened and why.

She addressed those who may have been wounded or embittered head-on. "For those of you who feel like we haven't done the best, I'm sorry," she said. "I think we did the very best we could. And I didn't want to go another day with this hanging over my head." She told them they couldn't have gotten a standing committee to attempt to make peace between the loggers and the activists, nor would the company have been in any mood to erect a memorial, had the case gone to trial, regardless of the verdict.

"I don't want you to think we sold out to Pacific Lumber," she said.

But, she said, "Y'all have to be open to some change, right? Am I right? I'm doin' this for y'all more than anybody else, because I don't want to see anybody else hurt or killed. But there's some hard issues we need to look at."

Somebody said the committee sounded like all talk and no action. Allsbrooks said she'd be there to hold it or its members accountable. Somebody else said not pressing on with the trial had allowed the company the chance to avoid taking responsibility. Allsbrooks said that, to her way of thinking, the company had admitted responsibility because it had agreed to the negotiated terms, financial and nonfinancial.

David Allen Chain, wearing a new T-shirt he'd gotten at the Harley shop in Eureka, told the forest warriors that interfering with a man's job was a sure way to piss him off.

"I don't think going out there and playing cat and mouse with the loggers is the answer to the problem," he said. "It's been tried, it's failed. I'm saying there are other ways to get this point across, and I hope this committee doesn't turn into a pile of bullshit and will be a real committee that answers some of y'all's questions."

But, he said, he knew he couldn't stop the activists from doing whatever they believed they had to do.

Then they all stood and held hands. They wore boots and sandals; some had bare feet pressing into the needles on the ground. In a moment that resembled a Quaker service, all were invited to contemplate, and say something if the spirit moved them. After a time, Ayr looked at Cindy.

"My heart goes out to y'all," he said softly. "I don't want you to feel defensive. I totally have faith that you're doing the right thing, as always, and I just want to thank you for that."

She thanked him back. She said there were nights when she felt she couldn't keep fighting, and then she thought of the Earth First!ers who kept fighting. And, she said, she felt Nathan's spirit was strong in them.

"As a parent," she said with a smile, "I couldn't be prouder of the people my son chose as his friends."

. . .

DAVID CHAIN THE ELDER LAID eyes on the spot where his son was killed for the first time that afternoon, when the family went up Gypsy Mountain together. A grandfatherly Pacific Lumber man unlocked the gate near the Van Duzen River bridge and slowly drove them up the rutted, narrow trail in a white Suburban. They parked on the flat landing and looked around. The day was warm and clear, and from the hillcrest it seemed they could see trees to infinity. Cindy Allsbrooks, her two daughters, and her ex-husband walked thirty yards down the skid road from the landing. "This is where the thing broke," Allsbrooks said. "This is where they found him, head facing down."

As part of the settlement, the company had agreed to not log within one hundred feet of the tree. The brush had grown up in just a few years. It seemed much steeper than even Allsbrooks remembered. It seemed as if the ground had shifted.

David Chain tended to have a rough time on the 17th of most every month, the date of David Nathan Chain's death, and here he stood on the mountain where the young man's life had been taken three years and one month before. He climbed around the precipitous hillside, with shale-gray soil so loose it might as well have been sand, and at last fully understood that it would have been physically impossible for his son to have gotten out of the way once the tree started coming down. Running was out of the question on that slope, and even moving slowly made a man breathe hard.

He made his way some ninety feet down the trunk that A. E. Ammons had scrambled up. He stepped carefully, reaching out for branches as handholds. Then he stepped on the stump and looked around. Behind him it was clear and he could see the mountain ridge. And growing out of and around the periphery of the stump were new redwood shoots, three years old and already seven feet high, well over David Chain's head.

"It's amazing," he said quietly, "how many trees can grow out of one stump."

Once back up the tree along the skid road, Gypsy's father stood on a broken section of the tree and looked in the distance, silent again. Allsbrooks watched him, sobbed, and asked softly, "How must that feel for a father?"

Next to where Gypsy died, they found the altar. It had been there since the free state was set up, the beneficiary of pilgrims since. They found a glass vitamin bottle, a rusted kazoo, beads, a rock in a hemp bag, a button that said "Protect Our Wild Areas." And a jade statue of the Earth mother Gaia, the name of the character Sarah had played in *The Gypsy Chain*. It seemed to Sarah no coincidence. She found a shard of the fatal redwood on which she thought the statue would look nice, but hesitated.

"If you take it, you have to leave something," Bridgett said.

"If she doesn't take it, I am, because I think it belongs to us," Allsbrooks said.

David Chain: "I think you should leave your sunshades if you're going to take it."

Allsbrooks: "Okay, I'll give up *my* sunshades."

Bridgett: "This isn't a white elephant party."

Cindy laughed at that. She stepped away to have the last smoke from her pack and thought about leaving the pack at the altar. Maybe she needed to start rolling her own to slow her down. Nathan had been the one who got her to switch to American Spirits, saying if she was going to smoke she might as well smoke something that didn't have all those additives.

Sarah smelled the cigarette and reacted as if her mother had just desecrated a shrine. "Are you *smoking*?"

"Don't y'all *even*," her mother shot back from her seat on the ground, raising an arm and a pointed finger. "Nathan came up here and rolled his own and they want to bitch at me?"

The debate about the statue wasn't over. "This statue either sits here and gets ruined by weather, gets taken by somebody else, gets destroyed by loggers, or whatever," Cindy said, "or we take it and cherish it. It's not about stealing."

"It's about respecting sacred space," Sarah said. "And I'm just trying to figure out what's the right thing to do."

Two weeks later, Pacific Lumber men were back up on Gypsy Mountain, marking trees for cutting.

Memorial
on the
Mountain

AMMONS WAS SERIOUSLY PISSED. MAYBE the kid's mom had been right—maybe Pacific Lumber had screwed him over, betrayed him, made him a patsy. Settling implied wrongdoing, and by God he and Reback hadn't done anything wrong. Now they wouldn't have their day in court. He felt betrayed by a company to which he'd been loyal. All he had to do was get up there on the stand and tell exactly what happened. Having the opportunity to do that wasn't asking so goddam much. Now the company had thrown a bunch of money at the thing to make the smell go away, although nobody knew how much—financial terms of the settlement were sealed. But Ammons, unlike the company, had nothing to hide. The whole deal was fucked. And Ammons didn't have much to do except be alone with his thoughts. He'd been on disability since March 2001 suffering from such a severe case of vertigo that the only way to get to the bathroom was crawling on his hands and knees. He was sick as hell, overweight, out of work, and now robbed of the chance to put this whole wretched episode to rest.

Reback shared Ammons's frustration. "It's like studying for a test, working your ass off, and then you don't get to take the test," he said one Sunday morning as he watched football in his living room. "It didn't give me and A.E. any satisfaction. It made me and A.E. look guilty as hell. I think me and A.E. had way more pain and suffering then they did, being drug through all this. Me and A.E. had nothing but the truth to tell. We stuck our necks out for the company and the company settled. It came down to a money thing. It didn't come down to the right thing."

Nor were Ammons and Reback the only ones feeling shafted by the company. At the beginning of the month, John Campbell, now a relic of the old regime, was demoted upstairs, relieved of his fifteen-year burden as president and CEO of Pacific Lumber, and installed on the company's board. The books had run red for three straight years, the company losing some $200 million. Worse, it was projected to lose another $85 million in 2001 alone. They'd shaved off two hundred jobs since Headwaters and the adoption of its attendant Habitat Conservation Plan, the guiding document that was supposed to make Pacific Lumber an industry leader in conservation and instead was proving to be a tome so detailed as to be practically unfollowable. Still they couldn't stanch the flow. They'd shut down the giant old-growth mill, Mill B, in Scotia because they weren't logging enough old-growth redwood to keep the place running. Once a massive symbol of a thriving company, the old mill was now a massive symbol of unrecoverable history and brutal bottom-line realities. Back when Campbell started, old growth was practically all they milled, and now it was either all but gone or off limits. They were reduced to cutting mostly second-growth redwood and Douglas fir, and the most regulated timber company in America was hurting. In practice, the HCP was a nightmare. There was no way the company could mill enough timber to nudge the numbers into the black, not even after trimming the employment rolls to 1,200. No company could sustain itself and follow all those regulations. Campbell had looked at buying the assets of the busted Eel River Sawmills, but backed away from the deal.

So Maxxam brought in a turnaround guy, Robert Manne, a former software honcho from Seattle with a background in timber. The guy wasn't quite as reliant on charm and persuasion as that old pussycat Campbell, but this was no longer a job for a pussycat. The dubious PR line went forth: John Campbell, after many years of loyal service, had been rewarded with a seat on the company's board and relieved of the burdens of running the company from day to day.

It was plain that Campbell had been whacked. He was stung, and he discreetly vented to friends. He'd been loyal to Hurwitz; his legacy had been cast in the crucible of strife and controversy and he had run the company well. He had stood fast, refusing to run away and let the hippies spin it as a victory. He had, in fact, just moved into a new house. (Noisy hippies were still showing up at the old place. The new owners were not amused.) On the regulatory front, the company had seen a tenfold reduction in violations and the California Department of Forestry had given the company a two-year license at the end of 1999. The entire company was dedicated to living up to the promises it had made and pledged to keep for the next hundred years. And this was his reward? But he and Manne smiled and made nice for the newspaper photographer. The company spokeswoman, Mary Bullwinkel, said John just felt it was time for a change.

His new office looked and felt like a space he didn't spend much time occupying.

Meanwhile, things were great in Houston. A couple of weeks before Manne's installation at PL, Charles Hurwitz scored big. The day after jets crashed into the World Trade Center, the Pentagon, and the Pennsylvania countryside, a federal administrative law judge recommended, with clear and emphatic language, that every claim that the Office of Thrift Supervision had made against Hurwitz be thrown out. Among other things, Administrative Law Judge Arthur Shipe said the OTS failed to produce "a scintilla of evidence" for some of its charges and engaged in "unseemly name-calling." Hurwitz had fought for ten years and it was estimated that his attorneys had logged some $30 million in billable hours in the savings-and-loan case, maintaining it was a politically motivated witch-hunt. Now the judge seemed to agree. Hurwitz issued a statement that wrapped himself in the cloak of righteousness, effectively saying he was brave enough to stand alone against the tyranny of corrupt government persecutors whose aim from the beginning had been to get him to cough up Headwaters.

The feds now had little or no legal remedy to recover the $1.6 billion that United Savings had flushed away.

Meanwhile, Hurwitz said his related suit against the FDIC was still a go. He wasn't done teaching them a lesson.

At the end of November, Mill A joined its big brother in dormancy, and it wasn't long before they were selling off the equipment inside. The company said the "regulatory burden had become too great"—that is, as with Hurwitz and the OTS case, the government was a malevolent entity whose purpose was to harass decent men of commerce. The restrictive timber harvest plan and a timber market that was in the tank had given the company no choice but to fire another 140 people, leaving just 1,060 or so folks relying on Charles Hurwitz for a paycheck, steady or otherwise.

It was a moment for history. The little but once-mighty mill town of Scotia, California, was out of the business of milling timber.

Among those laid off was Rhett Reback.

New guy Manne also cranked up the cut rate, enough to draw protests but not meaningful, sustained howls from the hippies. Acquiring new timberland was another alternative, and one to which he was not averse. It would in the long term mean more trees going to the remaining operational mills in Carlotta, Arcata, and Fortuna, but it also required a prohibitive capital outlay on the front end. No way, not now. Spending more money was exactly what he didn't need to be doing. Pacific Lumber was going to turn a profit, even if it meant the new company only faintly resembled the old operation. He fired all the remaining loggers and made deals with contract operations—saw jocks for hire. Same with the truckers. All of them were now independent operators, meaning Pacific Lumber wouldn't be paying for their benefits. He sold off a mountain of equipment and banked the cash. And in May 2002, Manne announced that he had done in a little more than eight months what Campbell hadn't managed in more than thirty-six: the Pacific Lumber Company, or what remained of it, had turned a profit. The company was going to be completely out of the old-growth business in a matter of a very few years, meaning it would have to turn its attention to milling smaller second- and third-growth timber. Smaller trees meant smaller profit margins, but so it would have to be. Pacific Lumber was here to stay. The environmentalists' claim—which they had been chanting for sixteen years now—that Hurwitz was going to cut all the old growth he could and then let the company bleed to death, was plainly what it always had been: a lie born of hysteria.

Not that things were perfect yet. The same month Manne was crowing about driving the company into the black, the CDF slapped Pacific Lumber with a $10,000 fine for spraying herbicide in a clear-cut on a watershed. To the environmentalists, this was a signal that the company would never effect true change, would never care about anything but its own land. Manne was going to have the company running in the black come hell or high water.

TOWARD THE END OF MAY, on a brilliant Friday afternoon that happened to be the twelfth anniversary of the day Darryl Cherney and Judi Bari were bombed, Cindy Allsbrooks stood at the foot of the mountain the activists named Gypsy wearing a somber black dress and shoes ill-suited for a hike. She walked down a path toward a stand of four redwoods growing in a rough semicircle and removed the boughs and branches covering the face of a slab of granite that had been set against them. Affixed to the boulder was a bronze plaque by a local artist whom Allsbrooks had asked to design her son's memorial after the lawsuit was settled. The artist, Joan Dunning, who also had written a book about the struggle, had thought the spot was perfect—four trees, one for each of David Nathan Gypsy Chain's names—a cool and dark space near a bend in the road, where people might come to contemplate the gravity of Gypsy's sacrifice. The memorial was certainly more grand, and the setting more scenic, than the cemetery back in Pasadena, where the marker was set flat in the ground like all the others.

Now, almost four years after she'd seen Bridgett walking toward her door bearing awful news—"I knew that one of my gifts had been taken," she would later write—they were here for another formal memorial, a reminder that her son could change people's lives even in death. As bereaved parents know, notions of closure are an insult and a lie when it comes to "getting over" the death of one's child, but today before the sparkling sun went down there would be a ceremony held, more words said. This day offered another milestone in a journey that began on a fall day in 1998 and had no discernible finish line.

Mike Avcollie; his wife, Calista; and Alder Nathan, the son they had named both in memory of Gypsy and the cause, were there. So was Schectman; his wife, Liz; and his onetime apprentice Jamie Romeo. David Allen Chain was there with his third wife as well as much of the extended Chain-Allsbrooks family. Allsbrooks's mother, Marjorie Trimm, was on hand, as was Gypsy's paternal grandmother, Meriam Chain; sisters Sarah and Bridgett; Bridgett's husband and their three children, Gypsy's nieces and nephews. It was the children's first time to fly, their first trip to California. In the wake of David Chain's death,

Bridgett's youngest, Mathew, had made up a story about Rocky Dave, who fought to save the tall trees. Rocky Dave was so strong that if a logger cut a tree, Rocky Dave would hold it up and it wouldn't fall and hurt anyone.

But that had been years earlier. Now, Bridgett said, the memory of their uncle was beginning to fade, an ebbing tide in the minds of Mathew and her other two children.

Rich Bettis from Pacific Lumber, one of several valued friends Allsbrooks had made in the company, and the one who had driven the family up the mountain, was there. Most of Gypsy's Earth First! friends arrived en masse, hooting up at the tree sitters on Gypsy Mountain as they walked down the trail. For a moment, they made it feel like a pep rally.

Then it began. They sat in a circle, about seventy in all, as Naomi Steinberg officiated once again. "I have the honor and joy of welcoming you to my home," she said. Again she told the story of the salmon— how they'd run in such numbers in the past, how logging and erosion from logging had more than decimated their population. She told the story of how she awoke each morning thanking a man she never knew for his sacrifice, and praised "the young people who are working so hard doing what needs to be done."

After Steinberg's eloquent opening, overcome with the gravity of a moment she had fought for, Allsbrooks broke down twice attempting to begin her remarks. Then she began reading, saying in a clear, determined voice she was "moved beyond words."

She said she had thought for a week about what she'd say. "I have said so much over the last three years and eight months that everything becomes repetitious and I begin to wonder who has not heard the story not only of his untimely death but also of all the little childhood stories I have told. Then this morning I woke up and realized that I will spend the rest of my life telling those stories to anyone who will listen and want to hear them." Stories about how Nathan would hum himself to sleep in church. How he would say, when he was exasperated with his sisters, "The gwirls are giving me a headache" and put a hand to his forehead. She said he was grumpy in the morning and told the story of how she got him out of bed by making a snake with her arms. How he turned into a babe magnet as a teenager. How she was grateful she was hundreds of miles away "when my boy took his last breath."

Gypsy's grandmother Marjorie Trimm spoke, saying, "Sometimes in death we attain what we couldn't in life."

Mike Avcollie stood up and stepped away from Calista and Alder Nathan. He said a few words about what happened the day Gypsy died, and there was pain, relief, and a hope of explanation on his face when he said them. He said he felt good about what they'd done, and wondered whether in fifty years people would talk about them like they talked now about Laura Mahan, who'd shut down the bulldozers in Founders Grove in the 1920s—and who also had a plaque in the woods in her honor. But mainly he talked about losing a friend: "If I never would have known him," he said, "I would have lost so much more."

Steve Schectman addressed the still-bruised feelings of many activists, some of whom were stung that the litigants had settled—short-circuiting a showdown they felt could have been nothing less than a trial of Pacific Lumber's post-takeover history and practices. They might have won, they might have lost, Schectman said, but they certainly wouldn't have a memorial—"something that was paid for in blood," he said—on Pacific Lumber land.

"Do we have justice?" Schectman asked. "I don't know."

IT WAS NATIONAL NEWS IN JUNE of 2002 when a 96-foot, 460-year-old oak tree showed its age and fell in a violent Maryland thunderstorm. The Wye Oak, Marylanders' beloved state tree, drew thousands of mourners to the tiny state park named for it. They cried. They prayed. State officials collected samples in an attempt to clone the Wye Oak, while others contemplated how best to use the wood in a manner appropriate to its historical significance. The governor issued a respectful statement, saying that any tree dating to fifty years after Columbus and remained upright for twice as long as this republic has stood was remarkable. But all this fuss over a tree? For timber fallers working the woods in coastal northern California and elsewhere, cutting big redwoods more than twice the oak's size—

sacred elders in some activists' eyes, cash money in those of the lumber companies—that's nothing more or less than a good day on the job. True, once the Wye was indisputably magnificent, an explosion of healthy foliage, but in recent decades it could hardly be celebrated for its conventional beauty—it was rotten and hollow on the inside, a habitat for snakes, effectively on life support. Why did its falling resonate with so many people? Because it represented a living connection to the natural world? Because it put the relatively brief lifespan of humans in perspective even as it underscored how much we have altered the landscape to suit our needs? Because, through some fluke of inattention, we had failed to kill it during all these hundreds of years and eventually it attained a kind of graybeard novelty status? Look, a really, really old tree.

In fact, it was celebrated and mourned because Marylanders chose to single it out for preservation, and they devised a plan without precedent to do that. In 1939, the state bought the Wye Oak from its last owner, the only time a governmental body had purchased a single tree. Two years later the state turned the twenty-seven acres around the tree into a state park specifically to protect it. The Wye Oak would be preserved so that generations would come to regard it as a piece of their home, a piece of the past. The preservation also brought into sharp relief the fact that less impressive specimens of white oak had not been spared the saw, and the Wye Oak was the biggest and best one that remained. Singling out one tree for preservation, of course, isn't quite the best way to maintain the diversity and integrity of the larger ecosystem, but it's a not insignificant start. As John C. Sawhill, the late president of the Nature Conservancy, would later put it, "In the end, our society will be defined not only by what we create, but by what we refuse to destroy."

That quote happens to be the epigraph to Edward O. Wilson's *The Future of Life*, in which the brilliant and widely influential scientist and author presents a lively and altogether compelling argument that, among other things, environmental and economic interests need not be at odds, as they seem so intractably to be in Humboldt County and elsewhere. In fact, new conservation methods can be plenty profitable.

Wilson, who has two Pulitzer Prizes, closes the book with a favorable assessment of protests groups that

> gather like angry bees at meetings of the World Trade Organization, the World Bank, and the World Economic Forum. They boycott insufficiently green restaurants. They mass on logging roads. In response the executives and trustees they target ask, Who are these people? What are they really after? The answers to these questions are simple. They are people who feel excluded from the conference table by faceless power, and they distrust decisions secretly made that will affect their lives. They have a point. The CEOs and governing boards of the largest corporations, supported by government leaders committed to an expanding capital economy, are the commanders of the industrialized world. Like princes of old, they can, in the realm of economics at least, rule by fiat. The protesters say: Include us, and while you're at it, the rest of life.
>
> The protest groups are the early-warning system for the natural economy. They are the living world's immunological response.

Harvard professors tend to regard such groups more warmly than do guys like Rhett Reback, guys who work with their backs and see protesters as a clear threat to their jobs. One night after dinner at the brew pub in Fortuna, Reback leaned against his pickup and brooded over the long-term prospects for the timber industry in the area. "Not good," Reback said, "and bad for me personally."

"What about college?" I asked.

"Ah, it's too late for me," he said.

When he said that, Rhett Reback was twenty-four years old, the same age as David Chain at the time of his death.

Rhett Reback is now married and working as a tree climber for a logging company that contracts with Pacific Lumber. He's going to need a paycheck for a long time, considerably longer than the timber industry is likely to keep him making his monthly house payments. The resource-based economy in his part of the world is in a steady and seemingly irreversible decline. The work people did for one century and for half of another is going away. When even more of the mills are shuttered, the people who work in timber are going to be looking for jobs—and then what? They can't all turn their Victorian fixer-uppers into bed-and-breakfasts. And if we save all the remaining old-growth redwood? Fine, I'd love for my kids to see them. But the hard truth is they will have to serve some purpose our capitalist-minded policymakers will understand in a visceral way, and while only a fraction of the old growth remains, it's still too many trees for folks to be willing to pay to drive through every one. (I've done it; the novelty wears off rather quickly.) Meaningful jobs that pay adequately will be critical as the trees become smaller in both number and size. If that doesn't happen, we may well have a class war. And somewhere, Judi Bari will be smiling, reaching for her bullhorn.

While the pitched battle between environmentalists and capitalists rages in northern California, variations on this cacophonous and ceaseless theme are playing across America—in the Chesapeake Bay, the Arizona desert, the Louisiana bayous, and the Florida swamps. And so it will be for decades to come. It isn't helpful to suggest that the answer is hurling the Earth and its human inhabitants back in time, moving people out of the Midwest and Western Plains, for instance, and re-populating Chicago with prairie grass and bison. Yet the desperation of such measures is inherently part of their appeal, especially when the current Bush administration announces, as it did in June of 2002, that, yes, global warming will take a toll on our environment; and, yes, it's caused by the emission of heat-trapping gases; and, yes, it's going to cause more deadly heat waves and the drying up of marshes and water sources from snowmelt; but, no, there's nothing we can do but adapt to the changes. Should the environmental apocalypse come to pass, anyone left to write the history will remember that this disaster was foretold well in advance, and we chose to do little but load up on sunscreen.

At the risk of offending partisans, I will confess here to being a raging moderate. I enjoy breathing clean air when it can be had, admiring exquisitely tall trees where they still grow, and honoring the right of working people to earn a living wage. I am a radical environmentalist exactly once a week, when I put on my hiking boots and haul the recycling to the curb. Yet the air in my state, Texas, is demonstrably dirtier than it was when George W. Bush became governor, in part because of actions he took before he left abruptly to pursue the finer pleasures of the presidency. In Austin, we produce such a bounty of smog that the city regularly offers free bus rides on "ozone action days," and the southerly breeze exports this noxious stew to the north, to the countryside not far from Bush's Crawford spread, where old-timers wax wistful and angry about the blazing blue skies that are a thing of the past. And in Houston, where both Charles Hurwitz and Bush's parents reside, the air is filthier than anywhere in the country.

In response, we dither.

ACKNOWLEDGMENTS

PRINCIPALS IN THE CHAIN CASE AND the surrounding, seemingly perpetual controversy spoke candidly and at greater length than an outsider such as I could ever have hoped. I'm grateful to all of David Chain's family, particularly Cindy Allsbrooks, who has endured my questions for years. Better than most people thrust into an at times bizarre and horrific situation, Allsbrooks and her family grasped the complexities of this story, and neither she nor her family expected or desired this book to be a hagiography of David Nathan Chain. Furthermore, neither Allsbrooks nor anyone in her family—and I would include Ron Allsbrooks here—made any effort to influence the shape, substance, or tone of this work. That is an act of stupendously courageous restraint, one of which I'm not sure I'd be capable if the roles had been reversed. Any time a journalist drags the lake of a source's soul (in the memorable phrasing of *The Washington Post*'s Anne Hull), the infliction of pain, intended or otherwise, is always a possibility; I can only imagine what it's like for someone to endure having outlived one's child. Cindy Allsbrooks made a great leap of faith. She was as undemanding of me as I was demanding of her, and I will never adequately repay that kindness. Allsbrooks has paid a terrible price, and if anyone is entitled to be absolutely positive about where she stands, it is she. She is both an outsider and an empath, and as such she is sometimes skeptical when she comes across one of Humboldt County's bumper crop of myths, lies, mistaken assumptions, and superheated opinions: that the pre-takeover Pacific Lumber didn't clear-cut and that it did not plan to be out of the old-growth business by now if not before; that the radical environmentalists want a complete end to logging rather than the sustainable forestry most of them advocate; that Earth First! does not value human life; that, to a man, the workforce of Pacific Lumber—such as that remains after the company fired all its drivers and loggers—despises the activists and longs to do them bodily harm. For anyone willing to take the time to seek out answers, as Allsbrooks has, these presumptions are all provably untrue. Nevertheless, they have formed the bedrock for what's closing in on two decades of acrimony, sporadic violence, and white-hot rage, a kind of homegrown intifada whose origins actually predate the first Palestinian uprising in 1987.

As if one death wasn't enough, Allsbrooks has been forced to grieve anew: two tree sitters fell to their deaths in 2002, one in Oregon and one near Santa Cruz. She spoke with at least one longtime tree sitter in the winter of 2002–2003, urging the woman to return to ground safely and continue her work from there. She didn't, but a Pacific Lumber–contracted tree climber accomplished what Allsbrooks's cell phone call couldn't. In addition to continuing and legitimate concerns about activists' safety, Allsbrooks has become suspicious of tree-sit-as-career-move, à la Julia Butterfly Hill. Look at what Hill has accomplished since she came down, Allsbrooks notes, much of it in the service of good causes that have little to do with saving the planet. Allsbrooks remains weary but committed to the near impossible task of keeping the environmentalists and the loggers talking through the Forest Peace Alliance, a condition of the lawsuit's settlement and something that certainly wouldn't have happened had the case gone to trial. Pacific Lumber pledged to chip in $5,000 for five years' funding, Allsbrooks would fly in at least half a dozen times a year, and she and her hand-picked representatives would meet with their Pacific Lumber doppelgangers. If diplomacy is the art of preventing the escalation of a crisis by prolonging it, the alliance appears to be performing adequately—although Allsbrooks has seriously considered dissolving the group because of still-simmering tensions. Her regular trips to the North Coast have been a financial and emotional drain.

Ironically, after attending a four-day class on mediation at Humboldt State University in the summer of 2003, she returned to Coldspring as weary and dispirited as she had ever been. On the second day of class, she had an epiphany and realized her position was untenable: no one with so much invested in a conflict could be an effective shuttle diplomat. The Forest Peace Alliance, which she had hoped would provide meaning to her son's death, had lost more ground than it had gained in two years. "I am still committed to the FPA," she wrote in her diary, "but I have also decided that if we cannot make something productive come from it soon, it will be time to let it go . . .

"Maybe it is time to get real. Maybe Nathan is even watching me from afar and saying, 'Enough, Mom.' I have lost too much time. Why did I do it? . . . And the bigger question that I can't seem to answer is, was it just a self-serving venture that has left me feeling empty and all alone?"

While Allsbrooks was instrumental in helping me tell this story, she was by no means alone. David Allen Chain, whom I wrongly expected to be somewhat reticent in responding to my questions, opened a vein from the first time we spoke. Allsbrooks's daughters, Sarah and Bridgett, were of great benefit. To tie up the Gaia story: after mulling it over, Sarah left the statue where it was the day of the memorial. Activist Jake Wilson, by then going by the forest name Shunka, later presented it to her. But after hearing Sarah's reasons for leaving it in the first place, they took the statue back up the mountain together.

David Nathan Chain's aunt and uncle Karen and Mike Ripple were also helpful. This book might have been possible without the family's help, but it's much better for having had it.

At Pacific Lumber, John Campbell sat for a pair of interviews and answered questions old and new with patience and detail. Campbell is now retired from PL and, in a perversely fitting grace note, nearly had his retirement party in Scotia disrupted by activists.

The Manne regime, meanwhile, is proving to be much more aggressive in its dealing with protesters, just as it was in pushing the company ledger into the black. In April of 2002, Manne went to the county board of supervisors to float the trial balloon of going after money from the newly created and then still-unnamed Department of Homeland Security to combat activists "who have boldly proclaimed themselves eco-terrorists." (A small group of protesters did little to dispel the image that following August, when they drove a car up to the front door of Pacific Lumber's headquarters and locked down. Jittery employees inside worried the radicals might have a bomb.) Predictably, the activists howled that Manne was trying to monkey-wrench the Forest Peace Alliance. Manne then issued a clarification, but refused to back away from his core position: that people in Humboldt and the nation regarded the "coordinated and often clandestine activities of groups like Earth First! to be a security threat." Manne has also been much less tolerant of tree sitters than his predecessor. There will not be another Julia Butterfly Hill on Manne's watch.

I believe Mary Bullwinkel, one of Pacific Lumber's spokespersons, has fielded queries from me as long as anyone involved in this story, and her reserve of good humor seems to be holding. Rhett Reback and A. E. Ammons were fairly chomping at the bit to tell their side of the story after *Chain v. Pacific Lumber* settled, and both endured multiple interviews. "The last three years have been the absolute fuckin' pits," Ammons told me just after the settlement. "And I've had a hard life." He'd been off work for six months already when he said that because of his debilitating vertigo. He has good days and bad days, but he hasn't been able to go back to work.

Bill Bragg and Steve Schectman continue to practice law in Eureka. In addition to sitting for many hours of interviews, Bragg and Schectman each installed me in their offices and allowed me to spend time there following the legal thread of this tale. The thousands of pages of depositions taken in preparation for the trial proved an inexhaustible resource. Jamie Romeo and others who had worked in Schectman's office told me of the camaraderie they felt there and of what happened when things fell apart. Some of Schectman's former workers sued him for back wages, interest, and penalties. The case settled the week before it was to go to trial.

Ed Moriarty invited me to spend a few days at his ranch, where his assistant, Jeanella Mathis, ably guided me through Moriarty's end of the case. Early on, Jerry Bosch was the case's navigator, and he recounted that history with photographic precision and detail. Earlier still, Jay Moller advised the Earth First!ers in the heat of the criminal investigation and provided details on his involvement. At the Humboldt County district attorney's office, Terry Farmer and Andrew Isaac provided a good deal of vital material relating to the county's investigation of Chain's death. Farmer, a twenty-year incumbent, was upset in 2002 by local attorney Paul Gallegos, whose campaign included promises to revamp county policy on prosecuting small-time dope users and to better enforce environmental laws. Not long after taking office, Gallegos sued Pacific Lumber for submitting allegedly fraudulent data during the Headwaters negotiations, seeking damages that could easily bankrupt the company. Humboldt County residents responded by mounting a recall effort just four months into Gallegos's term.

Juan Freeman proved, contrary to convenient stereotype, that the Humboldt County Sheriff's Department is not staffed entirely by knuckle-dragging, hippie-stomping stooges in the employ of Charles Hurwitz. (Sheriff Dennis Lewis, whom protesters regarded as the head of Charles Hurwitz's private security force, also lost a reelection bid to his chief deputy in 2002—by a three to one margin.) The volume of paper these lawyers and investigators made available to me, which I subsequently copied and shipped home to Texas, likely made the owner of the Mail Boxes Etc. store in Eureka a happy franchisee indeed. Upon our first meeting, Naomi Steinberg spent almost an entire day recounting her involvement in events before and after David Chain's death, and then sent me off with a reading list that gave me a richer understanding of the controversy's underlying causes.

The word "polarizing" is used so often when talking about Darryl Cherney it almost seems to be the man's middle name, but his indefatigability demonstrates the depth of his convictions. He is a living link to Earth First!'s past and he continues to stir the pot, most dramatically in June 2002 when, twelve years after Redwood Summer and the car bombing, a federal jury in Oakland rendered a $4.4 million verdict for the plaintiffs in *The Estate of Judi Bari and Darryl Cherney v. FBI Special Agent Frank Doyle, et al.* The jury agreed that the pair's First and Fourth Amendment rights had been violated and that Bari had been subjected to false arrest. "We're blocking the FBI from clear-cutting the Constitution," Cherney crowed, positioning himself as a man who had stood up against a power-drunk government—not unlike Charles Hurwitz in his legal tussle with the feds. Cherney is always adept at the care and feeding of media types. That's true of Josh Brown, too. Jennifer Walts, Carey Jordan, Erik Eisenberg, Mike Avcollie, Gabriel Deutsch, and many other Earth First!ers overcame a sometimes-reflexive mistrust of a guy in the employ of an international media conglomerate and spoke with me about their experiences in and out of the woods. Jake Wilson is perhaps the gentlest and most trusting soul I've ever met. He's also much braver than I am. My telephone rang one or two days before Christmas 2002, and it was Shunka, high up in a tree on Gypsy Mountain, having just ridden out a rough winter windstorm. I'll leave the debate over some of Earth First!'s tactics to others, but these people have thought long and hard about what they're doing.

David Chain's adult life was a work in progress at the time of his death, and many of the people who knew him at various stages paint him as an altogether different person from the one others describe, up to calling him by different names. For helping me craft a coherent version of a man I didn't know I am grateful to Josiah Hardagon, Stephanie Kirby, Ravyn Erlewine, and Laura Somers, among many others. Somers, who co-wrote and directed *The Gypsy Chain*, the play about her friend, has been rewriting ever since and is developing the project into a film.

Charles Hurwitz is still making deals in Houston. Maxxam Inc.—with its interest in aluminum, forest products, real estate, and horse tracks—racked up a $14.6 million loss for the last quarter of 2002, a substantial improvement from the $508 million the company lost in the same quarter of 2001. Charles Hurwitz declined to be interviewed for this work, but certain Maxxam officials in Houston did speak to me on background. I thank them.

Long before I had heard of Pacific Lumber or knew much about Earth First!, a few canny writers saw a tremendous story brewing and told it well. I'm particularly indebted to two authors whose past efforts made mine richer and more complete: David Harris's *The Last Stand* is a nonfiction thriller that tells the story of the Pacific Lumber takeover and its aftermath in exceptional, novelistic detail; Susan Zakin's *Coyotes and Town Dogs* is a thorough account of the early days of Earth First! Harris and Zakin were among the first to smell a story here, and their works have preserved events and details that might otherwise have been lost to history. John Driscoll at the *Eureka Times-Standard* covers the environmental beat for the paper with a solid understanding of the issues and an outsider's willingness—not unlike Allsbrooks's, come to think of it—to challenge natives' long-held assumptions. Both sides regard Driscoll as fair, straight down the middle, and so do I. Driscoll first reported some of the events detailed in this book, and his unblinking eye deserves credit here. Mike Geniella at the *Santa Rosa Press-Democrat* has covered the timber business for a long time and provided vital historical perspective, especially observations about how the North Coast has changed since the mid-1960s. This book also benefited from stories first published in the *San Francisco Chronicle*, the *San Francisco Examiner*, the *Houston Chronicle*, and other publications both mainstream (or "corporate," as some of the activists would characterize them) and alternative.

Several wise friends and colleagues helped guide this project from vague lunchtime chat to finished manuscript. Robert Draper, the most fearless writer I'm pleased to call my friend, was among the first, tutoring me by example in the craft of the book proposal. Jim Hemphill, my friend for more than twenty years, read portions of the book with a lawyer's eye and spared me innumerable embarrassments. Three of the best newspaper editors I've ever worked with, Rich Oppel, Fred Zipp, and Melissa Segrest, first dispatched me to Humboldt County, unwittingly dropping me into a project that would take me almost six years to finish. My thanks go to all of them and everyone at the *Austin American-Statesman* for the chance to begin the story then and for the time off to report and write this larger version of the tale.

Stephanie Land's early enthusiasm for my proposal is a big reason this book exists. After Stephanie left Doubleday before our work together was finished, the manuscript enjoyed the careful attention of Kendra Harpster, whose praises I could sing for a hundred pages. Doubleday editor-in-chief Bill Thomas's editorial guidance was reassuring and confident throughout the process. Copyeditor Karla Eoff rescued me from errors of grammar, syntax, spelling, and fact. Jim Hornfishcher is a very rare breed—a literary agent who promptly returns the calls of even his most fretful, angst-paralyzed, high-maintenance client. He is a tireless cheerleader, champion, and advocate, not to mention a perceptive reader and an elegant writer. Most important, we were friends before we had a piece of paper binding us together, and so, I hope, we remain today.

My young sons, Adam and Joe, are simply the joy of my life. Adam wrote dozens of books in the time it took me to write this one. He suggested I could have speeded things up if I'd used fewer words and more robots, and I have little doubt he is right. My wife, Allison, proved to be the consummate master of the most thankless occupation in existence, that reductive cliché, the author's spouse. (She is also a fine editor.) Allison is remarkable for much more than just her tolerance of me, but anyone living in a writer's house knows that a book is a less-than-equal partnership—with the spouse pressed into service to such a degree that it must surely violate federal labor laws. Not once did Allison utter the mildest of complaints, even when my duties kept me on the North Coast for months at a time. For her patience and devotion wildly in excess of what I will ever deserve, she has my undying love.